CHILDREN AND THE POLITICS OF CULTURAL BELONGING

Conversations about multiculturalism rarely consider the position of children. Yet providing care for children separated from their birth families raises questions central to multicultural concerns because they frequently find themselves moved from communities of origin through adoption or foster care, a practice that deeply affects marginalized communities. This book explores the debate over communal and cultural belonging in three distinct contexts: domestic transracial adoptions of non–American Indian children, the scope of tribal authority over American Indian children, and cultural and communal belonging for transnationally adopted children. Understanding how children "belong" to families and communities requires hard thinking about how cultural or communal belonging matters for children and communities, who should have authority to inculcate racial and cultural awareness and under what terms, and, finally, the degree to which children should be expected to adopt and carry forward racial or cultural identities.

Alice Hearst is an Associate Professor of Government at Smith College, where she teaches courses in American politics and public law. In addition, she has been a visiting or adjunct professor at Cornell University Law School and the University of Utah Law School. Her research interests focus on state regulation of the family. She has published essays in the *Law and Society Review* and the *Journal for the History of Childhood and Youth* (for which she is the contemporary issues editor).

Children and the Politics
of Cultural Belonging

ALICE HEARST

Smith College

CAMBRIDGE
UNIVERSITY PRESS

CAMBRIDGE UNIVERSITY PRESS
Cambridge, New York, Melbourne, Madrid, Cape Town,
Singapore, São Paulo, Delhi, Mexico City

Cambridge University Press
32 Avenue of the Americas, New York, NY 10013-2473, USA

www.cambridge.org
Information on this title: www.cambridge.org/9781107017863

First published 2012

Printed in the United States of America

A catalog record for this publication is available from the British Library.

Library of Congress Cataloging in Publication Data

Hearst, Alice.
Children and the politics of cultural belonging / Alice Hearst, Smith College.
    pages   cm
Includes bibliographical references and index.
ISBN 978-1-107-01786-3
1. Interracial adoption – United States.   2. Interethnic adoption – United States.
3. Intercountry adoption – United States.   4. Adopted children – United States.
5. Ethnic identity.   6. Indian foster children – United States.   I. Title.
HV875.64.H43   2013
306.874–dc23   2012012620

ISBN 978-1-107-01786-3 Hardback

Contents

Acknowledgments

My interest in the issues discussed in this book began many years ago when I worked as a law clerk on a case, *In re Adoption of Halloway*, involving the Indian Child Welfare Act (ICWA), at the Utah Supreme Court. The court had to decide whether an adoption decree entered by a Utah trial court should be set aside and the case transferred to the Navajo Nation for resolution under ICWA. Although there was no question in that case that the child was an Indian child under the terms of the Act, nor was the legal question particularly difficult, there was considerable concern about setting aside the decree because of the length of time that the child had spent with his adoptive parents, with whom he had developed affective ties. In the end, however, the court returned the case to the Navajo Nation, and the reasoning and language in the case were later cited extensively in the U.S. Supreme Court's decision in *Mississippi Band of Choctaws v. Holyfield*. The case left a number of issues unaddressed, including the question of who decides who is an Indian child; although those issues had generated some passing discussion, they did not need to be resolved in order to issue the decision in the immediate case. Accordingly, once that case was finished, I put questions about culture and belonging on the shelf.

Much later, however, the questions reemerged in a slightly different context: a student in my office for an advising appointment spent most of her time discussing not her academic program, but her frustrations as a babysitter. The student had grown up in Zimbabwe and was working several hours a week tending two grade-school children whose white American parents had adopted them from somewhere in West Africa. The parents told her she had been hired to introduce their children to their African roots and to customs like Kwanzaa. As the student pointed out, she knew nothing about Kwanzaa – a celebration of African American heritage, with which she was not familiar – and little about West Africa; the children, in the meantime, seemed primarily concerned with playing video games and, at ages eleven and eight, expressed little interest in their original connections to Africa. She wanted to honor the parents' good intentions but felt placed on the spot as the communicator of culture for the children in her care. That conversation, coming on the heels of much discussion among academics of multiculturalism and cultural belonging, allowed me to begin developing the questions that inform this book.

Those questions have, at times, seemed endlessly complicated. What seems to be a straightforward proposition – that the interests of cultural groups and communities should be considered in the placement of children – continuously bumped into other considerations. Marginalized groups may have compelling claims for recognition, but deciding who belongs to such groups – or who speaks for such groups – is not an easy matter, nor is it obvious how those claims might be put into effect. In addition, it seems critical that children's voices should matter, although how to incorporate such voices presents difficulties. Nonetheless, it seems clear that discussions about multiculturalism, which are after all about generational connections, need to think about the position of children, especially those moved through adoption and foster care.

In the course of writing this book, I was assisted by several able undergraduate research assistants: Eliza Bryant, Allyson Hawkins, Claire Stein-Ross, and Margaret Woodman-Russell. Each brought her own questions to the table, and those questions helped shape the final project. A grant from the Feminist Legal Theory Project at Emory Law School, directed by Professor Martha Fineman, allowed me to spend a semester at the School of Law at Queen's University in Belfast, Northern Ireland, where I was able to discuss the issues with a new group of associates and begin putting together my thoughts, particularly about transnational adoption. Several supportive colleagues at Smith College and elsewhere helped me clarify my thinking. Kristin Bumiller, Michael Clancy, and Greg White read parts of the manuscript at different times and provided thoughtful assistance. Cecelia Cancellaro, of Idea Architects, was immensely helpful as the book took final shape, and John Berger, at Cambridge University Press, was both a patient and thoughtful editor.

The commitment associated with writing a book about families and children inevitably required understanding from my own family, Tom and Daniel McCormick. Their affection and good humor supported me when I needed it, and I realize how fortunate I am to have them in my life.

Introduction

Helping build families one miracle at a time.
              – Adoption Network Website

Providing families for children in need is unquestionably a worthy goal. Adoption conjures soft-focus images of abandoned and vulnerable innocents welcomed into families who can love and nurture them. People who choose to engage in stranger adoptions – adoptions that do not involve kin or stepparents – are typically motivated both by a desire to become parents and by a wish to do good in the world. The families thus created are, in fact, miraculous, and these families often work hard not only to provide for a found and chosen child but to give back to the communities from which the child originated.

The uplifting story of family creation enabled by adoption, however, tows a darker story of marginalization and loss in its wake. Historically, adoption in the United States was not simply about providing care for needy children; it was also explicitly driven by the desire to move children from unsuitable to suitable families. Charles Loring Brace, founder of the Children's Aid Society of New York, argued, for example, that placing poor and immigrant children with American farm families via orphan trains provided "the cheapest and most efficacious way of dealing with the 'Dangerous Classes' of large cities, . . . draw[ing destitute youth] . . . under the influence of the moral and fortunate classes, [enabling them to] grow up as useful producers and members of society, able and inclined to aid it in its progress."[1] Similar motives were evident in the federal government's Indian Adoption Project[2] in the

---

[1] Charles Loring Brace, *The Dangerous Classes of New York, and Twenty Years' Work Among Them* (New York: Wynkoop and Hallenbeck, 1872): i–ii.

[2] The Indian Adoption Project operated from 1958 to 1967 and was administered by the Child Welfare League of America under a contract with the Bureau of Indian Affairs in the U.S.

mid-twentieth century, and as recently as 1994, former U.S. House of Representatives Speaker Newt Gingrich argued for the reinstitution of orphanages as a way of ending the welfare dependency of poor women.[3]

However, even when the separation of children from their biological families and communities is not propelled explicitly by efforts to control so-called deviant families, adoption entails a loss for communities and families separated from children. Whether by design or happenstance, the children of disadvantaged communities are more likely than children of privileged communities to find themselves tangled in adoption and foster care arenas, with the result that the loss of children is borne disproportionately by such communities. Marginalized communities view this loss of children with alarm and sometimes despair. As a result, claiming – or reclaiming – such children is freighted with significance as those communities strive for equality, recognition, and respect.

Another current in the darker story of adoption concerns the universe of adoptable children. The adoption wars are fought over relatively few children: healthy infants are a highly prized item – some might say a commodity – in the context of stranger adoptions, where the focus tends to be on adopting the youngest, and thus presumptively least traumatized, child. As the number of white infants available for adoption has declined over the last few decades, more prospective parents have become interested in adopting infants and very young children across racial, ethnic, and national boundaries. However, the vast majority of vulnerable children, both domestically and internationally, stand on the sidelines; they are older, children of color, belong to sibling groups that should not be separated, or have intellectual, emotional, or physical problems that make them difficult to place.

This is the yin and yang of adoption and foster care. A child who gains a family through adoption, whether as an infant or older child, has also lost a family, a history, and a community. A community that opens its arms to a child finds its counterpart in a community that has lost or failed that child. An adopted child is shadowed by legions of children who have been left behind.

The fact that adoption entails gains and losses for individuals, families, and communities means that adoption is a volatile political issue, particularly when adoption and foster care placements cross racial, cultural, and national boundaries. It is, as one commentator has noted, a "crucible" issue into which a lengthy history of subordination and deprivation has been compressed and

Department of the Interior and the U.S. Children's Bureau. www.adopting.org/uni/frame.php?url=http://www.uoregon.edu/~adoption/topics/IAP.html.

[3] Jason DeParle, "Abolishment of Welfare: An Idea Becomes a Cause," *The New York Times* (April 22, 1994).

submerged.[4] To be sure, the number of children adopted both domestically and internationally is small in real terms and most of the communities from which they are removed do not face extinction as the result of the practice – although this claim has more potency in connection with the history of some indigenous communities. At the same time, the intrusion of the privileged into the intimate spaces of poor and marginalized communities cuts to the bone.

Some might argue that in adoption, the only interest that carries moral weight is the interest of the child and that adult members of a community of origin do not sustain a cognizable loss when children are placed outside of that community. There is truth in that assertion; as discussed in later chapters, some communities have stronger claims than others. But all communities place a value on "their" children, and communities that have long suffered from social and political disadvantage are quite understandably resentful when children appear to become commodities to be picked over by others. Whether their future survival as a community is placed at risk by the removal of such children may be debatable, but appreciating the symbolic impact of the loss is critical to understanding how such communities view their place in the world.

In addition, marginalized communities are acutely aware of how adoption can be used by a privileged community to domesticate difference: children of different races and cultures become exotic specimens on display, even when the idea of such a display is repugnant to the families who adopt them. A *New Yorker* cartoon captured this concern in 1997, depicting a well-to-do white woman at a party exclaiming, "We're so excited, I'm hoping for a Chinese girl, but Peter's heart is set on a Native American boy."[5] It is understandable, therefore, that marginalized communities in these circumstances often suspect advantaged communities of applauding transracial, transcultural, and transnational placements as no more than a ploy to secure children for their own members. Thus, while the primary focus in adoption and foster care placements should be on serving the best interests of the child, considering the child in isolation from the communities from which the child originates is frequently viewed by less well-off communities as an expression of callous indifference to the structural conditions that place such children at risk in the first instance.

To create equitable systems of care for vulnerable children, it is critical to understand that marginalized communities experience the loss of children keenly and to account for those concerns in the legal and policy regimes

[4] Janet Farrell Smith, "Analyzing Ethical Conflict in the Transracial Adoption Debate: Three Conflicts Involving Community," *Hypatia* 11 (1996): 1–33, 2.
[5] William Hamilton, *The New Yorker*, July 7, 1997, 31.

governing both domestic and international adoption and foster care. This communally aware position does not mean that adoption and foster care should not cross racial, cultural, or national boundaries. It does mean, however, that the goal of placing every child with a traditional nuclear family must not automatically trump all other forms of care, even for some young children. A communally aware position means, for example, that there must be some retreat from the position that the best option in caring for vulnerable children always entails placing a child through adoption into a "real" family of his or her own. Rather, there must be a range of options available, such as creating small group homes with stable caregivers that allow some children, where appropriate, to remain in the communities into which they have been born or have grown up, or making better use of guardianship options rather than adoption to avoid the total alienation from a child's origins that occurs in formal adoption proceedings. These types of communally aware options are too often dismissed out of hand by adoption proponents because of their institutional overtones.

Being attentive to the concerns of marginalized communities, moreover, does not mean that every community should always be given exclusive or even primary authority to place "its" children. Many children "belong" to more than one racial, ethnic, or cultural group, or have ties to communities that are exceedingly weak. Efforts to draw rigid boundaries of belonging that grant irrevocable authority to one group to determine who belongs only generates ill will, creating endless jurisdictional disputes that produce racial, ethnic, or cultural winners and losers, while children's interests fall by the wayside. Indeed, the concept of belonging – especially cultural belonging – can dissolve into incoherence when talking about children because culture is acquired, not innate. To talk about a child's culture or community of origin – when that child has been moved among families, communities, and nations – and to use that concept to set fixed jurisdictional boundaries creates as many problems as it resolves.

Communities that seek to revitalize themselves by reclaiming children whose connections are highly attenuated must be willing to seek an accommodation with competing communities. Moreover, disadvantaged communities must be realistic about their own abilities to cope with large numbers of vulnerable children. Although the precarious position of many children in such communities can typically be traced to a series of historic injustices, not every injustice is easily or immediately remediable, and providing immediate care for vulnerable children is a problem of such magnitude in many communities that it may be difficult, if not impossible, for marginalized communities to respond adequately in the moment. At the same time, privileged communities must not jump to the conclusion that the best solution is always to remove children through adoption or foster care, and make more than illusory efforts to alleviate the problems that lead to large numbers of abandoned and needy children in the first place. Providing support for families and in-place care is a critical part of the equation.

This kind of compromise and accommodation is largely absent from the political contests over adoption currently being waged on both the domestic and international fronts. The factions in the adoption debates can be roughly divided between groups that advocate for relatively unlimited access to adoption for children in need and those who view adoption or placement outside of a community's boundaries as an option of the last resort. Although this discussion refers to the former as *adoption proponents* and the latter as *adoption opponents*, positions of the various actors are located along a spectrum rather than a single, unambiguous axis.

Adoption proponents are typically a diverse group, consisting of persons who have adopted or are seeking to adopt a child, many of the public and private agencies that provide adoptive or child welfare services, and others who believe that adoptive families provide children with their best life chances. Proponents are quick to point out that many studies suggest that children adopted across racial and cultural boundaries develop without significant difficulties attributable to racial or cultural difference and, while not naïve about asserting that "love is enough," they argue that the benefits accruing to children by virtue of permanency far outweigh any trauma that children might experience as the result of movement through adoption or foster care. Adoption proponents rarely acknowledge that *communities* whose children are transferred may experience the transfer of children as a tangible injury. Moreover, as a group, adoption proponents have tended to dismiss concerns about trafficking and baby-selling or have treated such scandals as isolated incidents, despite mounting evidence that such practices are widespread and that the concerns are legitimate. They often view efforts to slow the rate of transnational transfers through laws or policies that give communities some degree of control over the placement process as nothing more than misguided nationalist games using children as pawns.

Genuinely concerned about the trauma that can ensue when children are placed in institutions, drift aimlessly through inadequate foster care systems, or are simply left to seek their own way on the streets, proponents seek to speed the process by which children at risk become available for adoption, and bridle at both domestic and international regulatory schemes that appear to impede the process, including the Hague Convention on Intercountry Adoption, discussed in Chapter 5. Domestically, proponents express frustration with social policies stressing across-the-board goals of family reunification, which in many cases keep children shuffling back and forth between incompetent or abusive families and an equally problematic state child welfare system. Internationally, proponents argue that calls for community-based care make little sense in impoverished communities overwhelmed by vulnerable children. They point out that placing orphaned or abandoned children in informal or kinship care systems often re-victimizes them and may even threaten their very survival.

Adoption opponents are an equally diverse group: some of the most strident critics are mothers who felt compelled to surrender children because of social stigma or economic necessity and are now challenging the system, as well as adoptees who were adopted when the practice was shrouded in secrecy and families were advised not to be open about the process.[6] Of concern in this book, however, are communities and organizations that argue that the practice exploits poor parents, mothers in particular, and historically marginalized communities. These opponents argue that adoption is an exceedingly limited fix to the problem of caring for vulnerable children – a fix that allows the privileged to camouflage their appropriation of the youngest and most adoptable of children behind a veil of compassion while ignoring the conditions of inequality that create vulnerability in the first place. These critics argue, in particular, that transracial, transcultural, and transnational adoption and foster care placements stigmatize whole communities as unfit to care for children and thwart efforts to create community-based care systems that would ultimately redound to the benefit of both children and the communities themselves. Rather than providing families for children in need, they argue, adoption today has become a market system of boutique baby-shopping focused on providing children for elites who feel entitled to select children to parent.

The conflicting philosophies that underlie these two positions can be illustrated by examining two pieces of federal legislation in the United States: the Multiethnic Placement Act of 1994, as amended by the Interethnic Placement Provisions of 1996 (MEPA-IEP)[7] and the Indian Child Welfare Act of

---

[6] One of the most difficult issues in analyzing the effects of adoption on children and communities lies in the fact that practices have changed dramatically over the past sixty years. Adoption rules during 1950s and 1960s, when the practice was often a family secret, vary considerably from practices today, where open adoption permitting continued contact with families and communities can do much to help a child navigate his or her identity across racial and cultural boundaries. Similarly, parents who adopted transnationally and transracially in the late 1960s assuming that issues of race and ethnicity would be easily overcome are often among the first today to recognize that such placements raise unique issues for both parents and children.

[7] Multiethnic Placement Act of 1994, Pub. L. No. 103–382, sec. 551, 108 Stat. 3518, 4056 (codified as amended at 42 U.S.C. secs. 1996b, 5115a (2006), *repealed in part by* Small Business Job Protections Act of 1996, Pub. L. No. 104–188, sec. 1808(d), 110 Stat. 1755, 1904 (codified at 42 U.S.C. sec. 1996b (2006)).

1978 (ICWA),[8] both of which continue to generate bitter disputes. MEPA-IEP prohibits race-matching[9] in adoptive and foster care placements for non-American Indian children except in compelling circumstances. The Act and its amendments were passed in response to what adoption advocates argued was an unconscionable reluctance on the part of public and private placement agencies to place children transracially, either because of formal policies or because of social workers' discomfort with such placements. MEPA-IEP has generated pointed criticism, largely from the African American community, for undercutting the cohesiveness of minority communities to the detriment of both those communities and the children placed outside of them. Critics also argue that the law removes any incentive for agencies to actively solicit potential adoptive and foster care families from minority communities.

ICWA, on the other hand, represents what might be called a culturally or community sensitive approach. Broadly speaking, ICWA grants tribal courts exclusive jurisdiction over the adoptive and foster care placement of children who are, or are eligible to become, members of an American Indian tribe and presumptive jurisdiction over other categories of children. Indeed, construing ICWA in a 1989 decision, *Mississippi Band of Choctaws v. Holyfield*,[10] which has been widely lauded by indigenous communities, the U.S. Supreme Court recognized that tribes have a distinct *communal* interest in the placement of Indian children. Other provisions of the Act require state courts placing Indian children to comply with preferences that require such children to be placed with kin or in other Indian families before considering non-Indian families. ICWA has been praised by supporters not only because it allows Indian children to grow up Indian, but redresses, in part, the efforts to erase native populations that occurred openly until at least the mid-1970s. Critics argue that it grants tribes unfettered authority to reach out and disrupt adoptive and foster care placements based on connections to a tribe or community that may be no more than a whisper.

ICWA, of course, is rooted in the unique political history of Indian tribes in the United States and rests on considerations of sovereignty unique to tribal status. In fact, scholars who have argued that non-Indian minority communities should be granted authority akin to that granted to tribes have earned sharp rebukes from American Indian scholars who scoff at the idea that African American communities, for example, should be granted exclusive authority to

[8] Indian Child Welfare Act of 1978, Pub. L. No. 95–608 (codified at 25 U.S.C. secs. 1901–1963 (2006)).
[9] In the adoption context, race, ethnicity, and culture are often used as proxies for one another, although such a conflation raises its own problems, discussed *infra*.
[10] *Mississippi Band of Choctaws v. Holyfield*, 490 U.S. 30 (1989).

place African American children, as discussed in Chapter 4. On a more general level, ICWA has drawn fire from adoption proponents, who argue that it dooms children to live in tribal communities where alcohol and substance abuse problems are epidemic, effectively extinguishing such children's life chances.

Similar controversies pervade the transnational adoption arena, where a host of declarations and conventions endorse a variety of human rights protecting individual, family, cultural, and national identity with the potential to affect adoption practices. Many nongovernmental organizations (NGOs) concerned with the plight of large numbers of vulnerable children, as well as sending nations (those whose children regularly find their way into the transnational adoption arena), talk about transnational placement as an option of the last resort, as opposed to adoption service providers and potential adoptive parents who worry that increased regulation of the adoption process and a focus on community-based care will constrict and eventually eliminate access to adoptable children. Sending countries, as well, are now taking steps to privilege domestic over transnational adoption, both to counter the impression that "their" children are available for export and to create opportunities for potential adoptive families in their own communities. The success of such efforts varies, of course, as many sending nations face overwhelming obstacles that make providing for vulnerable children a Herculean task.

In receiving countries, however, the pressure to eliminate considerations of race or ethnicity in making transnational adoptive placements has increased. In the United States, as noted, MEPA-IEP specifically forbids the consideration of such factors except under special circumstances; supporters of MEPA-IEP have argued strenuously that such a race or ethnicity blind approach is constitutionally required under the Equal Protection Clause of the U.S. Constitution. Other receiving countries have expressed similar concerns. In an interesting twist, Italy's highest court recently issued a high profile decision endorsing only racially and culturally neutral approaches to adoption. The decision rejected the adoption application of a family who sought a child only of "European" descent, holding that adoption applications from families who designate a racial, cultural, or ethnic preference for a child must be dismissed and observing that families specifying such preferences may be assumed to be bigoted and thus unsuitable to adopt at all.[11] The case has generated interest as nations, NGOs, and child welfare professionals have begun to grapple with the consequences, including worries about placing children with families who

---

[11] Bock, Erin, "Italy high court rules adoptive couples cannot request children based on race, ethnicity," *Jurist*, June 3, 2010, http://jurist.org/paperchase/2010/06/italy-high-court-rules-adoptive-couples-cannot-request-children-based-on-race-ethnicity.php.

may not be prepared to deal with the issues raised by parenting a child who obviously differs in race or ethnicity from his or her adoptive parents.[12]

Adoption and foster care placements that transfer children among communities with disparate resources and distinct cultures raise a number of issues relevant to broader debates about multiculturalism in political scholarship. The first set of issues relates to the nature of group claims to recognition and the preservation of cultural integrity. While some theorists argue for the recognition of group interests as third-generation solidarity rights, there is considerable debate over whether these types of group interests can ever be formulated as rights, a debate that is often carried out at a relatively abstract level. The claims of marginalized communities for the protection of cultural integrity in the adoption and foster care arena starkly illustrate some of the problems in this area: the boundaries of communities are notoriously difficult to fix, and the position of children, whose identities are malleable, raises genuine concerns about who ought to be allowed to designate membership and the process by which such membership decisions are made. Although understanding claims for cultural continuity as enforceable rights may be problematic, there are nonetheless significant justice concerns that warrant consideration because of the vulnerable position of such groups, which concerns are often elided in current debates over adoption and foster care.[13]

A second issue central to broader discussions of multiculturalism concerns the child him or herself. Liberal arguments about multiculturalism tend to center on the concerns of adult actors; claims for recognition typically issue from communities composed of adults whose identification with a particular community is not in doubt. When individuals or groups demand accommodation for religious practices or language differences, for example, rights can often be relatively easily formulated and enforced, even if they are staunchly

---

[12] This decision, interestingly, reflects the thought experiment articulated by Fogg-Davis in *The Ethics of Transracial Adoption*. In that book, Fogg-Davis reflects on how the adoption universe might be changed if all adoptive placements were race-blind, so that children and parents would be matched without considering the race of either, and explores how such a practice might affect the ways in which Americans consider race altogether. H. Fogg-Davis, *The Ethics of Transracial Adoption* (Ithaca, NY: Cornell University Press, 2002).

[13] This book does not examine the claims of religious groups as distinct cultural communities. While in the history of adoption, religious matching was the norm, with separate charities dealing with, e.g., Protestant, Catholic, or Jewish children, that is no longer the case. E. Wayne Carp, *Adoption in America: Historical Perspectives* (Ann Arbor: University of Michigan Press, 2002). Today, when religion is raised as a concern in adoption or foster care proceedings, it is often a coded reference to ethnic difference: should a Muslim child be raised in a Protestant home? When a child is older and has grown up in a particular religion, it may serve the child's best interests to be placed in a foster or adoptive home of the same background to provide continuity for the child.

opposed by those opposing "special" treatment for minorities. Moreover, adults who disagree with the values of a particular community often have exit rights, in law if not in fact.

Children, however, have no such rights of exit: where they are placed will largely determine the identities that they develop. Arguably, these children have been subjected to a forced exit from a particular community; they are, as Bergquist has noted, "involuntary immigrants," even when such placements have been made to further their best interests.[14] Compounding the analytical problems, in adoption and foster care across transracial and transnational boundaries, community and culture are often configured as flowing through the child him or herself. These expectations play out differently for different children. Some children feel genuinely stricken by the loss of the families and communities from whom they have been separated, regardless of the age at which they were adopted or the love they feel for their adoptive families. Others may resent the efforts of either their adoptive families or originating communities to forge connections, whether through culture camps, roots trips, or more sophisticated arrangements for exchange and reconnection.

The movement of children through transnational and transracial adoption also shifts, to some extent, the ways in which the development of children's moral agency is understood, since moral agency, and the degree to which we can exercise that agency,

> depends on the forms of life we inhabit, the niche we occupy in our par-
> ticular society; the practices and institutions within the society that set the
> possibilities for the courses of action that are open to us; the material, cul-
> tural, and imaginary resources at our disposal; . . . [and] the shared moral
> understandings that render our actions intelligible to those around us.[15]

For children in adoption and foster care, it is difficult to chart the tangled interaction of the environmental factors that shape the child's development from the imperatives that the child might feel to belong in one place or another or both. Children moved across traditional boundaries of belonging thus confound assumptions about parental authority to shape children's identities and children's own perceptions of how they develop those identities.

Concerns about moral agency run in another direction too. Disadvantaged communities often assert that children are their futures: the removal of children therefore impairs any possibility of cultural and communal continuity.

[14] Kathleen Ja Sook Bergquist, "International Asian Adoption: In the Best Interest of the Child?" *Tex. Wesleyan Law Rev.* 10 (Spring, 2004): 343–349, 343.
[15] Hilde Lindemann Nelson, *Damaged Identities, Narrative Repair* (Ithaca, NY: Cornell University Press, 2001): xi.

Children, however, inevitably disrupt, resist, and reshape cultural and communal norms as they become agents of their own identity. If community connections are to be forged, it is critical to understand how children themselves navigate among different spheres of belonging and to grant them the opportunity to shape their own identities as they mature.

Although sound adoption practices today emphasize the importance of allowing children to explore their origins, adoption is often seen, at the same time, as giving children a new start, especially if they have experienced trauma at an earlier point in their lives. Placing children in stable, loving homes is presumed to be part of an overall corrective strategy for helping children overcome early mistreatment or neglect. Yet it is important to realize that children often have strong ties to parents and other caregivers even when those parents or caregivers are incompetent or abusive, as is often the case with children whose adoptive and foster care placements have been effected through state child welfare systems. Policies focused on hastening adoption eligibility, such as that articulated in the Adoption and Safe Families Act of 1998 (ASFA),[16] may negatively affect children who are moved into permanent adoptive families at the cost of legally erasing the biological family and eliminating community ties. Under those circumstances, children may feel considerable grief at losing any ability to connect to a parent or original community. Those children, however, may nonetheless be the lucky ones; many children whose parental ties are severed by the operation of ASFA – especially those who are older or have special needs – will never find a permanent placement, and will drift through foster care until they attain majority.

Thus, the argument that adoption proponents must recognize the real injury imposed by the removal of children from disadvantaged communities who must, in turn, be realistic about their abilities to claim and care for children ties into a subsidiary argument that children themselves need to be granted a voice in determining where they "belong." Increasingly, children's advocates have argued that children's voices should be heard as identity rights. The scope and existence of children's identity rights is a matter of considerable debate, despite the fact that documents such as the Convention on the Rights of the Child suggest that such rights exist: identity rights are difficult to articulate with any specificity and children's abilities to make decisions about their identities shift over time. As communities seek avenues to connect with "their" children, either through claims for protecting cultural integrity articulated under international human rights covenants and conventions or through

---

[16] Adoption and Safe Families Act, Pub. L. No. 105–89, 111 Stat. 2115 (codified as amended in 42 U.S.C., various sections).

domestic laws that grant them authority to determine or intervene in a child's placement, the impact of such arrangements on children themselves needs to be carefully assessed. Both communities seeking connection and foster and adoptive parents must be attuned to children's desires, and possibly rights, to either create or resist such connections.

   This book explores the debate over communal and cultural belonging in three distinct contexts: the debate over domestic transracial adoptions of non-American Indian children, the debate over the scope of tribal authority over American Indian children, and the debate over cultural and communal belonging for transnationally adopted children.[17] Unfortunately, looking at those three arenas does not lead to the development of an elegant set of principles that can be applied to resolve questions of belonging for children located in and between cultures. Indeed, the reverse becomes clear: different policy prescriptions are necessary depending on the circumstances of particular children. At the same time, exploring these issues can deepen the ways in which cultural and communal belonging is configured. Understanding how children "belong" to families and communities requires hard thinking about the extent to which cultural or communal belonging matters for children and communities, who should have authority to inculcate racial and cultural awareness and under what terms, and, finally, the degree to which children should be expected to adopt and carry forward racial or cultural identities.

---

[17] Other authors have certainly noted that "culture" figures prominently in discussions about adoption and foster care, although the primary focus has been on how culture and community matter for children rather than for the communities from which they originate. *See* Madelyn Freundlich, *The Role of Race, Culture, and National Origin in Adoption* (Washington, D.C.: Child Welfare League of America, Evan B. Donaldson Adoption Institute, 2000). Freundlich notes that claims about culture arise in different ways under MEPA-IEP, the ICWA, and in transnational placements, using the same broad categories discussed in this book. *See also* Madeline H. Engel, Norma Kolko Phillips, and Frances A. DelleCava, "Cultural Difference and Adoption Policy in the United States: The Quest for Social Justice for Children," *International Journal of Children's Rights* 18, no. 2 (April 2010): 291–308. Janet Farrell Smith, *supra* n. 4, explores questions of community in the context of the debate over the domestic transracial adoption of African American children by white parents, looking at how the issue reflects historical tensions around race relations in the United States.

1

Children, Law, and Belonging

During the last three decades, claims for cultural and communal integrity have been made forcefully by a number of groups. Debates over the nature and scope of such claims typically center on disagreements about the degree of political self-determination that distinct communities should be accorded or the extent to which differences should be accommodated or supported in public policies. These claims may be framed as individual rights, communal rights, or both. They raise questions about the legitimacy of state power over distinct communities, as well as questions about how groups themselves define and exercise power over membership. Providing a voice for marginalized communities has become a moral imperative in liberal democracies where such groups have been systematically disempowered.[1]

Questions about communal belonging are particularly poignant when centered on children because the removal of children is often one of the chief injuries such groups have sustained. Because of the disproportionately high rates at which children in marginalized communities have been removed through adoption and foster care, these children may comprise a diverse diaspora. Even when the connections between such children and a particular community are attenuated, the children nonetheless often stand as markers for that endangered group, longed after as carriers of a culture that the community hopes to reassemble or revive. Cultural vitality and community flourishing

---

[1] Not all groups have the same moral claim to recognition. One would not assume, for example, that a group favoring the subjugation of women should have a cognizable claim to engage in sexist practices, even though such practices might be integral to its self-definition. In the adoption and foster care context, however, it is easy to trace a deliberate history of political and economic discrimination against particular racial, ethnic, and cultural communities that have left the children of such groups particularly vulnerable to family disruption and left those groups themselves without an effective political voice.

become closely linked to the child as the representative of the community's future.

In conversations about belonging and group rights, however, children are rarely mentioned. As John Eekelaar has noted, children present a "hard case" when talking about identity and rights because they require adult guidance, but at the same time, must be allowed sufficient latitude to shape their identities as they mature.[2] In mainstream theorizing about groups and identity, however, children are typically relegated to the shadows. Children are presumptively nested in families who are, in turn, nested in communities; families are presumed to be best positioned to protect and advance children's interests, and children's interests, not incidentally, are assumed to be congruent with those of the family. Moreover, families themselves are assumed to hold fixed loyalties to the identity groups in which they are rooted and to the nations in which they are located.

When family boundaries are stable, those assumptions may be largely correct. However, when those boundaries are breached and children are removed or separated from their families and communities for adoption or foster care, the same assumptions are tossed into the air: for the child standing alone, both what constitutes "the family" and what constitutes "belonging" become points of contestation. Indeed, because children ordinarily find themselves subject to adoption or foster care *because* the family or community has "failed," issues of belonging can be acute.[3] If a child is removed from a family and community early in his or her life, does the child still "belong" to that community? On what terms? On whose authority and under what lived experience? The questions are different for each child and each group, and there is no simple formula for weighing all of the interests.

Children have always posed problems for liberal theorizing about personhood, autonomy, and belonging because they are not and cannot be the rational individuals around whom liberal regimes are created. As Sue Ruddick notes, "The family or caregiving arrangements for children [are]...a site where aspects of the fully Hobbesian subject are distributed across a collectivity – 'held in trust' by caregivers... until such time as [the child] is deemed

---

[2] John Eekelaar, *Family Law and Personal Life* (New York: Oxford University Press, 2006): 167. Eekelaar goes on to note that families and communities have a strong interest in ensuring that children learn the values of that community, which can often lead to conflict as children may challenge or alter those values as they mature.

[3] Whether children are voluntarily or involuntarily surrendered for adoption, they are nonetheless often presumed to be so placed because of a character defect attributable to the parent – typically a mother, because of careless or wanton sex – rather than because of a structural factor such as poverty.

fully competent."[4] This ever-present problem of imagining children increases when children move to new families and new communities via the state, and when assumptions about the typical allocation of authority for socialization and responsibility for dependency are upended.

When adoption created "as if" families – families matched by race, ethnicity, and religion to appear "as if" the family were "natural" or biologically related – questions about belonging could be evaded because the adoption itself was shrouded with secrecy. Today, the adoption landscape has changed. With a push toward more openness around adoption in general, with transracial and transnational adoption making the creation of families through adoption more visually obvious, and with cultural and ethnic groups demanding more consideration in and control over the process, questions about belonging take on a sense of urgency. As Kenneth Karst has noted, fears about children's socialization often drives cultural politics, and have arisen repeatedly in disputes over both gay/lesbian and transracial adoption. Those fears are compounded, he points out, when questions about the status of distinct cultural or communal groups are added to the mix, because the issue then becomes not just whether a particular child will learn socially acceptable values, but what kinds of families and communities themselves will be validated.[5]

Where the debate over the protection of cultural identity writ large often pits "multiculturalists" against "cosmopolitans," as discussed in Chapter 2, the arguments take on a distinctive twist when centered on the placement of children. Transnational and transracial adoptees are often "celebrate[d] . . . as bridges between cultures, symbols of interethnic harmony, and embodiments of postmodern cosmopolitanism."[6] That view, however, tortures the notion of cosmopolitanism. Children may belong in multiple ways to multiple groups, but must in the first instance be rooted in a set of personal attachments that provide them with a context in which to grow. Cosmopolitanism champions *choices* to unanchor oneself and to be self-conscious about transcending the ties that bind, whereas children cannot be self-conscious about making such choices (if choice is indeed involved) when they are moved without their consent or understanding.

[4] Sue Ruddick, "At the Horizons of the Subject: Neo-liberalism, Neo-Conservatism, and the Rights of the Child, Part Two: Parent, Caregiver, State," *Gender, Place, & Culture: A Journal of Feminist Geography* 14, no. 6 (2007): 627–640, 628.

[5] Kenneth Karst, "Law, Cultural Conflict, and the Socialization of Children," *California Law Review* 91, no. 4 (July 2003): 967–1028, 977–978.

[6] Tobias Hubinette, "From Orphan Trains to Babylifts: Colonial Trafficking, Empire Building, and Social Engineering," in *Outsiders Within*, eds. Jane Jeong Trenka, Julie Chinyere and Sun Yung Shin (Cambridge, MA: South End Press, 2006): 139–149, 139.

These issues converge at an interesting historical moment. Domestic and international laws and conventions protecting personal, familial, and communal identity have multiplied over the past quarter century, at the same time that laws and policies protecting children's status and recognizing children's rights have emerged in full force. Sometimes these laws and policies complement each other; at other times, they articulate rights, aspirations, and obligations that conflict. Article 3 of the United Nations Convention for the Rights of the Child,[7] for example, declares that the "best interest of the child" shall be the fundamental principle governing interpretation of the Convention as a whole; the best-interest standard is also the standard used to allocate custody in contested divorce cases under U.S. law and has been imported into most child welfare statutes. Imbuing the best-interest principle with content, however, proves difficult in specific circumstances, as there is no consensus about what that standard means in varying contexts; distinct communities and cultural groups may legitimately emphasize different child-rearing values.[8] Nor is there any straightforward means of resolving conflicts when different human rights instruments appear to confer contradictory rights or there are conflicts with domestic laws.[9] As a result, children subject to adoption and foster care, and the communities in which they are located, may be pulled in several directions at once.

To understand how communal belonging might matter for children subject to adoption and foster care, it is first necessary to understand how children's belonging is framed when the child is part of an intact family. This chapter explores how children are imagined as political subjects and looks briefly at how children's belonging is discussed in international human rights conventions. It then examines more closely how children's connections to families and communities are understood in U.S. law. Finally, it looks at how communal belonging can matter for children unanchored from families and communities and at how children's own understandings about the need for connection might be shaped in law, with the proviso that children may reject or resist such connection as well. This chapter lays the groundwork for a lengthier discussion of group rights to recognition in Chapter 2.

---

[7] Convention on the Rights of the Child, G.A. res. 44/25, annex, 44 U.N GAOR Supp. (No. 49) at 167, U.N. Doc. A/44/49 (1989), entered into force Sept. 2, 1990, www2.ohchr.org/english/law/crc.htm.

[8] Abdullah An-Na'im, "Cultural Transformation and Normative Consensus on the Best Interests of the Child," *International Journal of Law, Policy and the Family* 8, no. 1(1994): 62–81, 64.

[9] *See, e.g.,* Brian Sloan, "Conflicting Rights: English Adoption Law and the Implementation of the UNCRC" (May 16, 2011). University of Cambridge Faculty of Law Research Paper No. 30/2011; http://ssrn.com/abstract=1853385 or doi:10.2139/ssrn.1853385 (used by permission).

ATTACHING A CHILD TO FAMILY OR COMMUNITY

It seems hackneyed to observe that children need secure connections with one or more caretakers to grow into well-adjusted, productive members of any community. Nonetheless, that psychological commonplace is critical to understanding the politics of belonging for children without parents. As Nancy Rosenblum has argued,

> [p]arental authority and the shared rules of conduct maintained by their authority are crucial to developing [a child's moral sense]. . . . What we get exclusively from early relationships with parents or caretakers is love and the capacity to form intimate attachments. Emotional security does not lead inexorably to good character or good citizenship. But insecurity interferes with the formation of every social connection in which moral awareness is sharpened and translated into responsibility. [Insecurity] increases the chance that we will react to others with avoidance, fear, anger, or hostility.[10]

To say that children need stability and secure relationships is not to suggest that children must connect only with a biological parent or only with a particular community in a prescribed way: children can and do thrive in circumstances that bear no resemblance to the Ozzie and Harriet families of 1950s' American television. The point is that the need to be connected to – indeed, embedded in – a consistent set of interpersonal relationships is at the heart of discussions about adoption and foster care. "Every child needs a family" is a phrase found in the literature of virtually every organization that provides services to children, from the United Nations Children's Fund (UNICEF) and international charities such as SOS Children's Villages internationally to private and public adoption providers in the United States. As a matter of fact, this concern with providing a child with a family or, at the very least, with a secure relationship with one or more adults who provide care and unconditional love, is central to the Convention on the Rights of the Child. Its Preamble declares unequivocally that

[10] Nancy L. Rosenblum, "Democratic Families: 'The Logic of Congruence' and Political Identity," *Hofstra Law Review* 32 (2003): 145–170, 158. Rosenblum does not address issues connected to adoption or foster care. Rather, she challenges the assertion that equality in the family is essential to creating citizens who understand concepts of justice and fairness. Although equality within the family might be a laudable goal, she argues, children can develop an understanding of justice and fairness even if gender roles in the family are uneven. *See also* James G. Dwyer, *The Relationship Rights of Children* (New York: Cambridge University Press, 2006), 105: "Without a solid foundation of interconnectedness with persons who love and value us in a special way, we cannot feel secure and valuable, pursue our life projects effectively [or] achieve a sense of fulfillment."

the family, as the fundamental group of society and the natural environment for the growth and well-being of all its members and particularly children, should be afforded the necessary protection and assistance so that it can fully assume its responsibilities within the community, [and] ... the child, for the full and harmonious development of his or her personality, should grow up in a family environment, in an atmosphere of happiness, love and understanding.[11]

The emergence of a children's rights movement both in the United States and internationally largely reflects the view that placing children with nuclear families is of paramount importance if the child is to develop into a fully realized adult.

At the level of international human rights, there is strong support for creating avenues that allow children to develop and maintain stable relationships with permanent caregivers. Many of the rights articulated for children in the Convention on the Rights of the Child, for example, specifically respond to children's needs to make secure emotional connections – they acknowledge children's dependency and facilitate the creation and maintenance of affective attachments.[12] What that rights discourse does not address, however, is the dilemma that arises when placing a child with an immediate family – as in the process of adoption – requires severing ties to a larger community or extended kinship network with whom that child may be interested in maintaining ties.

The panoply of rights critical to understanding children's belonging may be broadly captured by the term *identity rights*, referring to rights that allow a child to make and maintain connections with families or communities. In the Convention on the Rights of the Child, these concerns range from guaranteeing a child the right "to know and be cared for by his or her parents," to "preserv[ing] his or her identity, including nationality, name and family relations," and, where a child is separated from one or both parents, "maintain[ing] personal relations and direct contact with both parents on a regular basis, except

---

[11] Convention on the Rights of the Child, Preamble, *supra* n. 7. The UN General Assembly has recently adopted "Guidelines for the Alternative Care of Children" to reiterate this position. That document, however, appears to strongly endorse community-based care for children over the alternative of transnational adoption. Guidelines for the Alternative Care of Children, A/Res/64/142 (Feb. 24, 2010); www.crin.org/docs/Guidelines-English.pdf. This issue is discussed in Chapter 5.

[12] These are often referred to as "relational" rights because they are grounded in relationships to others and tie children to caregivers in complicated ways. *See* Martha Minow and Mary Lyndon Shanley, "Relational Rights and Responsibilities: Revisioning the Family in Political Theory and Law," *Hypatia* 11, no. 1 (Winter, 1996): 4–30. *See also* Mary Lyndon Shanley, *Making Babies, Making Families: What Matters Most in an Age of Reproductive Technologies, Surrogacy, Adoption, and Same-Sex and Unwed Parents* (Boston: Beacon Press, 2001) and Dwyer, *supra* n. 10.

if it is contrary to the child's best interests."[13] Some commentators have read these and other provisions in the Convention as potentially conferring a right to cultural or communal identity for children as well.[14] Rights and interests of this nature provide stability for the families and communities of which children are members as well as providing security for children themselves.[15] No document formally articulates children's rights in the United States; the United States has signed but not yet ratified the Convention. Indeed, as discussed later, children in the United States have relatively few rights that stand in isolation from the rights of their caretakers.

Articulating identity interests as rights for children, however, is problematic for several reasons, and is at least as difficult as articulating identity rights for groups, discussed in Chapter 2. First, *identity* for both children and adults is an inherently fluid and ambiguous concept. Children's identities are particularly malleable; those identities are, as Stuart Hall has observed about identity in general, "never completed, never finished."[16] Second, because children are "inevitably dependent,"[17] their rights are deeply entwined with the rights of their caregivers – typically their biological parents – whose decisions have indelible effects on identity.[18] In most jurisdictions, for example, there are few restrictions on a legal caregiver's choices to move children in and out of communities or even in and out of affective relationships.[19]

For all of these reasons, it is difficult to frame a specific right of a child to shape his or her identity, and it is even more complicated if that right might

---

[13] Convention on the Rights of the Child, *supra* n. 7, Articles 7, 8, & 9.

[14] George A. Stewart, "Interpreting the Child's Right to Identity in the UN Convention on the Rights of the Child," *Family Law Quarterly* 26 (1992–1993): 221–233, 225–226. *See also* Sonia Harris-Short, "Listening to 'the Other'? The Convention on the Rights of the Child," *Melbourne Journal of International Law* 2 (2001): 304–350 (discussing the need for cultural sensitivity in interpreting children's rights).

[15] Joel Feinberg, "The Child's Right to an Open Future," in *Whose Child? Children's Rights, Parental Authority, and State Power*, eds. William Aiken and Hugh LaFollette (Totowa, NJ: Rowman & Littlefield, 1980); reprinted in Feinberg, *Freedom & Fulfillment: Philosophical Essays* (Princeton, NJ: Princeton University Press, 1994): 76–97. Feinberg has argued in favor of recognizing the right of children to "an open future." Those rights obligate adults to deal with children in ways that allow children to become autonomous in the future. In other words, adults may not treat children in ways that close off significant life opportunities. A similar position was articulated by Justice Douglas in his dissent in *Wisconsin v. Yoder* (1972), discussed *infra*.

[16] Stuart Hall, "Old and New Identities, Old and New Ethnicities," in *Culture, Globalization and the World-System*, ed. Anthony D. King (Minneapolis: University of Minnesota Press, 1997): 41–68, 47.

[17] Martha A. Fineman, *The Autonomy Myth: A Theory of Dependency* (New York: The Free Press, 2004): 35.

[18] Ruddick, *supra* n. 4.

[19] *See, e.g., Michael H. v. Gerald D.*, discussed *infra*.

be invoked to create or maintain ties to a family or community of origin after a child has been placed elsewhere through adoption or foster care. The issue becomes particularly difficult if maintaining such connections may appear to limit the choices of a child's new caregiver or adoptive family. As Barbara Woodhouse has observed, there is substantial discomfort with the idea of "preserving children's cultural or ethnic identities [because it seems] to conflict with liberal conceptions of parents' and children's individual rights, ideals of colorblind equality, and a peculiarly American kind of liberty embracing the freedom to reinvent oneself as a new citizen of a new world."[20]

Although children are often absent from discussions about identity politics and multiculturalism at a meta-level, there is nonetheless a lively conversation about the identity interests of children in the adoption context. Some scholars, such as Woodhouse and Stewart, argue that children's interests in their cultural or communal background should be among the constellation of rights or interests recognized in law and policy.[21] Woodhouse, for example, suggests that a child should have a legally cognizable right "to know and explore, commensurate with her evolving capacity for autonomy, her identity as a member of the family and group into which she was born."[22] Others, such as Carol Sanger, find that notion unworkable, as children's daily ties to a "community" are likely to be amorphous and presume too much about how fixed communal boundaries are.[23] Still others, such as Ya'ir Ronen, would recognize a child's identity right but limit it to protecting only ties "meaningful" to the child – those ties of interdependence to significant others, primarily immediate caretakers. Ronen, in fact, argues that any broader reading harms children: "Preferential protection of the child's ties to a minority culture or to individuals affiliated to that culture . . . violat[es] the [child's] right to identity . . . signifying a politicized selectivity of compassion."[24]

Ultimately, it may be impossible to frame an interest in identity and origins as a fully articulated right for children. Nonetheless, recognizing such an interest and accounting for that interest in some way in the legal regimes

[20] Barbara Bennett Woodhouse, "'Are You My Mother?': Conceptualizing Children's Identity Rights in Transracial Adoptions," *Duke Journal of Gender Law and Policy* 2 (1995): 107–129, 108.
[21] *Id.*, and Stewart, *supra* n. 14.
[22] Woodhouse, *supra* n. 20 at 129.
[23] Carol Sanger, "Placing the Adoptive Self," in "*Nomos XLIV: Child, Family, and State*," eds. Stephen Macedo and Iris Marion Young (New York: New York University Press, 2003): 58–97, 66–72. Sanger may underestimate the importance of such connections as children mature and are better able to understand their positions vis-à-vis a particular community, although she acknowledges that taking factors such as race or ethnicity into account may matter depending on the age and situation of a particular child.
[24] Ya'ir Ronen, "Redefining the Child's Right to Identity," *International Journal of Law, Policy, and the Family* 18, n. 2 (2004): 147–177, 148.

governing adoption and foster care is critical if children's well-being is to be realized. That position can be adopted without necessarily framing the interest as a right. As Woodhouse notes in arguing for the recognition of a right, adults should be seen as trustees for children's interests, which requires that all adults concerned with the child's welfare – "adoptive and biological parents, cultural and racial groups, states and nations [–] have a duty to recognize and protect the child's access to this heritage, as well as recognizing and protecting the young child's need for continuity in her psychological or social family."[25] Even without reaching Woodhouse's conclusions about the need for rights in this context, understanding adults as fiduciaries entrusted with children's welfare means that those adults must be attuned to children's interests in understanding, and if necessary coming to terms with, their origins.

It may seem odd to retreat from the language of rights in arguing for a greater recognition of children's interests, but children's rights are a hybrid animal, deeply entwined with and often subsumed within, the rights and obligations of caretakers. Understanding how those interests are imbricated is fundamental to understanding the needs of children whose circumstances place them in foster or adoptive care. It is axiomatic in American family law (and in the family law of all liberal democracies, for that matter) that parents have the primary authority to determine a child's upbringing. In the United States, the Constitution has long protected the rights of parents to rear their children as they see fit, absent a showing of harm to the child. Thus, the United States Supreme Court has protected the right of parents to send their children to parochial school or to study in a foreign language,[26] to withdraw children from public school after the age of fourteen,[27] to limit visitation with grandparents,[28] or even (in restricted circumstances) to sever ties to an alleged biological parent.[29] All of these cases have endorsed broad parental authority to shape their children's lives.

---

[25] Woodhouse, *supra* n. 20 at 128.
[26] *Pierce v. Society of Sisters*, 268 U.S. 510 (1925); *Meyer v. Nebraska*, 262 U.S. 390 (1923).
[27] *Wisconsin v. Yoder*, 406 U.S. 205 (1972).
[28] *Troxel v. Granville*, 530 U.S. 57 (2000).
[29] *Michael H. v. Gerald D.*, 491 U.S. 110 (1989) *Michael H.* involved a dispute between a woman and her husband, the child's presumptive father, and the alleged biological father, Michael, with whom she had had an affair. California law at the time created an irrebuttable presumption of paternity in a woman's husband when a child was born during the course of a valid marriage; the woman in this case had not divorced her husband, although she had moved in with Michael before and for three years after the child's birth (off and on). The presumption of the husband's paternity contained in California law precluded anyone other than the mother or her husband, the presumptive father, from challenging the husband's paternity, and when the child's mother chose to reunite with her husband and raise her daughter in that family, Michael was barred from introducing evidence of his paternity, either biological or psychological.

Interestingly, many of these cases have been tied into parents' preferences for ethnic or religious belonging; they illustrate how the family is viewed by the state as the channel through which appropriate socialization can be secured. The earliest Supreme Court cases articulating parental rights to rear their children as they see fit involved efforts by state legislatures to limit children's attachments to suspect ethnic or religious groups. In *Meyer v. Nebraska*, the Court limited the efforts of the Nebraska legislature, shortly after World War I, to require that children of German immigrants be educated in English. Shortly thereafter, in *Pierce v. Society of Sisters*, the Court held that the Oregon legislature's fears about Catholic children's political loyalties could not justify a law altogether prohibiting the education of children in parochial schools.

Wisconsin v. Yoder is particularly compelling for the ways in which both the majority and the dissent struggled to define the right of parents to raise their children in accordance with a distinct set of beliefs, and to evaluate the importance of children's belonging to a particular cultural – in this case, religious – community. In *Yoder*, the U.S. Supreme Court excused Amish parents from complying with Wisconsin's compulsory school law when those parents sought to remove their children from public schools at the age of fourteen. The parents argued that by fourteen, their children had been sufficiently educated to succeed in the Amish community, and that further public schooling undermined their very way of life:

> [Requiring Amish children to attend a public high school] not only . . . places Amish children in an environment hostile to Amish beliefs with increasing emphasis on competition in class, work, and sports and with pressure to conform to the styles, manners, and ways of the peer group, but [it also] takes them away from their community, physically and emotionally, during the crucial and formative adolescent period of life.[30]

The Supreme Court accepted the parents' argument that Amish adolescents had to be removed from the "worldly" influence of public high school in order to "acquire Amish attitudes favoring manual work and self-reliance and the specific skills needed to perform the adult role of an Amish farmer or housewife."[31]

Yoder was decided on the grounds of religious freedom for the parents, who argued that the Wisconsin law violated their rights under the First Amendment's Free Exercise Clause. At the same time, the opinion was a paean to Amish culture and illustrates how the legal regime governing the family has

[30] *Yoder, supra* n. 27, at 211.
[31] *Id.* at 221.

been invoked to shape communal belonging. Justice Burger, for the majority, spoke glowingly of the Amish way of life:

> Whatever their idiosyncrasies as seen by the majority, this record strongly shows that the Amish community has been a highly successful social unit within our society, even if apart from the conventional "mainstream." Its members are productive and very law-abiding members of society; they reject public welfare in any of its usual modern forms.[32]

Yoder thus underscored the importance of protecting the community in which the children and their families were embedded – so long as that community was, as the Court noted, "productive and law-abiding." Indeed, the majority opinion acknowledged that the community's well-being itself *depended on* sequestering children from the world at large, and upheld the authority of the children's parents to segregate their children as necessary to secure the community's continued existence.

Of course, the Court reached this conclusion by protecting the right of the parents to rear their children without undue interference, whereas children subject to adoptive or foster care placement, as noted earlier, are typically in that position because their parents are no longer available to provide care. In addition, the community at issue in *Yoder* had easily definable boundaries, unlike some of the groups who are now claiming interests in the placement of children by virtue of ascriptive traits such as race or ethnicity. Nonetheless, the case stands as an important statement of the value that the law might place on the importance of children to a community's continued existence.

The dissenting opinion took issue with the majority's willingness to allow parents to dictate a child's life course by limiting the child's education. Justice Douglas argued that children should be heard on matters that could dramatically affect their futures:

> While the parents, absent dissent, normally speak for the entire family, the education of the child is a matter on which the child will often have decided views. He may want to be a pianist or an astronaut or an oceanographer. To do so he will have to break from the Amish tradition.[33]

Moreover, Justice Douglas disdained the majority's focus on extolling the virtues of an Amish way of life, noting that "the law and order record of this Amish group of people is quite irrelevant. A religion is a religion irrespective of what the misdemeanor or felony records of its members might be."[34] The

---

[32] *Id.* at 222.
[33] *Id.* at 245.
[34] *Id.*

determinative question for Douglas was the extent to which parents could make decisions that limited the child's life options, a concern shared, incidentally, by three of the six Justices in the majority:[35]

> If a parent keeps his child out of school beyond the grade school, then the child will be forever barred from entry into the new and amazing world of diversity that we have today.... It is the student's judgment, not his parents', that is essential if we are to give full meaning to what we have said about the Bill of Rights and of the right of students to be masters of their own destiny. If he is harnessed to the Amish way of life by those in authority over him, and if his education is truncated, his entire life may be stunted and deformed.[36]

Yoder nonetheless continues to stand today as a statement about parental authority to shape a child's cultural identity and the law's role in protecting the boundaries of both family and community authority.

As a general rule, of course, it makes sense for the law to defer to parental wishes in child-rearing; to develop secure and healthy relationships with children, parents need significant latitude to rear their children in accordance with their own values and the values of the identity groups to which they belong. This strong tradition of deference to parental decisions about upbringing means that courts and legislatures in the United States have had few opportunities to specifically address children's identity interests independent of parental wishes.[37]

In only one case aside from its 1989 ruling on the Indian Child Welfare Act in the aforementioned *Mississippi Band of Choctaws v. Holyfield* has the U.S. Supreme Court addressed concerns about the importance of a cultural

---

[35] The case was decided by only seven of the nine justices on the Court. Three of the six justices in the majority observed that the record provided no evidence that the children either disagreed with their parents or had their life opportunities unnecessarily limited by their parents' decisions. Those three justices were thus unwilling to join Justice Douglas's dissent. Had they found such evidence, their concurring opinions suggest that the decision might have swung in the other direction, allowing children to override parental prerogatives.

[36] *Yoder, supra* n. 27, at 245–246.

[37] Aside from cases arising under the Indian Child Welfare Act discussed in Chapter 4, courts have been asked to evaluate the importance of communal ties primarily in contested custody cases where biological parents are at odds over a child's upbringing. Unlike cases involving adoption or foster care placements where parents are typically altogether absent from the placement decision, parents in contested custody cases presumptively have equal claims to custody of the child. Claims of community in those cases take a seat behind parental interests, if they are noticed at all, and the courts rely solely on a best-interest analysis to resolve those disputes.

community in a child's upbringing.[38] In the 1984 case of *Palmore v. Sidoti*, the Supreme Court rejected a father's claim that a mother should lose custody of her daughter because the child's background differed from that of the community to which her mother allegedly was exposing her. The case involved an effort by a Caucasian father to secure custody of his Caucasian daughter when his ex-wife became involved with, and later married, an African American man.[39] The trial court, as the Supreme Court noted, had granted the father's request on the basis that the mother "ha[d] chosen for herself, and for her child, a lifestyle unacceptable to the father *and to society*. . . . The child . . . is, or at school age will be, subject to environmental pressures not of her choice."[40] The Supreme Court emphatically reversed the trial court's decision, holding that although

> [i]t would ignore reality to suggest that racial and ethnic prejudices do not exist, or that all manifestations of those prejudices have been eliminated. . . . [t]he question is whether the reality of private biases and the possible injury they might inflict are permissible considerations for removal of an infant child from the custody of its natural mother. We have little difficulty concluding that they are not. The Constitution cannot control such prejudices, but neither can it tolerate them. Private biases may be outside the reach of the law, but the law cannot, directly or indirectly, give them effect.[41]

In other words, the Court in *Sidoti*, as in *Yoder*, endorsed the position that a fit parent could make choices about where to raise a child, even if the child might be subjected to stresses associated with living in a racially mixed household and despite the father's claim that the child would be stigmatized as a result.

A recent case from the Eleventh Circuit further illustrates the imperative that courts feel to permit parents to shape a child's belonging. *Furnes v. Reeves* involved a custody dispute between parents living in Norway and the United States, respectively, and required the federal court to interpret the International Child Abduction Remedies Act.[42] The couple's five-year-old child was born in Norway and had lived in Norway all of her life. Following a divorce obtained in Norway, which granted joint custody to the mother and her Norwegian ex-husband, the mother moved to the United States with her daughter. The court

---

[38] Of course, most cases raising such claims will not be found in federal courts, as the vast majority of domestic relations cases are handled in state court systems and do not raise constitutional concerns.

[39] *Palmore v. Sidoti*, 466 U.S. 429 (1984).

[40] *Id.* at 431, emphasis added.

[41] *Id.* at 433.

[42] *Furnes v. Reeves*, 362 F. 3d 702 (2004).

found that the custodial father had a right, under Norwegian law recognized by the United States, to veto the mother's decision to move their child out of the country without his consent. The court noted that under a valid custody order, the father was entitled to

> ensure that [the child] will speak Norwegian, participate in Norwegian culture, enroll in the Norwegian school system, and have Norwegian friends. That is, [the father] effectively can decide that [his daughter] will *be Norwegian*. The right to determine a child's language, nationality, and cultural identity is plainly a right "relating to the care of the person of the child" within the meaning of the Convention.[43]

These rights did not unduly denigrate the rights of the child's American mother, where the custody dispute had been fully adjudicated by a Norwegian court with proper jurisdiction. The case thus turned on the rights of parents – even where they disagreed – to determine a child's identity, rather than recognizing any independent right of a child to connect to or maintain ties with a culture of origin.

These cases reinforce the position that decisions about where to raise a child should be made by those closest to the child – ordinarily, the child's biological parents. An intact family provides the child with his or her cultural (racial, ethnic, or religious) bearings. Indeed, as noted earlier, Carol Sanger has noted that children's connections with families ordinarily are more important than vague ties to communities, which provide few supports for everyday living.[44] In *Palmore*, as noted, the Court refused to allow the modification of a child custody order solely because the child might encounter difficulties growing up in a transracial environment, especially where the trial court had specifically found "no issue[s] as to either party's devotion to the child, adequacy of housing facilities, or respectability of the new spouse of either parent."[45] In other words, unless a parent is clearly shown to be unfit, the Court concluded that the state should not throw its power into determining where and how a child should

---

[43] *Id.* at 716.

[44] For this reason, both Sanger and Shanley have argued strongly for deferring to a parent's – particularly a mother's – choices about where a child should be placed in adoption. Sanger, *supra* n. 23; Mary Lyndon Shanley, "Toward New Understandings of Adoption: Individuals and Relationships in Transracial and Open Adoption," in "*Nomos XLIV: Child, Family, and State,*" eds. Stephen Macedo and Iris Marion Young (New York: New York University Press, 2003). That discussion, however, centers primarily on voluntary adoptions – where a child is voluntarily surrendered at birth – rather than adoptions resulting from an involuntary termination of parental rights in state child welfare systems, which raise a different set of issues. Of course, even in an involuntary proceeding, it may be important to give at least some consideration to a preference expressed by a biological parent, depending on the circumstances of the case.

[45] *Palmore v. Sidoti, supra* n. 56 at 430.

be raised – a position that finds support in most commentary on children's rights.[46]

THE UNANCHORED CHILD

If a child's parents are not available, however, determining where a child should be placed becomes more problematic. When a child is subject to adoption or foster care, how should the default calculus be changed? A child removed from parents typically goes into the custody of the state if a voluntary or involuntary termination occurs during the course of a child welfare proceeding or into a private agency licensed by the state if the child is surrendered for adoption outside of a child welfare system. It is in that moment – as the child passes from the care of a biological parent into the custody of the state or an agency – that many communities want to be heard.[47] Unless the adoption involves an American Indian child, there is no system in place to refer the child to families within a particular community.

The issue here is not just whether the community in which the child is originally situated should be consulted about or empowered to control the placement of the child. An equally important question is whether the child him or herself should be granted a voice in determining where he or she belongs. The claims invoked in such a context are ambiguous: children's dependent status means that they cannot assert interests as adults do. Furthermore, fashioning such an interest as a right, for the reasons noted earlier, might well be unworkable.[48] As Sue Ruddick has observed, children occupy a "ventriloquist position [in] . . . relation to liberal ideas of [the subject and of] rights . . . [which] has produced a bizarre topography around the child – a ballooning exteriority of groups who speak for the child and an internally

[46] *See also Troxel v. Granville*, 530 U.S. 57 (2000). For an interesting, if ultimately unconvincing, counterargument, *see* Dwyer, *supra* n. 10, who argues that children should have a cognizable legal interest in being embedded in a family that can provide a secure and loving environment. In making that argument, Dwyer substitutes a best-interest analysis for children's voices: he would make licensing parents a requirement. In fact, Dwyer endorses adoption precisely because it provides a check on who may be a parent.

[47] In the United States, foster care systems are run by individual states, who assume guardianship of the child and exercise legal authority over the child's temporary or permanent placement; adoptions from the foster care system are administered by states. All states also allow independent or private adoptions subject to varying degrees of regulation, that is, some require that adopters work through a licensed agency while others allow the adoption to be handled by an attorney.

[48] For a discussion of whether the cultural rights of children should be recognized in general, which recognizes many of the complications noted throughout this book, *see* Laura Zagrebelsky, "Rights, Children, and Culture," manuscript on file with author.

differentiated interiority that filters children's wishes through adult interpretive strategies."[49]

To sidestep the conundrum posed by children's immaturity, courts and policy makers simply invoke the "best interest of the child" standard to guide them in making foster and adoptive placements. The problem, of course, is that the best-interest standard is culturally dependent; what constitutes a child's best interest can vary considerably from community to community.[50] Philip Alston has pointed out, for example, that

> in some highly industrialized countries, the child's best interests are "obviously" best served by policies that emphasize autonomy and individuality to the greatest possible extent. In more traditional societies, the links to family and the local community might be considered to be of paramount importance and the principle that: "the best interests of the child" shall prevail [must] therefore be interpreted as requiring the sublimation of the individual child's preferences to the interests of the family or even the extended family.[51]

In making decisions affecting a child's welfare, authorities ordinarily look to local conventions to give content to their judgments about what placement will serve a child's best interests. Nonetheless, "the choice of criteria is inherently value-laden; all too often there is no consensus about what values should inform this choice. These problems are not unique to children's policies, but they are especially acute in this context because children themselves often cannot speak for their own interests."[52]

When the child is moving from family to family, community to community, or nation to nation, then, conflict over what constitutes a child's best interest is inevitable: deciding who has *authority* to make decisions about what placement serves a child's best interests becomes a tangled political dispute that must be settled prior to resolving a particular case on its own facts. Disagreement over what constitutes the child's best interest becomes particularly charged when, as in the adoption and foster care context, children are likely to be moved from less affluent to more affluent communities or nations. In these circumstances, originating communities may legitimately feel resentment as their children appear to be whisked away to more privileged environments. Children, too, may yearn for a connection to their past, particularly if their

---

[49] Ruddick, *supra* n. 4 at 639.

[50] Philip Alston, "The Best Interests Principle: Toward a Reconciliation of Culture and Human Rights," *International Journal of Law, Policy, and the Family* 8, no. 1 (1994): 1–25. *See also* An-Naim, *supra* n. 8.

[51] Alston, *id.* at 5.

[52] *Id.*

adoptive status is clear because of racial or ethnic differences from adoptive parents.

For these reasons, it is simply insufficient to ignore the child's origins in adoption and foster care placements. As anthropologist Barbara Yngvesson has eloquently argued in discussing the issue of belonging for transnationally adopted children, children are tied in complicated ways to their beginnings. They have connections beyond their adoptive families that are both inside and outside, and it is imperative to provide them with both social and biogenetic narratives.[53] Woodhouse makes the same point in arguing that children's interests in their origins should be protected in law:

> Race and culture of origin, no matter how hard to define . . . matter to children and therefore should matter in adoption law. They may well be contingent and socially constructed, but children's awareness of race and group identity indicate that they are "real" for the purposes [of] . . . fostering and protecti[ng] . . . children's identity.[54]

This is not to say that the child's origins are or should be the concluding factor in determining where a child should be placed or by whom a child should be raised. Rather, it is an argument for recognizing the child's own experience and creating avenues that will allow the child to come to terms with that experience. Acknowledging the child's interests in defining his or her identity along multiple dimensions means that any debate over children's cultural and communal identity must at the very least give serious consideration to familial and communal interests in maintaining connections to a child as he or she is settled into a new family.[55]

Of course, giving children a voice in shaping their belonging raises interesting complications on its own. Children shape their identities through interactions with others, so *where* children are located is critically important for

[53] Barbara Yngvesson, *Belonging in an Adopted World* (Chicago: University of Chicago Press, 2010): 12 *et seq.* Yngvesson's work is discussed in greater depth particularly in Chapter 5.

[54] Woodhouse, *supra* n. 20 at 114.

[55] It may seem remiss not to talk about the interest of adoptive parents in shaping the child's identity because adoptive parents acquire the full panoply of parental rights on adoption and therefore legally have full authority to determine where and with what values a child will be raised. But cultural groups are typically interested in securing a voice during the adoption or foster care placement process *before* the rights of adoptive parents vest. For a child, the interest in understanding her origins may arise at a number of points: during the initial placement process, while in foster care, and/or subsequent to a formal adoption. It is, of course, critical to be attentive to the rights of adoptive parents, who acquire all of the rights of biological parents, it is nonetheless important to recognize that adopted children, no matter how loved and wanted, have experienced losses; that fact provides a basis for slightly shifting the position of the adoptive parent's rights to ameliorate that loss, especially when the adoption is in process.

imparting a set of cultural or communal connections. Culture is acquired through lived experience and, as Barbara Yngvesson notes, while children are "rerooted" on adoption, it is a multiple belonging that may involve both belonging and not belonging in different directions.[56] A child adopted from Bangladesh, for example, may feel herself, from time to time, an outsider in an adoptive family living in an all-white suburb of Cleveland, but she will not be Bangladeshi either. She will create her own identity by moving among various sites of belonging, and any identity interests she lays claim to must be framed to reflect that process. Although a community may seek to sustain or create a connection with a child, the child's own interests in creating her identity must be accounted for. In some cases, those interests may run counter to a community's expectations.

DISRUPTING FAMILY AND GROUP IDENTITY

Cultural and communal groups seeking a voice in the placement of their children can often make the compelling argument that children are their very future. But children actively shape their identities from the very beginning of their lives: "At a time so early that the questions of how to socialize and educate the child have not even arisen yet, the twig will be bent in a certain definite direction."[57] Wherever children grow up, they can be counted on to do nothing so much as push the envelope of belonging and test the boundaries of communal norms. More than adults, children are consistently changing and, as Allison James and her colleagues have noted, that fact makes them an enigma; "they are unstable, systematically disruptive and uncontained."[58] Children "'habitually and disturbingly emigrate from the world of their parents'."[59] In the same manner, they inevitably emigrate from the values of the communities in which they are located, even if they have never been moved from that community.

To say that children will unsettle norms and challenge communal understandings, however, is not to suggest that communities are not justified in seeking some form of consideration in the placement of "their" children.

---

[56] Yngvesson, *supra* n. 53. Yngvesson first discussed these issues in Barbara Yngvesson, "'Going 'Home': Adoption, Loss of Bearings, and the Mythology of Roots," *Social Text* 21, no. 1 (Spring 2003), 7–27. *See also* Derek Kirton, *"Race" Ethnicity, and Adoption* (Buckingham, UK: Open University Press, 2000).

[57] Feinberg, *supra* n. 15 at 238.

[58] Allison James, Chris Jenks, and Alan Prout, *Theorizing Childhood* (Cambridge: Polity Press, 1998): 198.

[59] Karst, *supra* n. 5, 990–991, *citing* Peter L. Berger, et al., *The Homeless Mind: Modernization and Consciousness* (New York: Random House, 1973): 92.

What it does do is sound a warning note about the expectations that legitimately may be placed on children as vectors of cultures, and to carve out a space that will allow children themselves to be heard. Disadvantaged communities can make powerful statements about how dominant communities have mistreated them, often directly through the appropriation of their children. At the same time, in the debate over adoption and foster care, it is well to be wary of the romance associated with the idea of recreating a cultural community in a pristine form as though such communities are capable of being easily revived and reestablished;[60] it is equally unrealistic to assume that children can be counted on to carry forward any set of communal norms in an unadulterated form.

One of the central criticisms leveled at proponents of group rights to cultural identity has been that communities may unduly constrain the actions of their members in the name of an elusive (and sometimes nonconsensual) ideal of cultural integrity, as discussed in Chapter 2. Scholars of childhood have expressed similar concerns: Sharon Stephens has pointed out that

> [w]hile many argue that international cultural rights discourses further the best interests of children themselves, in some contexts these discourses may be linked to significant risks to the physical, psychological, and social well-being of children. . . . [I]t might be argued that children . . . have rights not to be constrained within exclusionary cultural identities and not to have their bodies and minds appropriated as the unprotected terrain on which adult battles are fought.[61]

Veena Das has argued that cultural identity rights for children must include the right to engage in "cultural innovation," similar to the right to "cultural dissent" that Mahdavi Sunder suggests is a necessary corrective for women

---

[60] The idea that a culture or community that has been diminished may be "revived" raises interesting questions in itself. Communities and cultures change, not always in ways acceptable to all or even a significant majority of its members. Indeed, as Jack Donnelly has noted in his work on human rights, a community may "choose" to die out – that is, its members may choose not to follow traditional ways or to change their norms so that, in the end, there is no cultural community to claim distinction. Jack Donnelly, *Universal Human Rights in Theory and Practice*, 2nd ed. (Ithaca: Cornell University Press, 2003): 218 *et seq.* It is difficult to imagine a "people" "choosing" to disappear; such a disappearance is more likely to occur through the (non) choice to assimilate or by (sometimes) unjust pressures exogenous to the group – but it is still possible to imagine that a group could quite consciously decide to consign some norms permanently to the dustbin. That notion of choice, however, doesn't work when talking about children, who have no choice to stay within or leave a particular community.

[61] Sharon Stephens, ed., *Children and the Politics of Culture* (Princeton, NJ: Princeton University Press, 1995): 4.

located in cultural communities in which women's status is diminished.[62] As Sunder notes, "Law's valiant effort to rescue a culture's *nomos* – by effectively taking a culture back to a time when it was more distinct, insular and internally homogeneous – significantly diminishes the possibilities for greater [individual] autonomy and equality within culture."[63] Richard Ford, too, has argued for the right to *resist* the strictures imposed by a normative community.[64] Thus, as children are moved among families and communities, it is important to understand that children must be granted the space to pursue their own modes of belonging.

As noted, Justice Douglas's dissent in the *Yoder* case was explicit about the need to listen to children – and, in some cases, to support their dissent – as they create their lives, a position endorsed in the two concurring opinions in that case. Justice Stewart observed that the case "in no way involve[d] any questions regarding the right of the children of Amish parents to attend public high schools, or any other institutions of learning, if they wish[ed] to do so," acknowledging that different facts might raise that "interesting and important" question.[65] Justice White, joined by Justices Stewart and Brennan, agreed, noting that parents had no authority to "replace state educational requirements with their own idiosyncratic views of what knowledge a child needs to be a productive and happy member of society."[66] White expounded on the nature of the State's interest in educating children with particular attention to enhancing the child's life options:

> In the present case, the State ... is ... attempting to nurture and develop the human potential of its children, whether Amish or non-Amish: to expand their knowledge, broaden their sensibilities, kindle their imagination, foster a spirit of free inquiry, and increase their human understanding and tolerance. It is possible that most Amish children will wish to continue living the rural life of their parents, in which case their training at home will adequately equip them for their future role. Others, however, may wish to become nuclear physicists, ballet dancers, computer programmers, or historians, and for these occupations, formal training will be necessary.... A State has a legitimate interest not only in seeking to develop the latent talents of its children, but also in seeking to prepare them for the lifestyle that they may

---

[62] Veena Das, cited in Hall, *infra*, n. 71 at 224; Mahdavi Sunder, "Cultural Dissent," *Stanford Law Review* 54, no. 3 (Dec. 2001): 495–567.
[63] Sunder, *id.* at 549.
[64] Richard T. Ford, *Racial Culture: A Critique* (Princeton, NJ: Princeton University Press, 2005).
[65] *Yoder, supra* n. 27 at 238.
[66] *Id.* at 241.

later choose, or at least to provide them with an option other than the life they have led in the past.[67]

Like Justice Stewart, however, Justice White found no evidence in the record that upholding the parents' wishes either unduly limited the life options of the children concerned or ignored any children's wishes contrary to those of their parents.

Suggesting that children should be granted the ability to dissent from cultural or communal expectations may seem a bit far afield from the central discussion of the interests of groups and/or children to create or maintain connections. After all, the concern about cultural and communal identity that so stridently threads itself through foster care and adoption debates is in *which* community the child will find himself embedded – that of his community of origin or the community to which he or she is moved by foster or adoptive parents. In either case, the child is subjected to the strictures of a cultural community. Nonetheless, the idea that children should not be unduly burdened by the obligations of culture and community has unique significance for adopted and fostered children, and is closely tied to the idea of making or sustaining connections. Even in the most attentive families, adoptive and foster children often grow up acutely aware of a disjunction between themselves and their adopted families and communities, and they may seek guidance from a community of origin as they steer a path to maturity. Alternately, they may feel pressured to represent a culture of origin – by adoptive parents or by the communities of origin themselves – regardless of their own perceived attachment to that community.[68] There are, therefore, distinctive reasons to be concerned about the expectations placed on such children to carry forward a set of cultural or communal values with which they are not familiar. Even if children are imagined as carriers of culture, they become such carriers only through enculturation: they do not carry culture in their bones.[69] Children become adept at crossing cultural boundaries and often become acculturated in more than one group, plotting their own belonging in several dimensions.[70]

Studies of children living in immigrant communities illustrate the complex ways that children negotiate their identities in the space between their parents' cultural groups and the culture outside of family and community boundaries,

---

[67] *Id.* at 240–241.

[68] *See, e.g.,* Kirton, *supra* n. 56.

[69] Annie Bunting, "Elijah and Ishmael: Assessing Cultural Identity in Canadian Child Custody Decisions," *Family Court Review* 42 (July 2004): 471–484, 473–475.

[70] *See generally,* H. Fogg-Davis, *The Ethics of Transracial Adoption* (Ithaca, NY: Cornell University Press, 2002).

often reconfiguring communal norms. In her study of second-generation Sikh teenagers in Britain, Kathleen Hall observed the ways in which these children parsed their own identities – combining Bengali and Celtic music, for example – and concluded that their cultural identities were both multiple *and* hybrid, as they could both move with relative ease among groups and create a unique cultural space in between groups.[71]

The situation is similar for adopted children, but is complicated by the fact that in many cases, adopted children may have never lived in the cultural community of their birth; they may have been adopted as infants or as children too young to remember those beginnings. Their negotiation thus may be between the cultural community in which they have been raised and the *idea* of the culture from which they originated. Just as immigrant children must self-consciously pursue an ethnic identity as they move into the second and third generation,[72] adopted children may have difficulty creating or connecting to a cultural or communal identity that is not remotely familiar to them – in which they have not grown up – whatever their desires for connection may be.[73]

Of course, the situation differs for each child. Children adopted at or shortly after birth have experiences that differ significantly from children adopted later in their lives. In addition, children in foster care may spend months or even years moving in and out of cultural groups or communities while decisions about permanent placements are being made. Children placed in new families may leave siblings and other family members behind with whom they hope to maintain relations or to reconnect later in life. These facts of belonging, partially belonging, and not belonging, as children in adoptive and foster care move between cultural and communal spaces, must be fully considered as the law is invoked to allow children to traverse boundaries.

CHILDREN'S COMMUNAL BELONGING, RIGHTS, AND THE LAW

Legal regimes centrally define how persons are connected to families, communities, and nations. The law performs a critical role in children's lives

---

[71] Kathleen Hall, "'There's a Time to Act English and a Time to Act Indian': The Politics of Identity Among British-Sikh Teenagers," in *Children and the Politics of Culture*, ed. Sharon Stephens, *supra* n. 61: 243–264. Hall points out that these are not unbounded choices to live in one or another cultural community. She notes that these children ultimately run into divides that are unbridgeable: "the boundary between English and Indian is ultimately immutable . . . drawn in the relations of domination and subordination in British society," 260.

[72] *See, e.g.,* Alison Dundes Renteln, *The Cultural Defense* (New York: Oxford University Press, 2004).

[73] Kirton, *supra* n. 56.

by assigning responsibility for children's dependency and shaping children's belonging at the most intimate levels. But the law is often at cross-purposes with itself. As Martha Minow points out, the law tends to set up competing rather than combined or complementary categories of belonging: either one is a citizen or not a citizen, a parent or not a parent.[74] How the law shapes belonging for children subject to adoption or foster care varies depending on the circumstances – whether a placement is temporary or permanent, whether an adoption is voluntary or involuntary, whether a placement is transracial or transnational – and in each circumstance the concept of communal identity sounds a different note.

One of the problems of using the law to create identity categories lies in the fact that whereas in the real world, identities are incomplete and mutable, an identity once articulated in the law tends to become frozen.[75] For this reason, some prudence is required when invoking the law to create modes of belonging for children to ensure coherence between various identity categories and children's lives. This need for coherence is especially significant for adopted children: when the law creates a "new" family for a child via adoption, a former family and former community may be essentially erased for the child.[76] The question of concern is the manner and the degree of that erasure.

Before following out that question, however, it is important to understand that discourses around identity rights and claims for children have emerged primarily at the international level, as there has not been any particularly vigorous pursuit of such rights at the domestic level in the United States. For example, Article 8 of the Convention on the Rights of the Child (CRC), discussed in greater detail in Chapter 5, recognizes a variety of rights that touch on identity including "the right of the child to preserve his or her identity, including nationality, name and family relations as recognized by law without unlawful interference."[77] Stewart argues that this article may be interpreted

---

[74] Martha Minow, *Not Only for Myself: Identity, Politics, and Law* (New York: The New Press, 1997): 59 *et seq.*
[75] *Id.*
[76] As noted earlier, many adoptions today are "open," particularly private adoptions where the birth mother or birth parents select the adoptive parents. The particular openness of arrangements varies. Barbara Yngvesson, "Negotiating Motherhood: Identity and Difference in 'Open' Adoptions," *Law and Society Review* 31, no. 1 (1997): 31–80; Adam Pertman, *Adoption Nation: How the Adoption Revolution is Transforming Our Families – and America* (Boston, MA: Harvard Common Press, 2011): 43–46. Open adoptions generally allow a child to learn about and/or spend time with his or her biological family; connections with community are rarer.
[77] Convention on the Rights of the Child, *supra* n. 7, Art. 8.

as protecting four categories of identity: "familial, tribal, biological and political," where the "tribal" category includes "ethnic, religious and cultural"
identity.[78]

This "cultural identity" category in international law takes on particular
importance for children without families. Article 20 of the CRC provides that
a child "temporarily or permanently deprived of his or her family environment
or in whose own best interests cannot be allowed to remain in that environment" is "entitled to special protection and assistance," which assistance may
include foster and adoptive placement. Article 20 then specifically states that
"when considering solutions, due regard shall be paid to the desirability of
continuity in a child's upbringing and to the child's ethnic, religious, cultural
and linguistic background." To this end, Article 21 states that "inter-country
adoption may be considered as an alternative means of a child's care, *if the
child cannot be placed in a foster or an adoptive family or cannot in any suitable
manner be cared for in the child's country of origin.*"[79]

The extent to which Article 21 privileges community-based care over transnational adoption is the subject of considerable debate, discussed in Chapter 5.
For the moment, suffice it to say that the protection of family and community
ties is woven throughout the Convention on the Rights of the Child and other
international covenants and agreements, and those provisions might certainly
be read to accord a child at least an interest in creating or maintaining an
identity linked to a culture or community of origin. Article 5 of the Convention, for example, directs states to "respect the responsibilities, rights and
duties of parents or, where applicable, the members of the extended family
or community as provided for by local custom," suggesting a broader role for
communities in caring for children.[80]

But the provisions are murky, and there is no consensus on their precise
meaning.[81] Ronen has argued that the Convention protects the child's dignity

---

[78] Stewart, *supra* n. 14 at 223. Samantha Besson has argued that this provision means that all children have a right of access to birth records to effectuate a "right to know one's origins." Besson
does not, however, take that right of access to information about origins further. Samantha
Besson, "Enforcing the Child's Right to Know Her Origins: Contrasting Approaches under
the Convention on the Rights of the Child and the European Convention on Human Rights
Source," *International Journal of Law, Policy, and the Family* 21, no. 2 (2007): 137–159.

[79] Convention on the Rights of the Child, *supra* n. 7, Articles 20 and 21 (emphasis added).

[80] *Id.*, Article 5.

[81] Leslie Hollingsworth has asked whether the Hague Convention on International Adoption
specifically protects an adoptee's cultural identity, and concludes that at the very least, adoption
agencies have an ethical obligation to provide information about the adopted child's culture
of origin to the adoptee and the adoptive family. Leslie D. Hollingsworth, "Does the Hague
Convention on Intercountry Adoption Address the Protection of Adoptees' Cultural Identity?
And Should It?," *Social Work* (Oct. 2008): 377–379.

and important relationships that inform the child's understanding of him or herself, but argues that it does not guarantee a child the right to participate in any particular cultural community, except to the extent that that culture forms part of the child's life experience.[82] Indeed, she argues that recognizing a right *in the child* could cut both ways in protecting ties to a particular community because who is important to a child may not correspond to traditional understandings:

> Though the overall outcome of this approach would be greater legal protection of the child's ties to their family and community of origin, in certain cases law may protect significant ties a child has developed to a family and community which they were not born into, thus overriding the interests of biological parents and minority communities.[83]

Philip Alston agrees, arguing that while cultural and communal origins might matter for some children and thus be considered in determining a child's interests, neither culture nor community should become a "metanorm" that trumps the child's individual rights.[84]

These concerns have undeniable merit, but do not obviate the need to seriously consider the importance of communal connections for children. For each child, the considerations may be different, but it makes no more sense to dismiss them altogether than to give them conclusive weight. In the United States, for example, the law's recognition of a child's cultural or communal identity in adoptive and foster care placements errs in both directions. One legislative scheme forbids the consideration of race, color, or national origin in placing children; a second legislative scheme affecting children who are members of, or eligible to become members of, an American Indian tribe, requires absolute deference to tribal interests in some cases. Neither scheme

---

[82] Ronen, *supra* n. 41, at 155–157. This position has been endorsed at a broader level by Jeremy Waldron in his writings about cosmopolitanism in general; Waldron is understandably wary of claims of culture that try to fix human identities in irrevocable ways. *See, e.g.*, Jeremy Waldron, "What is Cosmopolitan?," *The Journal of Political Philosophy* 8, no. 2 (2000): 227–243. It may be, as Sharon Stephens has argued, that "the primary culture to which all children have a right is the international culture of modernity." Stephens, *supra* n. 61 at 37. Stephens is primarily addressing, however, the issue of children at risk from various cultural practices and is arguing against consigning children to communities in which they may be mistreated. Children growing up in different cultures are all growing up in cultures of modernity, whether it is a culture that claims to be espousing ancient traditions or not. Few marginalized communities are unaware of the pressures and demands of modernity, as noted earlier; in making claims over children, most are simply seeking a way to stem the outmigration of children, typically under circumstances of poverty and dislocation.

[83] Ronen, *supra* n. 24 at 156.

[84] Alston, *supra* n. 50 at 20.

works in all cases or recognizes the interests of children themselves in creating or pursuing a particular identity.

Questions of belonging are complicated when applied to the identity of diasporic populations; they are particularly brittle and fractious when those questions are raised about children whose identities are not yet fixed and will be shaped by factors too numerous to list. The nature and scope of such rights, if any, for groups whose existence is threatened or affected by the actions of a dominant group has generated significant struggle, usually framed in jurisdictional terms, which often leads to intractable conflict. Discussions of the importance of cultural and communal belonging and the fluidity of identity simmer underneath these jurisdictional disputes, as different communities vie for recognition and self-determination. Unfortunately, decisions to vest jurisdiction in one or another of these groups often reflect uninformed substantive conclusions about the value of different cultures and communities.

Authority over children is a particularly sensitive subject. Asking the threshold question about who decides where a child belongs is often reframed in terms of a child's best interests. Marginalized communities are likely to feel that their concerns carry little weight in disputes over a child's care, especially when those interests are being determined by a decision maker who has little or no knowledge of that community; such groups understandably mistrust how decision makers with little knowledge of their communities are likely to assess the importance of both belonging and the adequacy of care that can be provided by caretakers from within those communities. Moreover, disadvantaged communities are at a distinct handicap in asserting such claims; they are likely to look less capable, at a superficial level, of providing for a particular child's needs when compared to a dominant community, particularly if the dispute is being considered in a forum controlled by that latter community.

In fact, those marginalized communities may *not* have the same resources, having long been underserved by the dominant community, and that fact matters considerably when framing an adequate response to caring for vulnerable children. It is denying reality to assume that all groups are sufficiently distinct to be defined clearly, or have the resources to respond to pressing social issues. In some cases, the groups may be so diffuse that it becomes difficult even to decide with whom or what a child might connect, or there may be overwhelming problems that are beyond any single group's competence to remedy.

As complicated as these issues are in their own right, however, the debate over who decides who belongs at the group level is incomplete without engaging questions about the interests of children themselves. Recognizing such interests will significantly affect the shape of a group's claim as well as the interests of a child's adoptive or foster family. How such rights and interests can or should operate on the ground is particularly unclear when thinking about children. Thus, Philip Alston's claim that cultural identity cannot be conferred on an individual is not wholly satisfactory, inasmuch as a large degree of a child's identity *is* conferred based on where the child is placed and with whom.[85]

Clearly, defining the nature of a child's interest in connecting with a culture or community is diffuse. Creating a connection may make immanent sense when an older child is removed from a family who has been embedded in a distinct cultural group or when the child has connections to that group via language, shared traditions, or ways of viewing the world. It may also be felt as a need by children who, although perhaps placed outside of their communities of origin at a very early age, nonetheless feel – both as a result of their own perceptions and as the result of other's reactions to them in their everyday lives – that they are somehow different. For such children, having some form of access to a community or culture of origin can be of significant importance.[86]

Discussions about recognizing communal interests are complicated by the myriad ways that the narratives of cultural discrimination and belonging unfold. In the debates over adoption and foster care, how the various parties are framed in the dispute can make a difference for the outcome. Is the child a helpless innocent languishing in an orphanage or situated within a desperately poor community without economic and political resources, or is the child an individual who, although disadvantaged in some respects, nonetheless lives in a supportive environment whose strengths are simply misunderstood by others? Are the adoptive/foster parents well-off white parents who feel entitled to grab any child from any culture, or are they humane, well-meaning individuals simply concerned with providing a home for a child in need who are sensitive to a child's situation? In the adoption and foster care context, these conflicting images often dictate the responses themselves.

---

[85] *See generally* Alston, *supra* n. 50.

[86] As noted earlier, providing such avenues of access may be seen as unduly imposing on the prerogatives of adoptive parents. These concerns cannot be dismissed lightly. Not all families are interested in opening their families or exposing their adopted or foster children to communities of origin, although there is increasing consensus in the field that more, rather than less, openness is helpful for all affected parties. The issue of adoptive parents' interests is a compelling one, as noted earlier, but this discussion simply seeks to introduce another consideration into the legal regimes surrounding adoption, based on the needs of the children and communities affected.

Subsequent chapters explore these problems of children's interests in three contexts: the dispute over transracial adoption in the United States; the dispute over the placement of American Indian children; and concerns over the burgeoning practice of transnational adoption. Before moving to those substantive discussions, however, it is useful to explore the literature on multiculturalism in general to provide the space for folding dialogues on children and adoption into the broader discussion of group identity claims.

2

Community, Identity, and the Importance of Belonging

In both politics and law, the debate over protecting cultural and communal identity has forced participants to articulate how belonging matters. At one level, the answer to that question appears self-evident and trivial. Cultures and communities supply individuals with the tools necessary for making sense of the world. Rootedness – loosely construed – provides individuals with a base from which to think and act: belonging helps individuals to thrive. Individuals may revise or ultimately reject understandings acquired within a particular culture or community, but all begin their journey girded with understandings imparted by the culture within which they have been grounded.[1]

At another level, the question of how belonging matters is profound. Determining the boundaries of belonging can be an explosive matter because these disputes strike at the very heart of how individuals, communities, and nations understand themselves. At both the domestic and international levels, questions about identity generate intense disagreement. States may recoil at the idea of granting some form of sovereignty to distinctive subnational groups; communities may find that members are at odds with one another and with other groups in determining who has authority over what subject matter areas; and individuals may bristle at being excluded from, or equally, subjected to the strictures of a particular community.

In recent years, the argument for recognizing rights to culture and/or group identity has been espoused not only by communities seeking recognition, but

---

[1] Bhikhu Parekh, *Rethinking Multiculturalism: Cultural Diversity and Political Theory* (New York: Palgrave Macmillan, 2000): 142–154. This is not to suggest that "rootedness" is static, nor that belonging means the same thing for every person. Of course, there is more than one form of rootedness that can help individuals become fully actualized individuals. Parekh draws a distinction between culture and community when he notes that "one might retain one's culture but lose or sever ties with one's cultural community . . . [or] retain one's ties with one's cultural community but not one's culture." p. 154. The point is an important one, but not determinative of the issues discussed here.

by political and legal theorists concerned about the damage that minority groups have sustained as the result of dominant communities' efforts to undermine or override their membership and traditions, whether those actions have been deliberate or only incidental. These scholars have made a forceful case for protecting cultural and communal difference, arguing for policies that not only guarantee tolerance for distinct groups but affirmatively support the continued existence of such communities.[2] They argue that liberal societies ought not only to eliminate discrimination based on ascriptive or cultural group affiliations, but should positively support those connections via law and policy.

The argument extends well beyond an exhortation to tolerate difference: these theorists argue that states should both recognize distinct communities and accommodate group identities. That accommodation may range from relatively innocuous requirements, such as allowing members of groups to wear traditional clothing or speak their own languages on the job, to more radical forms of accommodation that require according such groups a grant of substantial political self-determination. Many of these scholars, Will Kymlicka most prominently, argue that contemporary nation-states need to rethink themselves as multi–nation-states, in which some groups – those with a "distinctive culture" or a history of marginalization – acquire a degree of authority to govern themselves in order to preserve their beliefs and way of life.

Modern nation-building has always been assimilationist, based on the assumption that creating a homogeneous civic identity is essential to weaving together tolerant and unified societies. Thus, nation-building during the last 200 years has centered on the creation of national "peoples" whose existence can trump local ties of community. Many of the political demands for recognition of group identity heard over the last several decades are driven by the sense – indeed, the fact – that groups have been unevenly incorporated into nation-states, creating all of the problems that deep inequality breeds. Indeed, modern nation-states have always found it difficult to fully accommodate significant diversity, and have privileged only particular social groups.[3]

---

[2] *See, e.g.*, Will Kymlicka, *Multicultural Citizenship: A Liberal Theory of Minority Rights* (New York: Oxford University Press, 1996) and *Politics in the Vernacular: Nationalism, Multiculturalism and Citizenship* (New York: Oxford University Press, 2001); Charles Taylor, "The Politics of Recognition," in *Multiculturalism: Examining the Politics of Recognition*, ed. Amy Gutmann (Princeton: Princeton University Press, 1994); James Tully, *Strange Multiplicity: Constitutionalism in an Age of Diversity* (New York: Cambridge University Press, 1995).

[3] Tully, *supra* n. 2, at 1. In the American context, for example, Rogers Smith has argued that American political ideology's commitments to equality have always been undercut by the belief that "true Americans are in some way chosen by God, history or nature to possess superior moral and intellectual traits, often associated with race[,] class, gender or ethnicity."

There is no doubt that the impetus to create a homogeneous community derives in significant measure from the need that all national communities have to "decid[e] . . . and . . . deliberat[e] together."[4] Historically, however, inventing national communities typically entailed subsuming individuals and groups in a process that was often undeniably brutal. The harm to outlying groups was substantial, and both the real and the symbolic erasure of entire peoples had devastating consequences. As they were conscripted into the nation-building process, these peoples were stripped of the languages, customs, and histories that anchored them, and left to fend for themselves without the social, political, and economic resources necessary to sustain themselves in a new world. That pressure to assimilate has not appreciably dissipated in recent decades, although it may not be proceeding at the same pace or with the same virulence.[5] For many historically marginalized groups, the demands for recognition of cultural and communal ties being asserted today arise in direct response to a lived experience of deprivation and disrespect that has arisen from these normalizing demands of nation-building.

As dominant groups inevitably universalized their cultures, they configured their own members as "normal" while marking others as different, rendering the latter therefore invisible and effectively excluded from full participation in political life.[6] More critically for the discussion here, that erasure was often accomplished by design or circumstance via the removal of children from families, whether by orphan trains that separated children from their immigrant families or by government policies both at home and abroad that sought to domesticate indigenous children by placing them in boarding schools located thousands of miles from their homes.

Until relatively recently, the importance of communal belonging was discounted in liberal political and legal theory. Political scholars traditionally worried about the relationship between the state and the individual, viewing group membership as a private matter. If rights to political, civic, and social equality could be secured to the individual, the argument proceeded, individuals would be free to belong to whatever groups suited them.

Rogers Smith, *Civic Ideals: Conflicting Visions of Citizenship in U.S. History* (New Haven: Yale University Press, 1999): 508, n. 5. This fundamental faith provided a framework for cohesion and order, asserting the primacy of an "American Way." That set of beliefs, of course, strongly influenced public policies concerning the family. Similar tacit assumptions about who is fit to rule undoubtedly occur in other nations.

[4] Charles Taylor, "Multiculturalism and Political Identity," *Ethnicities* 1, no. 1 (2001): 122–128, 123.

[5] In various parts of the globe, of course, the process is as potent and deliberate as it ever was, as evidenced by so-called ethnic cleansing efforts from the Balkans to Rwanda.

[6] *See generally* Iris Marion Young, *Justice and the Politics of Difference* (Princeton, NJ: Princeton University Press, 1990); Kymlicka, *supra* n. 2.

Guaranteeing rights to association and free speech, coupled with a broad range of rights to equal treatment, would allow individuals to sustain those communities from whom they drew support and understanding, an argument that continues to wield significant power.[7] Theorists in this camp worry that recognizing communal distinctions, especially when grounded in concepts as intrinsically murky and changeable as "culture" will lock individuals into rigid categories and construct false boundaries between individuals and groups. Indeed, for some theorists, the press of modernity itself makes it particularly difficult to talk about cultural or communal difference; especially in today's world, peoples are more alike than they are different. In her elegantly argued analysis, Anne Phillips points out that "[c]ultural difference is not as great as it is often said to be. It does not map neatly on to communities. [Problems of inequality] will not be resolved by ceding authority to cultural groups."[8]

Although those arguments are persuasive, it is, at the same time, exceedingly clear that the extension of individual political and civil rights has proved insufficient for moving many people and communities into conditions of equality. Widening the circle of individual political and civil rights has secured neither individual nor, by extension, communal well-being because of the inevitable fact that groups themselves are positioned in a broader social hierarchy that can be difficult, if not impossible, to transcend.[9] This inequality has affected not only individuals, but the communities within which such individuals are located; those communities have often been wholly discounted in political discourse.[10] Under these circumstances, marginalized groups have been more likely to be acted on than acting when seeking to participate in larger communities.[11]

These facts have given rise to a set of demands that can be loosely categorized as cultural or communal identity claims, many of which have begun to be articulated in human rights documents and the laws of some nations. These

---

[7] See, e.g., Brian Barry, *Culture and Equality: An Egalitarian Critique of Multiculturalism* (Cambridge, MA: Polity Press, 2002); Jeremy Waldron, "Minority Cultures and the Cosmopolitan Alternative" in *The Rights of Minority Cultures*, ed. Will Kymlicka (Oxford: Oxford University Press, 1995): 93–119; Jack Donnelly, 'Human Rights, Individual Rights, Collective Rights," in *Human Rights in a Pluralist World: Individuals and Collectivities*, ed. Jan Berting et al. (Westport, CT: Meckler Press, 1990): 39–62.

[8] Anne Phillips, *Multiculturalism without Culture* (Princeton, NJ: Princeton University Press, 2007): 180.

[9] See generally Parekh, *supra* n. 1, 190–238.

[10] See generally Anne Phillips, *The Politics of Presence* (New York: Oxford University Press, 1995): 8–21.

[11] See, e.g., Adeno Addis, "Individualism, Communitarianism, and the Rights of Ethnic Minorities," *Notre Dame Law Review* 67 (1992): 615–676.

group-based or, as Kymlicka prefers, "group-differentiated," rights both complement and transcend individual rights guarantees and have been viewed as critical to creating real power for marginalized groups. Historically excluded groups, as noted earlier, have little reason to trust that dominant majorities will be attentive to their ways of understanding the world or be sensitive to justice claims arising out of the group's history,[12] and have therefore argued that recognizing such rights is a necessity for securing fair treatment.

The emergence of claims based on group belonging has thus revived a political category largely eclipsed in the contemporary world. Shifting focus from the broad national community, these claims are grounded in the concrete relationships that shape an individual's everyday experience. As Bikhu Parekh notes, "'[o]ur' culture is one which we live, which has shaped us, and with which we identify. . . . Like all communities, cultural communities are not and cannot be, just imagined communities."[13] In other words, there is a reality to belonging, even if the individual sees it only obliquely, out of the corner of his or her eye.

The reintroduction of community as a significant political category complicates the range of identity claims being asserted today. Traditionally, the laws of most liberal states acknowledged three identity categories – personal, familial, and national – although the content of identity "rights" in those areas were not clearly articulated. Personal identity was guaranteed, presumptively, by rights to free association; family identity by rights to family privacy and autonomy; and national identity by a host of citizenship rights. The emergence of claims for cultural identity at a subnational level creates uneasiness, as these claims must be carved out of earlier categories of citizenship and family. In some cases, such groups may claim an identity that crosses national boundaries, as those boundaries were historically drawn with little regard for the affinity groups that they disrupted.

The argument for recognizing and enhancing the status of minority cultures has derived from concerns both for individual well-being and the well-being of society as a whole. Kymlicka and Taylor, for example, have argued, in distinct ways, that a politics of recognition is essential for reasons that are both

---

[12] Melissa S. Williams, *Voice, Trust, and Memory: Marginalized Groups and the Failings of Liberal Representation* (Princeton, NJ: Princeton University Press, 1998): 30–56.

[13] Parekh, *supra* n. 1, 155. Importantly for this discussion, Parekh notes that one's culture need not be the one into which one is born, as one may move or be adopted. This point is well taken, and raises questions about the extent to which having been "born" into a particular community should have any weight. However, if children are immigrants only by happenstance who feel a loss as the result of that move, and if the communities from which they have been moved also feel that departure as a loss, then it is reasonable to think about how the legal regime surrounding adoption might be framed to account for those facts.

individual and collective.[14] First, one can make a compelling argument that it is important to preserve diverse ways of life in an increasingly globalized world primarily to enhance individual autonomy. Autonomy, they argue, begins with being securely grounded in a community whose value is recognized by others. It is that grounding that imparts the self-confidence essential to becoming an autonomous individual; by affirming individual connectedness and according that connectedness credence in the wider political world, individuals can navigate their worlds with confidence, whether they ultimately accept or reject those origins.

More critically, however, the politics of recognition provide both individuals and groups with a *reason* to belong to larger communities. Stabilizing cultural or communal groups is thus critical to the security of the nation-state, which has an interest in shaping its institutions in ways that promote its citizens' identification with it: individuals whose communities are devalued are likely to be quite loosely attached as citizens of the nation-state in which they are located.[15] As Charles Taylor has observed, "Whoever is not part of the people, not party to the common understanding, lacks an important reason to feel bound by its decisions."[16] Failing to understand how relationships and connectedness are essential for both individual well-being and for social cohesion, these theorists argue, creates an impoverished political system incapable of resolving fundamental social and political problems.

Of course, the idea of recognizing group identity – and especially of articulating rights flowing from cultural identity – has not been embraced wholeheartedly. One of the primary critiques of claims for cultural identity stems from the fact that terms like "culture" and "identity" have no fixed meaning, either standing alone or linked as a single idea. In addition, even if a culture has an identifiable shape, its internal norms may be inconsistent. Given those facts, efforts to construct political boundaries are likely to dissolve in disputes over how to compose the community and what norms or traditions are essential for binding the community together.

---

[14] Kymlicka, *supra* n. 2; Taylor, *supra* n. 2.

[15] *See* Taylor, *supra* n. 4. Indeed, Parekh argues that respect for cultural differences creates, paradoxically, cultural openness, which in turn is essential as a bulwark against cultural fundamentalism. *See generally,* Parekh, *supra* n. 1, 196–238. Rogers Smith has argued, in a slightly different context, that people-building requires that individuals and communities be able to trust that political leaders will be attentive to their interests and that those leaders understand their worth; building those capacities involves, among other things, listening to those groups' constitutive stories – and cannot be built utilizing only the principles of liberal egalitarianism. Rogers M. Smith, "Citizenship and the Politics of People-Building," *Citizenship Studies* 5, no. 1 (2001): 73–96.

[16] Taylor, *supra* n. 4 at 125.

When political and legal theorists talk about cultural and communal groups, the definitions are often unwieldy because they cover both too much and too little. In his writing on the subject, Kymlicka defines a cultural group as "an intergenerational community, more or less institutionally complete, occupying a given territory or homeland, sharing a distinct language and history."[17] Iris Young defines such groups as "a collective of persons differentiated from another group by cultural forms, practices or ways of life."[18] These groups "have a specific affinity with one another because of their similar experience or way of life," with the result that the group is defined more by a *sense* of shared identity than a specific set of attributes.[19] Ayelet Shachar uses an idea drawn from Robert Cover's 1983 discussion of groups with a distinctive *nomos*: such groups "share a unique history and collective memory, a distinct culture, a set of social norms, customs, and traditions, or perhaps an experience of maltreatment by mainstream society or oppression by the state, all of which may give rise to a set of group-specific roles or practices."[20] Bikhu Parekh defines a cultural group as one that shares a set of historically developed beliefs that shape the ways in which its members understand and structure their lives.[21]

Amy Gutmann, summarizing the writing over the last several years, notes that those theorists generally agree that

> a culture [is that thing which] constitutes and constrains the identities (and therefore the lives) of its members by providing them with a common language, history, institutions of socialization, range of occupations, lifestyles, distinctive literary and artistic traditions, architectural styles, music, dress, ceremonies and holidays and customs that are shared by an intergenerational community that occupies a distinct territory. Actual cultures encompass the lives of their members in many of these ways but not necessarily all.[22]

Even with this broadly inclusive definition, identifying communal groups is no easy task, however. Subgroups within communities and cultural groups may have distinctly different histories and markedly different traditions. Determining how much tradition and shared history provides the requisite degree of commonality to warrant recognizing a particular collection of people as a distinct cultural group or community is an unanswerable question in the

---

[17] Kymlicka, *supra* n. 2 at 18.
[18] Young, *supra* n. 6 at 43.
[19] *Id.*
[20] Ayelet Shachar, *Multicultural Jurisdictions: Cultural Differences and Women's Rights* (New York: Cambridge University Press, 2001): 2, n. 5.
[21] Parekh, *supra* n. 1 at 154–156.
[22] Amy Gutmann, *Identity in Democracy* (Princeton, NJ: Princeton University Press, 2003): 40.

abstract. Those questions, in turn, are made even more difficult because individual group members may disagree with one another and with the norms of
the group. Moreover, these definitions provide little guidance for determining
which group ought to be considered "authentic" – even acknowledging the
impossibility of utilizing a term like authenticity.

Bringing children into this broader debate over multiculturalism further
complicates matters. Speaking about a culture or community of origin may
not be fully coherent in the context of a child placed through adoption or
foster care, especially when that child is placed at a very young age. Culture
by its very nature is something that is acquired; it is the lived experience of
a particular community that imparts one's outlook. Thus, a child placed for
adoption at birth may have spent no time "acquiring" a culture of origin, and
stands in a very different position from a child adopted when he or she is older.
For this reason, efforts to claim a child as a community member based solely
on the child's "original" affiliations will always be contestable.

BELONGING TO FAMILY, COMMUNITY, AND NATION

Another challenge for thinking through claims to protect communal belonging
for children moved in adoption and foster care is closely linked to the difficulty
of defining culture, identity, or community as analytical terms in their own
right. This related problem lies in the fact that identity can rarely be defined
along a single axis, nor does it remain static for either individuals or groups.
When culture is loosely defined, the notion of a "cultural group" collapses all
kinds of belonging into a single category, as Amy Gutmann's work points out.[23]
Some groups share ascriptive characteristics rather than a common history,
language, or way of life; others are united on the basis of voluntary association
or beliefs.[24] The simple fact is that hybridity and multiple belonging are
increasingly the norm rather than the exception. Nonetheless, in the politics of
belonging, communal identity is frequently invoked as a single, overwhelming
imperative.

Most scholars today dismiss the idea of a primal identity, recognizing the
fluidity of identity and the multiple factors that affect its development. At the
same time, this idea of primordiality carries considerable political weight with
historically disenfranchised communities. As Sheila Croucher notes, those
who recognize identity as fragmented and changeable

> must still contend with the powerful and seemingly irrational passion and
> embeddedness that often surround identity. [They] also confront a troubling

[23] *See generally* Gutmann, *id.*
[24] *Id.*

paradox of emphasizing the invented, constructed . . . nature of identity while individuals and groups . . . continue to fall prey to and commit unspeakable violence and hatreds all in the name of these "inventions."[25]

Croucher draws on Stephen Cornell and Douglas Hartmann's concept of "constructed primordiality," in which groups and individuals "construct . . . an identity that typically claims for itself primordial moorings – an anchor in blood ties or common origin – [and is] experienced as touching something deeper and more profound than labels or interests or contingencies,"[26] as a model for understanding the power of claims of belonging. The idea of constructed primordiality is important because it "preserve[s] an appreciation for the emotional appeal of belonging, while shifting . . . attention to the dynamic processes and politics of identity formation."[27]

This concept is particularly apt in the context of disputes over the treatment of children: it explains the deep longing that many communities express when children disappear through foster care and adoption. Communities must rely on identity as a point for organizing, which increases the pressure for the group to present its identity and that of its members as, if not fixed, at least coherent. Groups seeking to protect and rebuild their communities thus may stridently claim a child as one of their own, regardless of whether the child has spent significant amounts of time with the group. These feelings arise with particular force when the community perceives the child's removal as an illegitimate "taking" from the community.

Similarly, children displaced from their origins by foster care and adoption often talk about being pulled to their origins. Tim Moore, an adoptee from Mexico, for example, reported that while growing up, his soul "screamed for color [in his parents' sand-colored home]. . . . You like certain things because your ancestors liked certain things, and it is inside you."[28] Regardless of the logic of a claim that longings or preferences have such elemental origins, they are often constitutive for individuals, and cannot be lightly dismissed, especially for children who are searching for grounding after having been moved via adoption or foster care.[29] It is important to note, as well, that children may be interested in exploring cultural roots with or without exploring connections to birth families – a fact that must

[25] Sheila L. Croucher, *Globalization and Belonging: The Politics of Identity in a Changing World* (New York: Rowman and Littlefield, 2003): 38.
[26] Stephen Cornell and Douglas Hartmann in Croucher, *id.* at 39.
[27] *Id.* at 40.
[28] Jill Brooke, "Close Encounters with a Home Barely Known," *New York Times*, July 22, 2004.
[29] Annette Appell, "The Myth of Separation," *Northwestern Journal of Law and Social Policy* 6, no. 2 (Spring 2011): 291–299, 295.

be taken into account in determining how to allow such connections to be made.[30]

Belonging, however, is rarely all encompassing along a single axis such as culture or community of origin. As Gutmann points out, individual identity is complex, and a culture provides only one among many contexts for making choices; membership in identity groups is inevitably multiple.[31] People belong in overlapping and intersecting ways – an individual may belong to more than one ethnic or racial group, or hold beliefs at odds with those of the majority of his or her culture or community of origin. Few members of cultural communities, in any event, experience "pure" membership, that is, they rarely live their lives in total isolation from the larger world. It is the nature of cultures to collide and of people to mix; crossing borders is the norm in a world where global connections can be made with a simple tap on a mobile device.

Communities and cultures are, above all, dynamic: they are always in flux and their boundaries are infinitely porous. Stuart Hall has noted that while cultural identity is often imagined as a seamless whole, it is fundamentally unstable.[32] In addition, cultural and communal identity derives from engagement with a host of factors beyond simple location within a particular community. Charles Taylor, for example, has observed that although it is certainly possible to point to cultural groups whose experiences have been shared over long periods of time, the only authentic identity an individual can have is the identity that that person has developed on his or her own. Yet, while identity is ultimately personal, it is, as Taylor points out, developed only in dialogue with others.[33]

Arguing for the importance of group affiliations, then, is not to suggest that cultural groups and communities are or should be intransigent in utilizing identity as an organizing point nor that they are themselves blind to the culture of modernity as they seek to protect their cultures; they are not seeking to preserve themselves in amber. These are not, by and large, disputes over maintaining a community insulated from the intrusions of the outside world. Indeed, most of the groups seeking a voice in the placement of children – or in other arenas, for that matter – are only too aware of the imperatives of modernity. Most seek integration into that more cosmopolitan world; minority

---

[30] Janet Farrell Smith explores this question in the context of how educational institutions might approach questions of origins with adopted adolescents. Janet Farrell Smith, "Identity, Race, and Culture in Adoption," in *Adoptive Families in a Diverse Society*, ed. Katarina Wegar (New Brunswick, NJ: Rutgers University Press, 2006): 243–258, 248–249.
[31] Gutmann, *supra* n. 23 at 36–37.
[32] Stuart Hall, "Old and New Identities, Old and New Ethnicities," in *Culture, Globalization and the World-System*, ed. Anthony D. King (Minneapolis: University of Minnesota Press, 1997): 41–68, 47.
[33] Taylor, *supra* n. 2 at 32–35.

groups are typically acutely aware of how their own cultures must adapt. Rather than trying to preserve a culture or community untouched by the world outside their borders, these groups generally seek only some degree of control over the pace and direction of change. This search for a voice during the process of transformation is especially critical when change is driven by forces that threaten the very existence of groups who seek recognition to integrate on their *own* terms.

Acknowledging change and adaptation, however, does not make it easier to determine how to accommodate conflicting claims, especially when the individual subjected to – or asserting – those claims can legitimately lay claim to membership in a variety of communities. The fact of multiple and over-lapping identities is particularly problematic when determining belonging for children. Identities are particularly fluid for children; they often belong to more than one racial or ethnic group or may be eligible for membership in multiple communities. In the adoption and foster care context, the dilemmas multiply: children may inherit one or more community memberships from biological parents who may have participated in those communities or may have left them altogether; they may be moved into families whose identities do not coincide with those of the biological parents; they may be moved in or out of national cultures as well. Determining the group or groups to which a child belongs under such circumstances is a labyrinthine task.

VOLUNTARINESS, INVOLUNTARINESS, AND EXIT

In addition to definitional problems and the problems of overlapping identity categories, one additional critique of multiculturalism requires consideration because it bears strongly on issues of belonging for children. When laws and policies empower cultural groups, they may simultaneously disempower vulnerable persons within such groups. Adults theoretically have the ability to understand and evaluate the groups to which they belong and, in liberal societies, to exercise an exit option should they disagree with the group's practices. Of course, such an exit option is not universally available either in theory or practice, especially for subordinated individuals within a group, but at least adults have an ability to articulate that concern and perhaps work to put it into effect.

The potential for subordinating weaker members within communities has been central to the critiques of multiculturalism.[34] Feminists have been particularly outspoken in critiquing liberal multiculturalism when the protection of cultural groups sanctions practices that are deeply oppressive to

[34] *See generally* Barry, *supra* n. 7.

women.[35] Women in such circumstances often are unable to object to tyrannical practices and, as a practical matter, lack the resources necessary to effect an exit. As a result, laws and policies that transfer authority from the state or the dominant community to elites within particular sub-communities may end up depriving vulnerable members of the at least arguably neutral protections for human rights that citizenship in liberal states provides. Indeed, a state's decision to transfer power over some subject matter areas to cultural groups may critically affect vulnerable individuals within that marginalized subgroup. Moreover, because that transfer of power is often likely to relate to family and domestic relationships, which is the focal point for many distinct groups objecting to the imposition of a dominant community's norms, the potential for continuing or exacerbating subordination exists.

Brian Barry, for example, has argued that liberal democracies, with their ideal of universal citizenship, grant the greatest freedom to live in accordance with individual and group beliefs and precepts; attempts to protect or revive cultural groups are likely to enable groups to seriously impede basic human rights.[36] In contrast to the position that groundedness and cultural connection provide the essential context for the emergence of autonomous citizens, critics such as Barry and Waldron point out that granting authoritative status to particular cultural groups is likely to inhibit individual development by locking people into systems from which they cannot deviate.[37] Indeed, both argue that liberal democracies should strive to present a cosmopolitan option to their citizens. Individual identity development, for these and other critics, is quintessentially a private matter, and the state should not be involved in trying to manipulate the conditions for that development or in trying to manipulate social cohesion on this basis. Furthermore, these critics point out that proponents of multiculturalism should not assume that an individual's cultural or communal identity will in fact prepare that individual for interaction with the wider society.[38] The best way to maintain cultural diversity, according to these scholars, is to ensure that individuals have substantive equality rights that allow them to choose their own identities over their life course.[39]

[35] *See* Susan Moller Okin, "Is Multiculturalism Bad for Women?" in *Is Multiculturalism Bad for Women?*, ed. Susan Moller Okin (Princeton, NJ: Princeton University Press, 1999): 7–26; Shachar, *supra* n. 20; Phillips, *supra* n. 8.

[36] *See generally* Barry, *supra* n. 7.

[37] *Id.* and Waldron, *supra* n. 7.

[38] *See generally* Chandran Kukathes, "Are There Any Cultural Rights?" *Political Theory* 20, no. 1 (Feb. 1992)1995; Phillips, *supra* n. 8.

[39] Parekh points out, however, that "[human beings] shar[e] a common human identity but in a culturally mediated manner. They are similar and different, their similarities and differences

Many feminists have been particularly concerned with the extent to which the protection of cultural identities might be used to discriminate both against outsiders and insiders of a group, although not all have been squarely opposed to multicultural accommodation. These authors have pointed out that efforts to recognize and reconstitute cultural or communal groups typically are insufficiently attentive not only to the nuances of identity formation but to the real-life consequences of utilizing the law to create cultural boundaries that isolate at-risk individuals. Shachar and Sunder, for example, have both argued that in empowering cultural groups, states must create safeguards to prevent groups from compromising individual members' human rights and to allow those individuals to exercise the power to craft their membership on their own terms.[40]

Concerns about powerlessness have particular force when talking about children, who typically cannot make any choices about where they belong. In an intact family, as noted earlier, parents typically make choices about where a child is rooted. But for children subject to foster care and adoption, biological parents are often out of the picture altogether unless an open adoption has been negotiated,[41] and transferring the child to a new adoptive or foster family will significantly affect identity development. These children are uniquely subject to the determinations of those with the power to place them. Decision makers presiding over such cases often assert their authority with little concern for the nuances of identity and belonging and can be strongly biased against communities that have been subject to hardship and seem less than ideal: the decision makers often begin from the position that such-and-such child is *of course* better off away from "The Rez" or a traumatized country like Haiti or an AIDs-ravaged community in Africa. (Marginalized groups, on the other hand, are sometimes too quick to make sweeping claims about the child's need to remain in a community of origin even when that community has few or no resources to provide for the child.) The problem here is that for most children, their exit from a family or community of origin is typically *not* voluntary; their

do not passively coexist but interpenetrate, and neither is ontologically prior nor morally more important.... Equal rights do not mean identical rights, for individuals with different cultural backgrounds and needs might require different rights to enjoy equality in respect of whatever happens to be the content of their rights. Equality involves not just rejection of irrelevant differences ... but also full recognition of legitimate and relevant ones." Parekh, *supra* n. 1 at 239–240.

[40] Mahdavi Sunder, "Cultural Dissent," *Stanford Law Review* 54, no. 3 (Dec. 2001): 495–567, 555–567; Shachar, *supra* n. 20 at 117–145.

[41] There is increasing recognition that children can benefit from continuing ties with family and community, especially when those children have been moved out of families at an older age. *See* Appell, *supra* n. 31. This issue is taken up in Chapter 3.

departure has been imposed on them from the outside. Whose voices are heard in this debate – and how they are heard – matters.

In the politics of belonging, law is invoked as both sword and shield. Both Martha Minow and Mahdavi Sunder have pointed out that trying to shape laws and institutions around identity categories may unfairly confine individuals, significantly limiting their ability to create their own lives.[42] The law may also err in viewing persons as proxies for a cultural group or community, creating an onerous individual burden – an issue of particular concern when considering children. At the same time, efforts to scuttle identity claims altogether may improperly sap citizenship of its vitality, making it easy, as Minow points out, both to miss the importance of constitutive relationships and to ignore or erase the ways in which communal belonging may continue to work disadvantages for both the individual and the group in the larger political and social sphere.[43]

Invoking the law to steer a path through identity claims is not surprising. On one hand, liberal democracies claim to have pulled out of the identity sphere, leaving people to choose identities for themselves. On the other hand, as Minow points out, the law has always been intimately concerned with identity: how the law defines an individual significantly affects how individuals are recognized in the outside world.[44] In the United States, for example, the protection of individual identity has a long legal history that stretches from common-law protection for personal reputation to contemporary articulations of autonomy interests in the form of constitutionally guaranteed privacy rights. Through legal categories that define the relations among individuals, families, communities, and nations, the boundaries of belonging itself are delineated and communities of belonging are shaped.

The imperative to call on the law to impart shape to belonging has, paradoxically, intensified in part because cultural boundaries are so porous. The demands for laws and policies that protect cultures and communities have become more strident precisely because of the difficulty of maintaining cultural integrity in the contemporary world: "[I]nsularity does not come naturally.... One response to crumbling cultural fences and the rise of internal cultural debates ... has been to *turn to law* to protect against the dilution of

---

[42] Martha Minow, *Not Only for Myself: Identity, Politics, and Law* (New York: The New Press, 1997): 78; Sunder, *supra* n. 42, 548–555.

[43] Minow, *id.* at 20 *et seq.*

[44] Minow, *id.* at 57.

cultural traditions and to preserve stable cultural categories."[45] The very fact
that individuals and communities are increasingly appealing to courts and legislatures to determine the meaning and boundaries of cultural and communal
belonging means that the law's conception of culture is important.[46]

The law is a blunt tool, however. The very creation of identity categories can
ignore individuals' lived experiences and cannot account for how individuals
move *among* and *between* identities, as Minow points out. The law is then
forced to impose an allegedly coherent identity on one which is fragmented
and fleeting. And even when the law attempts to account for the fluidity of
identity, it may not be sufficiently attentive to how individual identities are
also fixed by cultural, religious, or ascriptive characteristics.[47]

For all of these reasons, there has been considerable resistance to recognizing *rights* to cultural or communal identity in any form. Rights, of course, are
a particularly inflexible kind of claim. As Waldron has argued, when identity
and culture are linked as rights, it may be difficult to negotiate when different cultures and communities come into conflict: If culture and community
prescribe a whole way of being and identity is inextricably bound to that
community, then "criticism and discussion . . . [become an] *affront* to some
aspect of one's cultural identity."[48] Under these circumstances, cultural identity rights become a barrier to working out differences and accommodating a
variety of interests in a given social setting. Waldron notes that all of us are
always engaged, as citizens, in the "difficult business of coming to terms with
those with whom we *have* to come to terms," and worries that policies that
allow individuals to impose a cultural identity between themselves as individuals and as citizens in a larger polity will foster divisiveness.[49] Given that
every larger society is also trying to solve the everyday problems of social life,
invoking "cultural identity" rights will simply create an intractable conflict.[50]
Phrasing that issue somewhat differently, to say that individuals have a right to

[45] Sunder, supra n. 42 at 501.
[46] *Id*. at 549.
[47] *See generally* Minow, *supra* n. 44.
[48] Jeremy Waldron, "Cultural Identity and Civic Responsibility," in *Citizenship in Diverse Societies*, eds. Will Kymlicka and Wayne Norman (New York: Oxford University Press, 2002):
155–174, 170.
[49] *Id*. at 174.
[50] Waldron argues that the idea of cultural purity and authenticity is problematic throughout
this whole discussion: there is something artificial about self-consciously asserting "roots" and
"identity" as though it is something external to oneself. *Id*. at 168–169. *See also* Helder De
Schutter, "Towards a Hybrid Theory of Multinational Justice," in *Accommodating Cultural
Diversity*, ed. Peter Tierney (Aldershot, UK: Ashgate Publishing, 2007), noting the hybrid
quality of cultural belonging that many individuals experience.

their own culture begs the question with children, because "their own" identity may flit between two or more groups, especially when they are adopted or
placed in foster care.

Against fears that cultural rights inevitably become "too tightly scripted,"[51]
however, other commentators argue that cultural and communal rights are
essential to guaranteeing equal treatment and respect. The position that broad
guarantees of individual civil and political rights are the best avenue for protecting cultural interests too quickly dismisses the extent to which minority groups
and individuals belonging to those groups have encountered discrimination
and abuse and the importance that rights may have for securing resources. As
Patricia Williams has pointed out, dominant communities have been aware of
the *needs* of various marginalized groups and individuals for many years; only
when those needs have been expressed as *rights* have those claims been taken
seriously.[52] For many marginalized groups and individuals, the harms that
accrue from the absence of rights, and particularly rights to cultural accommodation and respect, far outweigh the difficulties that might ensue from their
recognition. Waldron, for example, recognizes that this demand for respect –
and the search for some mechanism to enforce it – stems largely from the fact
that "dominant majorities make no attempt whatsoever to *debate* the merits
of . . . [the views of] members of groups which hold contrary views. They simply *impose a view*, and then disingenuously accuse the dissident minority of
failing to live up to its civic responsibility,"[53] even if he does not endorse the
notion of cultural identity rights per se.

Even among those who support enlisting rights to protect cultural and
communal identity, however, debates continue over how such a right might
be framed and to whom the right might attach. Many advocates claim that such
rights must be both individual and communal. Individual rights that protect
cultural or communal identity – the right to speak in a particular language or
to wear religious emblems at work, for example – are relatively unproblematic
when they fit neatly into the traditional framework as rights of association
or expression. Thus, both Jack Donnelly and Philip Alston, like Brian Barry,
argue for the recognition of individual rights that enable participation in
particular forms of cultural life, and argue that any cultural rights can only be

[51] K. Anthony Appiah, "Identity, Authenticity, Survival: Multicultural Societies and Social Reproduction," in *Multiculturalism: Examining the Politics of Recognition*, ed. Amy Gutmann
(Princeton, NJ: Princeton University Press, 1994): 149–163, 163.
[52] Patricia Williams, *The Alchemy of Race and Rights: Diary of a Law Professor* (Cambridge, MA:
Harvard University Press, 1992): 148–161.
[53] Waldron, *supra* n. 48 at 172. Waldron maintains, however, that this fact still does not justify
raising one's beliefs, conditioned by culture, as an absolute bar to discussion.

individual.[54] They note that all human rights have a collective dimension and operate in a social context, but the protection of cultural integrity can best be secured through rights that allow *individuals* to act collectively: "[C]ultural identity will best be protected when members of culturally distinctive groups are allowed to participate in their culture, both in public and in private and transmit it to their children, without fear of discrimination, retaliation or attack by the state or other groups."[55]

Others, of course, note that unless communal rights are recognized, individual rights often cannot be realized, because the connections between the individual and the community are mutually constitutive.[56] Most advocates for cultural rights express concern that unless cultural and communal groups secure some kind of authority that moves beyond individual rights – a right to self-determination, as it were – cultural integrity will be lost.

SECURING COMMUNAL VALUES VIA GENERATIONAL TIES

The difficulties of defining communities, defining culture, and defining boundaries pose enormous obstacles. It may be that trying to pin down such concerns with the language of rights is something of a futile enterprise. At the same time, the interests that lie at the bottom of claims for rights are worthy of considerable attention in framing legislative regimes that affect adoption and foster care.

Concerns about belonging have particular resonance in family law. In pre-modern empires, it was the norm rather than the exception to grant at least partial regulatory control over selected subject matter areas to distinct groups to be resolved according to local juridical customs or those local practices were incorporated into the juridical code of the new sovereign. Foremost among the areas delegated to local authority were the rules governing the family, because those rules were considered to be essential to maintaining social cohesion and allaying anxieties about a change in larger power structures. As new states often had to be constructed around an extant formal or informal legal system, this approach allowed a new sovereign to manage difference and often eliminated considerable conflict.

---

[54] *See generally* Alston, in Steiner and Alston, *supra* n. 148; Barry, *supra* n. 7; Jack Donnelly, *Universal Human Rights in Theory and Practice*, 2nd ed. (Ithaca, NY: Cornell University Press, 2003): 204–224.

[55] Alston, *id.* at 58.

[56] *See generally* Rudolfo Stavenhagen, "The Right to Cultural Identity," in Jan Berting et al., *Human Rights in a Pluralist World: Individuals and Collectives* (Westport, CT: Meckler Press, 2000); Kymlicka, *supra* n. 2.

This sort of arrangement continues to exist in a number of plural societies, especially in matters of family regulation, and generates complex questions.[57] Disputes over ceding authority in family matters to distinct religious groups has recently surfaced in Great Britain, for example, in disputes over the extent to which Sharia law may be invoked to resolve domestic disputes in British courts.[58] Regulation of the domestic sphere has always been a primary site for accommodation of communal and cultural difference because family and kinship arrangements are so closely tied to both an individual's and a people's conception of itself. It was only with the advent of the nation-state, and then relatively late in the game, that efforts to universalize and normalize a particular form of the family emerged as an integral aspect of nation-building.[59]

Even in contemporary liberal states committed to a rhetoric of family privacy and autonomy, the domestic arena is highly regulated. Indeed, contemporary liberal states often have a Janus-faced relationship with the family. Whereas respecting family privacy, for example, allows the liberal state to privatize the costs of dependency, the state often asserts its authority over that sphere to ensure that individuals, particularly children, are adequately socialized, especially when the families appear to deviate from dominant ideals. That oversight is typically exercised most stringently over families outside of the mainstream, leading members of marginalized communities to conclude that their own family relationships are more strictly policed than families whose structures and practices conform to dominant expectations.

It is, therefore, not surprising that disputes over identity and belonging are particularly sensitive in the family law arena. As Shachar has noted, family law serves a gatekeeping function in the construction of cultural identity because membership is typically tied to family affiliation and enculturation:

> A *nomoi* [or cultural] group's membership rules, encoded in family law, . . . provide the bonds which connect the past to the future, by identifying who is considered part of the tradition. This is particularly true of rules that define group membership by virtue of birth and marriage, and thereby demarcate a pool of individuals who are collectively responsible for maintaining the group's values, practices and distinct way of life. Group membership

[57] *See generally* "When Legal Worlds Overlap: Human Rights, State and Non-State Law," International Council on Human Rights Policy (2009), www.ichrp.org/files/reports/50/135_report_en.pdf.

[58] *See, e.g.*, "Sharia Law in UK is 'Unavoidable'," BBC Feb. 7, 2008, http://news.bbc.co.uk/2/hi/7232661.stm; *Sharia Law in Britain: A Threat to One Law for All and Equality* (One Law for All, 2010), www.onelawforall.org.uk/wp-content/uploads/New-Report-Sharia-Law-in-Britain.pdf.

[59] For a discussion of how the United States has regulated citizenship through the family, for example, *see generally* Nancy F. Cott, *Public Vows: A History of Marriage and the Nation* (Cambridge, MA: Harvard University Press, 2002).

rules, like state citizenship laws, cannot by themselves guarantee that all children born to a *nomoi* group will necessarily choose to remain active members of that group, or that they will decide to follow its tradition. But *nomoi* groups, like states, ultimately acquire the majority of their members by birth instead of through adult choice.[60]

That the family plays such an important role in replicating culture and community goes far in explaining why the movement of children is likely to be a sensitive issue for communities. As noted earlier, *where* children are placed in voluntary and involuntary foster care and adoption proceedings can significantly shape the child's belonging. Producing that initial identity, however transformed or transcended over the course of a child's life, is thus perceived as an absolutely vital aspect of a community's ability to continue in existence, whether the removal of a few or even many children *actually* threatens that continued existence.[61] The placement of children thus becomes the central point around which a host of sensitive issues converges, and it is worth inquiring into how such concerns about belonging are – and ought to be – addressed in the context of adoption and foster care.

Positioning children in the general conversation over multiculturalism often boils down to who has the power to place children and where. This question has been, in recent years, elided under the guise of recognizing the right of the cultural group to set its own membership standards: if a child is a member of the group, the group *ipso facto* has the authority to place the child if the child's family fails.[62] On the surface, that approach has some merit: recognizing the power of a cultural group to formulate the criteria for belonging seems to be a critical aspect of self-determination. At a deeper level, however,

---

[60] Shachar, *supra* n. 20 at 45–46.

[61] John Eekelaar, *Family Law and Personal Life* (New York: Oxford University Press, 2006): 167.

[62] An interesting example of the problem created when groups exercise exclusive authority over who belongs recently surfaced in Great Britain, and illustrates the explosiveness of considering these issues for children, although the controversy centered on religious belonging, distinct from the issues discussed here. On December 15, 2009, Britain's Supreme Court issued a ruling in a case challenging a decision by the admissions office of the Jews' Free School, the preeminent school in North London's Jewish community, denying admission to a twelve-year-old boy whose father was Jewish and whose mother had converted to Judaism. The family was quite religiously observant, and had been throughout the child's life. British law allows publicly funded schools to grant preference to applicants in their own faith. Under the definition used by the school, the child was not considered Jewish because the mother had not converted under Orthodox auspices. The Supreme Court declared that use of the traditional test was discriminatory under the Race Relations Act, and held that while the school could give preference to Jewish students, it must impose a religious practice test rather than the Orthodox test utilized. Sarah Lyell, "Who is a Jew? Court Ruling in Britain Raises Question," *New York Times*, Nov. 7, 2009, www.nytimes.com/2009/11/08/world/europe/08britain.html.

assigning authority to determine who belongs ignores the fact that children, in particular, can belong to many groups in many different ways; disputes over membership in such cases are simply converted into jurisdictional disputes between different groups seeking legal recognition and authority.

The following three chapters explore these issues as they arise in three distinct adoption and foster care contexts. Chapter 3 examines issues associated with the transracial adoption debate in the United States that, under the Multiethnic Placement Act, generally prohibits consideration of children's racial, ethnic, and cultural identities in placement decisions. Chapter 4 looks at the distinctive legal regime governing the placement of American Indian children, which, under the Indian Child Welfare Act, takes an approach diametrically opposed to MEPA-IEP, because it reflects considerable deference to the child's community of origin. Chapter 5 probes these same issues of belonging in the context of the emerging transnational adoption regime. Understanding that there are compelling concerns on all sides and that communities and individual children have tangible concerns that deserve recognition, the book nonetheless questions the adequacy of assuming that issues of children's identity can or should be resolved by any single group.

The specific disputes always become hard cases because the questions themselves are hard: What criteria should be used to determine children's identity, and who ought to have authority to decide? How should courts and policy makers understand the importance of cultural belonging and reconcile those interests with competing concerns for the child's placement in a "forever" family? Throughout the ensuing chapters, it should be clear that there is no unambiguously correct answer to these questions. Concerns about belonging for both children and the groups from which they originate must be treated contextually, as the possibilities for providing care range along a continuum, whether dealing with the needs of children without parents domestically or internationally.

Recognizing that such a continuum exists means that the solutions will not fall into neat categories. Intricate problems require intricate solutions. The discussions that follow attempt to expose the complexity of the issues and to focus attention on a wide range of possible responses that, taken alone or in concert, may create a more nuanced approach to the treatment of children without parents.

3

Rainbow Dreams and Domestic Transracial Adoption

In March 2010, actress Sandra Bullock received an Academy Award for her performance in *The Blind Side*, a movie adaptation of the story of Michael Oher, an African American boy who drifted for years between a troubled family and an equally troubled foster care system and found himself homeless and barely literate at sixteen. In 2003, he met and was later adopted by Leigh Anne Tuohy, played by Bullock, and her husband, Sean, a well-to-do white couple living in Memphis. By 2009, Oher had graduated with a degree in criminal justice from the University of Mississippi, making the honor roll on two occasions, and was drafted as an offensive tackle by the NFL's Baltimore Ravens.[1]

Just days after securing her Oscar, Bullock made national headlines in a different context as she announced her separation from husband Jesse James. At the time, Bullock and James were planning to adopt an infant African American boy, Louis, who had joined the family following his birth three months earlier in flood-ravaged New Orleans. For weeks, stories about James's extramarital exploits made tabloid headlines, including the disclosure that he had at one time posed in Nazi regalia in pictures posted on the Internet, which, he asserted, "was funny then."[2]

The Blind Side represented one narrative in the strained conversation about transracial adoption: against all odds, a seemingly doomed African American boy finds a loving home with a white family in a transcendent story of

---

[1] The movie was based on a story by Michael Lewis, "The Ballad of Big Mike," which appeared in *The New York Times Magazine*, Sept. 24, 2006.

[2] Vicky Mabrey and Steve Baker, "Jesse James Talks about Sandra Bullock Baby, Nazi Rumors," ABC News Nightline, May 25, 2010. http://abcnews.go.com/Nightline/jesse-james-sandra-bullock-adopted-baby-nazi-rumors/story?id=10730627&page=2#.TylvWoKwUQA. Bullock subsequently divorced James and adopted the baby.

belonging.[3] The other narrative emerged with the disclosures about Bullock's personal life: a well-to-do white celebrity adopts a child of color from a disastrously marginalized community, while married, moreover, to someone who seemed woefully unprepared for the task of parenting this particular child.

In the four decades since transracial placements began drawing public attention, the practice has been controversial. In the United States, the Multiethnic Placement Act, enacted in 1994 and amended by the Interethnic Adoption Provision in 1996 (MEPA-IEP), forbids the consideration of race and ethnicity in adoptive and foster care placement decisions except in exceptional circumstances.[4] MEPA-IEP's approach, reflecting what some argue is a commitment to equality and neutrality in U.S. law, represents one approach to considering communal belonging when fashioning foster and adoptive care solutions for dependent children, and is at the heart of a deeply divided conversation over domestic transracial adoption. MEPA-IEP reflects the belief that, with few exceptions, the best interests of children should be evaluated without reference to their race or ethnicity; the primary objective in making placement decisions should be placing children in stable, permanent homes as quickly as possible.

MEPA-IEP's scheme, however, is not appropriate for every child in need of temporary or permanent placement with a family because it bars social workers from considering racial and communal connections in child-placement decisions. Critics of the Act argue that it disserves children and undermines communities of color by suggesting that children of color should be raised by white families.[5] These scholars argue that the legislation allows the complexities of the racial issues embedded in transracial adoption to be simply glossed over.[6] MEPA-IEP's supporters, on the other hand, argue that disparagement

---

[3] The movie has not been above criticism because of the racial issues associated with privileged white families taking in black athletes, which occurs more frequently than is commonly known. *See, e.g.,* Josh Levin, "The Other Blind Sides: The Michael Oher Story May Have Been Amazing, But Was It Unique?" *Slate* (Oct. 14, 2010).

[4] Multiethnic Placement Act of 1994, Pub. L. No. 103–382, sec. 551, 108 Stat. 3518, 4056 (codified as amended at 42 U.S.C. secs. 1996b, 5115a (2006), *repealed in part by* Small Business Job Protections Act of 1996, Pub. L. No. 104–188, sec. 1808(d), 110 Stat. 1755, 1904 (codified at 42 U.S.C. sec. 1996b (2006)).

[5] Transracial placements overwhelmingly involve the placement of children of color with white families, rather than the other way around.

[6] *See, e.g.,* Lauren K. Pfeil, "Recognizing Race as a Reality, Not a Barrier: The Problems with Colorblind Adoption Policy within a Race-Conscious America," *Children's Legal Rights Journal* 29, no. 2 (Summer 2009): 34–46; Twila L. Perry, "The Transracial Adoption Controversy: An Analysis of Discourse and Subordination," *New York University Review of Law and Social Change* 21 (1993–1994): 33–108 (hereafter The Transracial Adoption Controversy); Dorothy E. Roberts, *Shattered Bonds: The Color of Child Welfare* (New York: Basic Books, 2003).

of the Act is based on faulty assumptions about the long-term impact of transracial adoption on minority children and that its critics ignore the needs of vulnerable children for stability and emotional attachment.[7]

MEPA-IEP was enacted in the mid-1990s in response to the claims of transracial adoption advocates that transracial placements had become a virtual impossibility because both state and private adoption professionals were too often seeking to match children with families of the same race or ethnicity. Because of social workers' reluctance or refusal to place children transracially, MEPA-IEP proponents argued, children lived in limbo, drifting between foster care placements or in and out of abusive or neglectful homes, while social workers vainly (or laconically) sought homes with "appropriate" (read: same-race) foster or adoptive parents. Supporters of the legislation asserted that color-blind assessments of potential adoptive and foster homes were essential as a matter of racial equality.[8]

Opponents reiterated – and continue to reiterate – the arguments that they had been voicing since transracial placements surged in the late 1960s and 1970s: that children placed with white parents are likely to become alienated from their own identities and their families and communities of origin and grow up without the tools necessary to live in a world shaped by pervasive and seemingly ineradicable racism. Moreover, they argued that the practice as a whole erodes the stability of minority families and communities and reinforces a bias against parenting by members of minority communities in general, particularly because children of color are overrepresented in state foster care systems, and more children are born to unmarried women of color than to white single mothers.[9]

---

[7] *See, e.g.,* Elizabeth Bartholet, "Where Do Black Children Belong?," *University of Pennsylvania Law Review* 139 (1991).

[8] Elizabeth Bartholet, *Family Bonds: Adoption and the Politics of Parenting* (Boston: Beacon Press, 1999); Elizabeth Bartholet, *Nobody's Children: Abuse and Neglect, Foster Drift, and the Adoption Alternative* (Boston: Beacon Press, 2000) (hereafter *Nobody's Children*); Randall Kennedy, "Orphans of Separatism: The Painful Politics of Transracial Adoption," *American Prospect* 17 (Spring 1994): 38–45; Richard Banks, "The Color of Desire: Fulfilling Adoptive Parents' Racial Preferences through Discriminatory State Action," *Yale Law Journal* 107 (1998): 875–964.

[9] Roberts, *supra* n. 6, and Dorothy Roberts, "Feminism, Race and Adoption Policy," in *Adoption Matters: Philosophical and Feminist Essays*, eds. Sally Haslanger and Charlotte Witt (Ithaca, NY: Cornell University Press, 2005): 234–246; Dorothy E. Roberts, *Killing the Black Body: Race, Reproduction, and the Meaning of Liberty* (New York: Vintage Books, 1999); Dorothy Roberts, "Adoption Myths and Racial Realities in the United States," in *Outsiders Within: Writing on Transracial Adoption*, eds. Jane Jeong Trenka, Julia Chinyere Oparah, and Sun Yung Shin (Cambridge, MA: South End Press, 2006): 49–56; Perry, *supra* n. 6, and Twila L. Perry, "Transracial Adoption and Gentrification: An Essay on Race, Power, Family and Community," *Boston College Third World Law Journal* 26 (2006): 25–60; Ruth-Arlene W. Howe, "Adoption

Although MEPA-IEP has been in place for almost two decades, transracial adoption, particularly the adoption of African American children by white parents,[10] continues to generate uncomfortable conversations and heated disagreements; there is, indeed, a vast scholarly literature on the subject. As Fogg-Davis has argued, transracial adoptive families upset traditional understandings of both race and family: transracial adoption renders the concept of race "flexible," and because families are critical to the development of identity, "we should expect the most intense exchange of ideas about racial self-awareness to occur within immediate families."[11] In point of fact, MEPA-IEP along with the Adoption and Safe Families Act (ASFA) appears to have increased the transracial adoption of biracial children, rather than African American children.[12]

Transracial adoption produces disagreement because it is inextricably enmeshed with the history of race and privilege in the United States, in the same way that transnational adoption raises those concerns on a global level. It is, as Janet Farrell Smith notes, a dispute in which neither side can claim the moral high ground; a position for or against the practice inevitably leaves behind an irreducible moral remainder, as there are compelling arguments on both sides.[13] The idea that a child should be placed in a permanent family as quickly as possible competes with concerns that placements should neither undermine a child's sense of identity with a particular community nor stigmatize the community itself.[14]

Beyond arguments focused specifically on transracial placements – whether white parents can adequately parent children of color and whether children, families, and communities of color are undermined by the practice – transracial adoption raises broader questions about multiculturalism itself. As

---

Laws and Practices: Serving Whose Best Interests," in *Baby Markets*, ed. Michele Bratcher Goodwin (New York: Cambridge University Press, 2010): 86–93.

[10] The debate over transracial adoption refers primarily to the placement of African American infants and young children with white parents, with the national conversation centered on the black/white divide. Of course, the adoption of children of Latino, Asian, and other backgrounds is also affected by these disputes. In addition, there is a long and complicated history involving the adoption by whites of American Indian children, which is taken up in Chapter 4.

[11] H. Fogg-Davis, *The Ethics of Transracial Adoption* (Ithaca, NY: Cornell University Press, 2002): 20.

[12] Adoption and Safe Families Act, Pub. L. No. 105–89, 111 Stat. 2115 (codified as amended in 42 U.S.C., various sections). Patricia K. Jennings, "The Trouble with the Multiethnic Placement Act: An Empirical Look at Transracial Adoption," *Sociological Perspectives* 49, no. 4 (Winter 2006): 559–581, 577.

[13] Janet Farrell Smith, "Analyzing Ethical Conflict in the Transracial Adoption Debate: Three Conflicts Involving Community," *Hypatia* 11 (1996): 1–33, 2; *also* Mary Lyndon Shanley, *Making Babies, Making Families: What Matters Most in an Age of Reproductive Technologies, Surrogacy, Adoption, and Same-Sex and Unwed Parents* (Boston: Beacon Press, 2001): 13–14.

[14] Smith, *id.*, at 2–3.

discussed in Chapter 2, multiculturalism typically envisions the creation of spaces that allow individuals and groups holding distinct values and practicing different lifestyles to live respectfully with other communities and individuals, in the hope that an open society will learn to value cultural and communal differences. But transracial adoption crosses social boundaries in a way that seems to betray the promises of multiculturalism: because it typically involves the placement of children of color with white parents, rather than the other way round, the community that stands to lose its distinction is inevitably the community of color.

As noted earlier, multiculturalism is subject to critiques from both the left and the right. On the right, many argue that national communities in particular are entitled to demand a significant degree of assimilation in order to forge a coherent society, and that multiculturalism simply balkanizes societies, pitting the needs and demands of one group against another. Left critics of multiculturalism argue that basic adherence to liberal norms is the best guarantee of equality and freedom for both individuals and groups, and that laws and policies constructing boundaries around particular ways of life or group affinities may end up supporting wholly illiberal and exploitive communities at the expense of individuals located within them.

Disputes over transracial adoption tap into both of those concerns, but raise the issues in ways that move between traditional liberal and conservative critiques. Those skeptical about transracial adoption argue, as noted, that the practice undermines communities and disserves children because the latter never learn the coping strategies necessary to flourish in the face of racism and lose touch with the identities that will inevitably be assigned to them, while the former's distinctive traditions, such as extended kinship and nonkinship networks of care necessitated by the institution of slavery, as well as the community's reputation for providing care for vulnerable children, are undervalued. Efforts by adoptive families to inculcate an awareness of racial and cultural difference, according to these critics, simply amount to a shallow kind of racial and cultural tourism.[15] Thus, acquainting white parents with Kwanzaa celebrations or teaching them to deal with kinky hair are superficial adjustments that ignore deeper issues; it is the constant assault of racism and understanding how communal traditions deflect that assault that can only be imparted by same-race caregivers.[16]

Transracial adoption advocates, on the other hand, note that communities and cultures are by definition constantly in flux, revising, absorbing, and

---

[15] This argument is voiced even more frequently in the context of transnational adoption, discussed in Chapter 5.

[16] *See generally* Roberts and Perry, *supra* n. 178.

discarding different ideas and influences. They point out, too, that multiracial families bring together a variety of traditions and communities to create new cultural and racial understandings and enhance social cohesion. Moreover, they argue, attempts to "fix" a child in any particular community restricts the child's ability to fashion his or her own identity, and may run counter to the traditional prerogatives accorded both biological and adoptive parents. Children raised in bi- or multiracial families, they argue, learn to transcend the separatism that critics of multiculturalism worry about.[17]

On yet another level, transracial adoption raises broad questions about how claims of race and culture are intertwined in the first place. When the concerns of minority communities are articulated as claims of culture or cultural identity rather than claims of race or racism, the use of race and culture as proxies for one another becomes problematic. As Shanley has pointed out, "[t]ransracial adoption pits values of integration or assimilation against multiculturalism, and individuality against racial-ethnic community. . . . All of these values are fundamental to pluralist democracy in the United States . . . [and raise] complex moral and policy issues."[18]

This chapter traces the development of legal standards governing domestic transracial adoption and foster care placement culminating in the passage of MEPA-IEP and, shortly thereafter, ASFA, both federal statutes that provide the contemporary framework for adoption and foster care programs. It explores how MEPA-IEP and ASFA attempt to meet the needs of children as well as how those statutes frame the communities and families from which children originate. Both statutes aim to facilitate the adoption of children, particularly children of color and children drawn into state child welfare systems (who are disproportionately children of color), in order to minimize the damage done when children are shuffled among foster homes while awaiting permanent placements. But neither statute is wholly satisfactory in its approach, and both have created as many problems as they have solved.

Examining how MEPA-IEP attempts to elide questions of race, and how ASFA attempts to move children quickly out of allegedly harmful environments and into "forever" families, illustrates how difficult it is to draw the boundaries of belonging for children. Even when a community is united by a stark marker like race, it is difficult to assess claims grounded on assertions of group harm when members of the group identify with the group in distinct ways and may experience harm, if at all, in dramatically different ways.[19] Evaluating group claims is particularly fraught when racial and cultural differences

---

[17] *See generally* Bartholet, *supra* n. 180.

[18] Shanley, *supra* n. 13 at 13.

[19] Smith, *supra* n. 13 at 17–19.

do not map seamlessly on each other. Although every racially marginalized group in the United States can legitimately claim historical and continuing injuries attributable to race discrimination, it is less clear that racial groups are *ipso facto* distinct *cultural* groups, as there may be considerable variation in social practices and history within groups broadly defined on the basis of race. Thus, assessing whether transracial placement threatens distinctive communities is complicated because groups have different degrees of cohesion, and that cohesion in any event may not coalesce around traditional indices of cultural distinctiveness.

On the other hand, a cultural group may be defined, as noted in Chapter 2, as one that shares a unique history and has developed specific patterns of behavior shaped by that history. Members of minority communities in the United States typically share a singular history of discrimination, and many have adapted by developing (or continuing) social practices that help in coping with those injustices – informal adoption was one way of responding to the cruelties of slavery, for example, and extended kinship or guardian care continues to be common in many African American communities.[20] By some accounts, then, racial groups may justifiably be considered distinctive cultural units. Alternately, given the fact that race discrimination in and of itself continues largely unabated for many communities, it may be argued that members of marginalized racial groups should be accorded protection on the basis of race alone, whether or not such group's distinctive "cultural survival" is threatened or adversely affected.

What sets transracial adoption apart and makes communal belonging arguments quite difficult – what leads to treating it differently than, say, the adoption of American Indian children or children adopted transnationally – has to do with the political fact that non-Indian minority groups in the United States are not self-governing. Political, as opposed to cultural or communal, boundaries make it easier (but not easy) to treat a child as "belonging" to one group over another. Thus, while Latino or African American communities may be distinct from mainstream white communities, American law does not recognize such groups as semi-sovereign, and the complications of defining communal boundaries multiply.

Another difficulty arises because many of the children subject to adoption and foster care are bi- or multiracial; as *The New York Times* recently reported, those groups presently comprise the fastest growing demographic in the United States.[21] As increasing numbers of people identify as multiracial,

---

[20] *See generally* Carol B. Stack, *All Our Kin: Strategies for Survival in a Black Community* (New York: Harper and Row, 1974).

[21] Susan Saulny, "Black? White? Asian? More Young Americans Choose All of the Above," *New York Times*, January 29, 2011, www.nytimes.com/2011/01/30/us/30mixed.html. A 2009 report

claiming that a child should be placed within a particular racial community because mainstream society will label the child according to his or her race becomes problematic. As Fogg-Davis notes, children themselves must – and do – engage in "racial navigation" and, over time, carve out their own spaces of belonging between cultures and communities.[22] Over time, then, any policy response in the area of adoption and foster care that tries to account for communal boundaries centered on an ascriptive characteristic such as race must recognize that the interests of individual children may, over time, accord with or diverge from the interests of the communities from which they originate.

Finally, the public argument over transracial adoption is typically conducted at an abstract level, speaking in broad terms about children of color, rather than differentiating among the various groups of children subject to adoption or foster care. When the particular population of children at issue is not specified, important nuances are lost. MEPA-IEP advocates talk often about the need to pull children out of the nightmare of foster care, but many children in foster care are not the children who find homes as a result of MEPA-IEP's "race-neutral" placement requirement. Nor is it clear that ASFA has significantly improved the prospects for many sub-populations of children in foster care. These problems are explored next and discussed in the context of how transracial adoption affects understandings of multiculturalism more generally.

THE ASSIMILATIVE ROOTS OF DOMESTIC ADOPTION POLICY

The early history of adoption and foster care placement in the United States provides ample support for skepticism about the motives behind transracial placements, even if those motives have shifted over time. Before the middle of the nineteenth century, formal adoption was rare in the United States; care for needy children generally fell to kin or members of the immediate community. Over time, local governments and private charitable institutions began to provide both indoor and outdoor relief on a limited scale. Early in the nation's

from the Pew Foundation noted, too, that one in seven marriages in 2008 now involve spouses from different races. Jeffrey S. Passel, Wendy Wang, and Paul Taylor, *Marrying Out One-in-Seven New U.S. Marriages is Interracial or Interethnic*, Pew Foundation, June 4, 2010. http://pewresearch.org/pubs/1616/american-marriage-interracial-interethnic. That fact is important for understanding how children adopted transracially may continue to be perceived as different.

[22] Fogg-Davis, *supra* n. 11 at 2–3. Kevin Maillard and Janis McDonald argue that transracial adoption creates a space within which to "challenge the immutability of racial boundaries." Kevin Noble Maillard and Janis L. McDonald, "The Anatomy of Grey: A Theory of Interracial Convergence," *Law & Inequality* 26 (2008): 305–352, 352.

history, arrangements such as apprenticeship, arranged voluntarily either by a parent or by an overseer of the poor, functionally resembled adoption. Apprenticeship typically entailed an agreement that the child would provide personal services in exchange for room, board, and sometimes education, but did not dissolve the legal ties of family. As Grossberg has pointed out, the system was driven primarily by concerns about protecting the public fisc: Poor families could not veto apprenticeship decisions if made by a local authority; black children could be indentured regardless of parental resources; and "by the 1840s, public indentures were simply a device to recruit and exploit poor children."[23]

With the abolition of indentured servitude following the American Civil War and the advent of the Industrial Revolution with its demands for vast quantities of urban, unskilled labor, apprenticeship became anachronistic. Consequently, especially as the demand for factory workers made it increasingly difficult to care for children, the mid-nineteenth century saw the rise of "orphan asylums" providing institutional care for indigent children. The majority of children in such institutions were not orphaned but had at least one parent still living; parents often kept in close touch with children so placed and expressed significant concern about their well-being.[24] The time children spent in institutional care varied: at the Albany Orphan Asylum in New York, for example, the average stay for children was two and one-half years.[25]

In addition to changes in caring for vulnerable children, the mid-nineteenth century also witnessed a significant cultural shift around how children themselves were viewed as moral agents. Calvinist ideas of children as beings who needed strict discipline to control their innate inclination to evil gave way to a Victorian idealization of children as innocents who needed to be nurtured and protected from the vagaries of a harsh and heartless world. That new Victorian imagining, however, ran headfirst into the reality of poverty and dependence. As populations of needy children grew, they came to be viewed as a menace. In 1849, for example, New York City Police Commissioner Matsell warned that the city was filled with "idle and vicious children . . . only destined to a

---

[23] Michael D. Grossberg, *Governing the Hearth: Law and the Family in Nineteenth-Century America* (Chapel Hill: The University of North Carolina Press, 1985): 259, 266.

[24] *See generally* Judith A. Dulberger, *"Mother Donit fore the Best": Correspondence of a 19th Century Orphan Asylum* (Syracuse, NY: Syracuse University Press, 1996); *accord*, Patricia Susan Hart, *A Home for Every Child: The Washington Children's Home Society in the Progressive Era* (Seattle: University of Washington Press, 2010): 36–69.

[25] Dulberger, *supra* n. 24 at 15.

life of misery, shame, crime and, ultimately, to a felon's doom."[26] At the time, 80 percent of all felony complaints were leveled at minors, who accounted for 25 percent of the city's prison population.[27]

Reformers, then, had to balance deep-seated fears of feral children against sentimental images of children as innocents in need of guidance. Indoor relief was costly, and perhaps more importantly, un-American.[28] Charles Brace, founder of the New York Children's Aid Society, argued for the necessity of moving children away from cities into healthy, hard-working American families and was instrumental in developing the orphan trains that operated from the middle of the nineteenth century through the first two decades of the twentieth. Placing children with farm families, not incidentally, removed them from contact with their parents and their old-world values: inheritance represented danger.

Whereas the eugenics movement advocated birth control to eliminate being saddled with degenerate children, most child-savers, often deeply religious, believed that poor children's natural predisposition to crime could be overcome through proper education into the "civilized" habits of middle-class American families holding American values.[29] Sophie Minton, a prominent New York child-saver, extolled the virtues of placing out, and was one among many who argued that institutional care for children spoiled them, as they became accustomed "to the comfort of steam-heated halls and to being waited on."[30]

Brace's orphan trains moved tens of thousands of children out of eastern cities into the countryside, but its proponents initially did little to determine the appropriateness of homes in which children were placed: potential families simply lined up to pick out children when the orphan trains came through town.[31] Over time, however, reformers began to focus considerable energy on

[26] Quoted in Miriam Z. Langsam, *Children West: A History of the Placing Out System of the New York Children's Aid Society, 1853–1890* (Madison: State Historical Society of Wisconsin for University of Wisconsin, 1964): 1.

[27] *Id.* at 2.

[28] Institutions were also dangerous places for children, especially infants, where the death rate could be as high as 80 percent. Barbara Melosh, *Strangers and Kin: The American Way of Adoption* (Cambridge, MA: Harvard University Press, 2002): 18.

[29] Hart, *supra* n. 24 at 106.

[30] Sophie Minton, "Family Life versus Institution Life," in National Conference on Social Welfare, *History of Child-Saving in the United States* (Boston: George H. Ellis, 1893): 37–53, 46; *accord*, Charles Loring Brace, *The Dangerous Classes of New York, and Twenty Years' Work Among Them* (New York: Wynkoop and Hallenbeck, 1872): 42.

[31] Marilyn Irvin Holt, *The Orphan Trains: Placing Out in America* (Lincoln: University of Nebraska Press, 1991): 41–79.

the suitability of placements. Because both urban and rural reformers sought to bring children into contact with Christian values, it became imperative to determine whether the families into which children would be placed were morally worthy and capable of transforming the child's very identity.[32] As reform efforts increased throughout the nineteenth century, potential adoptive and foster families began to be screened to ensure that they could introduce children to dominant conceptions of what constituted a good family environment.[33]

From its outset, then, providing care for needy children was propelled by profoundly assimilationist impulses. It was patently discriminatory toward the poor; although there is no question that poverty was the primary factor in rendering many children's situations desperate, poverty itself was often figured as a personal sin, and "cultural inferiority" was a frequent reason for determining that poor children's families were unsuitable.[34] Driven by the impulse to Americanize and civilize needy children, systems of care were intimately tied to the project of nation-building. Appropriate adoptive families had to fit the preconceptions of good families constructed by charity workers and an emerging class of professional social workers, fueled by the conviction that some Americans – white, Protestant, and middle class – were uniquely suited to raise children and to give shape to the community itself.

Not all needy children were the objects of this beneficence, however. Child-saving efforts were largely directed at white children; children of color were not routinely accepted by institutions or served by a reform movement peopled by white, middle-class women. Children of color largely fell beneath the notice of mainstream reformers altogether, with formal assistance, if any, coming from charities and families located within those communities.[35]

As the nineteenth century moved into the twentieth, adoption and foster care continued to be informed by the belief that family environments had to be carefully monitored. The rhetoric shifted, however: adoption was no longer primarily motivated by the need to remove children from degenerate roots. Instead, it came to be framed as a cure for consequences of reckless

---

[32] Hart, *supra* n. 24 at 7–128. The same concerns pervaded care for children without parents in other Western nations. *See, e.g.,* Sylvia Schafer, *Children in Moral Danger and the Problem of Government in the Third Republic of France* (Princeton, NJ: Princeton University Press, 1997).

[33] Hart, *supra* n. 24 at 103–128.

[34] Linda Gordon, *Pitied but not Entitled: Single Mothers and the History of Welfare* (Cambridge, MA: Harvard University Press, 1994): 24–35.

[35] *Id.* at 111–143.

sexuality – at least for the children of white mothers, whose purity needed to be policed and protected. Adoption proved the ideal solution to the problem of illegitimacy, and served three ends simultaneously, as Melosh points out: it protected mothers from the shame of sexual license, children from the shame of bastardy, and adoptive couples from the shame of infertility. Childcare professionals took the position that "[t]he healthy [white] unwed mother ought to be persuaded – if possible in advance of the birth of the child – that the best possible thing she can do for the child is to give him to eager, loving parents who will do for him what she, by her very circumstances, cannot do."[36] Although the evangelical fervor to place children in Christian homes had abated slightly, most adoption organizations were affiliated with particular religious groups, and the idea that children's needs could be met only in homes that fit middle-class ideals persisted. This is not to suggest that families seeking to adopt children consciously decided to do so in order to save the nation from degenerates; the vast majority were childless couples seeking a child to love. Nor were all social workers purposely seeking to elevate only middle-class values and perpetuate a particular idea of the good citizen; they sought stable, secure homes for children and naturally found that stability in the middle-class environments with which they were familiar.[37]

Adoptions of white infants increased as the twentieth century moved forward, reaching a peak between 1945 and 1960. Race-matching was the norm – indeed, it was assumed by adoption professionals and others that an adopted child should appear to be the biological offspring of the adoptive parents. Creating such "as if" families was considered essential to promoting the proper adjustment of both the child and his or her adoptive family in order to create a new family bound by ties of affection. The law in turn naturalized this family, absolutely extinguishing the legal ties between a child and his or her biological family and replacing them with legal ties to the adoptive family.[38] As Shanley has noted, the complex dysfunctions of race relations meant that illegitimate African American children generated less anxiety in the dominant community; their illegitimacy was to be expected in a community that was, by definition, less worthy than white society and their needs were simply beneath notice.[39] When children were biracial, social workers were often at pains to determine what the child "was" in order to make certain that the child would move seamlessly into his or her new family. In some cases, lighter

[36] Melosh, *supra* n. 28 at 35.
[37] Hart, *supra* n. 24 at 114–124.
[38] Grossberg, *supra* n. 23 at 271–278.
[39] Shanley, *supra* n. 13 at 16–17.

biracial children were hardest to place because they did not blend easily into unquestionably white or black families.[40]

ECLIPSING THE "AS IF" FAMILY

By the 1960s, adoption was a relatively common practice. By 1970, some 175,000 adoptions were occurring annually in the United States, approximately half of those being "stranger" adoptions, or adoptions not involving kin. About a quarter of those stranger adoptions were carried on through private agencies, while the remainder were effected through public child welfare systems.[41] The landscape of adoption altered considerably during the late 1950s, 1960s, and early 1970s, however. Infertile couples became increasingly open about their decisions to welcome adopted children as their own, although considerable secrecy continued to surround biological mothers, those "girls who went away."[42] Moreover, whereas adoption during the latter part of the nineteenth century had involved a mix of older and younger children – many families sought children over the age of ten who could assist with home and farm work – during the twentieth century, adopting families increasingly sought infants to rear as their own.

During the 1960s, however, the number of white infants available for adoption contracted sharply. Birth control became more effective and more widely available. In addition, the stigma attached to single parenthood declined for white women who chose to keep their babies. Finally, adoption itself began to come out of the closet as mixed-race adoptive families appeared on the scene and adoptees from other parts of the globe, particularly Korea, began to join American families.[43]

---

[40] Melosh, *supra* n. 28 at 93–104.
[41] Adoption statistics are difficult to track, because statistics were not routinely collected. Penelope L. Maza, "Adoption Trends: 1944–1975," *Child Welfare Research Notes #9* (U.S. Children's Bureau, August 1984), pp. 1–4, Child Welfare League of America Papers, Box 65, Folder: "Adoption – Research – Reprints of Articles," Social Welfare History Archives, University of Minnesota located at http://pages.uoregon.edu/adoption/archive/MazaAT.htm.
[42] Ann Fessler, *The Girls Who Went Away: The Hidden History of Women Who Surrendered Children for Adoption in the Decades Before Roe v. Wade* (New York: The Penguin Group, 2006).
[43] Although many children initially adopted from Korea were classified as abandoned, over time, increasing numbers of children came from "broken homes" or were born to unwed mothers; by the 1980s, that latter category dwarfed the number of children who had been abandoned. Elena Kim, *Adopted Territory: Transnational Korean Adoptees and the Politics of Belonging* (Durham, NC: Duke University Press, 2010): 25.

While adoption began to be more openly acknowledged, other changes in American society affected the adoption universe. The civil rights movement brought American race relations to the forefront of American consciousness; as legal apartheid began to be dismantled with the Supreme Court's opinion in *Brown v. Board of Education* in 1954, and both the Civil Rights Act of 1964 and the Voting Rights Act of 1965 came into force, many white Americans naively believed that the "race problem" would fade quietly into history. For historically marginalized racial communities, however, it was a time to recover and claim racial identity. It was also starkly apparent for these communities that race discrimination was not likely to disappear quickly, nor was mainstream American society likely to take meaningful steps to remedy the legacies of apartheid that had affected those communities on every level. It was against this backdrop that the current controversy over transracial adoption erupted.

LEGISLATING TRANSRACIAL PLACEMENTS

By the early 1970s, transracial placements had increased significantly in number; by some accounts, some 20,000 African American children had been placed with white families over the previous decade.[44] It was not commonplace, however; even at its peak, transracial adoption constituted only between 1.5 and 2 percent of all adoptions annually.[45] But the practice attracted significant attention, coming as it did on the heels of the unfulfilled promises of the civil rights movement, the emergence of a vocal Black Nationalist movement and increasing moral panic about the disintegration or undermining of the black family.[46]

---

[44] Constance Pohl and Kathy Harris, *Transracial Adoption: Children and Parents Speak* (New York: Franklin Watts, 1992).

[45] Data on the precise number of transracially adopted children are limited. One study of transracial adoption placements in 1972 reported that, nationally, of some 6,000 African American children adopted, 4,500 were placed in homes with African American parents while the remaining 1,500 were placed with white parents. The figures were not broken down to indicate the number of same-race placements that were kin or stepparent adoptions. Opportunity: National Survey of Black Children Adopted in 1972, September 18, 1973, Viola W. Bernard Papers, Box 162, Folder 7, Archives and Special Collections, Augustus C. Long Library, Columbia University, http://pages.uoregon.edu/adoption/archive/OpportunityNSBCA.htm.

[46] Daniel Patrick Moynihan, working for the Johnson administration, issued a report in 1965 that argued that black families were mired in a "tangle of pathology" comprised of unmarried mothers and welfare dependency. The idea of a "culture of poverty" emerged from that report; because it was viewed as labeling African Americans as morally deficient, it touched a deep nerve and was widely criticized. Daniel P. Moynihan, "The Negro Family: The Case For National Action," Office of Policy Planning and Research, United States Department of Labor, March 1965, www.blackpast.org/?q=primary/moynihan-report-1965.

In 1972, the National Association of Black Social Workers (NABSW) issued a policy statement strongly condemning transracial placements in both adoption and foster care. Because that statement often forms the starting point in the debate over transracial adoption, it is worth quoting at length:

> [The NABSW] affirms the inviolable position of black children in black families where they belong physically, psychologically and culturally in order that they receive the total sense of themselves and develop a sound projection of their future. . . .

> In our society, the developmental needs of Black children are significantly different from those of white children. Black children are taught, from an early age, highly sophisticated coping techniques to deal with racist practices perpetrated by individuals and institutions. . . . Only a black family can transmit the emotional and sensitive subtleties of perception and reaction essential for a black child's survival in a racist society. . . .

> We fully recognize the phenomenon of transracial adoption as an expedient for white folk, not as an altruistic humane concern for black children. The supply of white children for adoption has all but vanished and adoption agencies, having always catered to middle class whites, developed an answer to their desire for parenthood by motivating them to consider black children. . . .

> We know there are numerous alternatives to the placement of black children with white families and challenge all agencies and organizations to commit themselves to the basic concept of black families for black children. . . . Black families can be found when agencies alter their requirements, methods of approach, definition of suitable family and tackle the legal machinery to facilitate inter-state placements. . . .

> We denounce the assertions that blacks will not adopt; we affirm the fact that black people, in large number, cannot maneuver the obstacle course of the traditional adoption process. This process has long been a screening out device. The emphasis on high income, educational achievement, residential status and other accoutrements of a white middle class life style eliminates black applicants by the score.

> The National Association of Black Social Workers asserts the conviction that children should not remain in foster homes or institutions when adoption can be a reality. We stand firmly, though, on conviction that a white home is not a suitable placement for black children and contend it is totally unnecessary.[47]

[47] National Association of Black Social Workers, "Position Statement on Trans-Racial Adoption," September 1972, in Robert H. Bremner, "Children and Youth in America: A Documentary History," Vol. 3, Parts 1–4 (Harvard University Press, 1974): 777–780, http://pages.uoregon.edu/adoption/archive/NabswTRA.htm.

Following the issuance of this position paper, policies abjuring transracial placements began to appear in both state and private placement agencies. Mia Tuan has argued that these policies reflected the position that a child's best interest was understood to include "preserving a child's racial and cultural heritage,"[48] a position that tracks the NABSW assertion, albeit less emphatically. Alternately, those policies may have simply reflected a continuing adherence to the idea that children should be placed in "as if" families, without focusing specifically on the need to "preserve" race and cultural heritage. It is clear, however, that many adoption professionals worried about the developmental effects of transracial placements on minority children; there is some evidence that many social workers worried, as well, about censure by other professionals in the field if they pushed transracial placements. By 1975, the number of reported transracial placements had dropped dramatically, although the data are incomplete, and transracial placements continued to be limited over the next two decades.[49]

Over the ensuing twenty years, the NABSW position was reiterated, albeit with a shift in focus to preserving African American families, as several studies suggested that transracially adopted children did not suffer disproportionately from identity and self-esteem problems.[50] In 1994, the organization issued a second statement, titled "Preserving African American Families," expanding on its concerns about transracial adoption and highly critical of child-protection policies that lead to the overrepresentation of African American children in child welfare systems. The 1994 statement also argued that transracial placement should be considered only after "documented evidence of unsuccessful same race placements has been reviewed and supported by appropriate representatives of the African American community."[51] The organization now advocates for policies that stress family reunification, kinship placement, or placement with "families of the same race and culture," that emphasize more effective recruitment of families of African

---

[48] Mia Tuan, "Domestic and International Transracial Adoption: A Synopsis of the Literature," *Sociology Compass* 2, no. 6 (2008): 1848–1859.

[49] C. A. Bachrach, P. F. Adams, S. Sambrano, and K. A. London, "Adoption in the 1980s," *Advance Data from Vital and Health Statistics* (Hyattsville, MD: National Center for Health Statistics, 1990) report that adoptions of African American children dropped to approximately 1,400 in 1987 from a high of almost 2,600 in 1971.

[50] Melosh, *supra* n. 28 at 306; Rita J. Simon and Howard Altstein, *Adoption, Race and Identity: From Infancy to Young Adulthood*, 2nd ed. (New Brunswick, NJ: Transaction Publishers, 2002): 111–170.

[51] *Id.* Today, the NABSW emphasizes the need to expand recruitment of foster and adoptive families in the African American community, but does not explicitly endorse the 1994 assertion that transracial placements should be reviewed by community panels.

ancestry, and that encourage the development of "culturally relevant agency practices."[52]

As empirical work has largely supported the claim of adoption advocates that children placed transracially are not significantly more likely than other children to suffer long-term harms to identity development or self-esteem,[53] the stronger argument in favor of race-matching has focused on the negative impact that transracial placements impose on African American families and communities, as discussed later. Other work, however, has suggested that while transracially placed children may not be harmed by such placements, many do feel displaced and at times struggle to "belong" to one or another community.[54] Thus, in evaluating the dispute, it is important to be attentive to both the concerns of communities and of children themselves.

By the early 1990s, pressure to address race-matching through federal legislation emerged, as many (largely white) adoptive families felt that their efforts to adopt infants, in particular, had been stymied by race-matching programs. A considerable black/white divide developed, with the result that the 1994 NABSW statement emphasizing the need to be race-conscious in adoption and foster care placement emerged almost concurrently with the introduction of federal legislation to eliminate racial matching in adoption and foster care under the Multiethnic Placement Act.[55] As originally enacted, MEPA made it unlawful to "categorically" rely on race in determining the appropriateness of particular adoption or foster care placements; that is, race or ethnicity could not in itself provide a reason to delay or deny placement. Senator Howard Metzenbaum, MEPA's sponsor, did not assert that transracial placement was the primary goal behind the legislation; rather, he stated that the legislation was intended to promote "transracial adoption when an appropriate same race

---

[52] National Association of Black Social Workers, "Preserving Families of African Ancestry," adopted by the NABSW Steering Committee, Jan. 10, 2003, www.nabsw.org/mserver/PreservingFamilies.aspx.

[53] *See* Simon and Altstein *supra* n. 50.

[54] *See generally* Barbara Yngvesson, *Belonging in an Adopted World* (Chicago: University of Chicago Press, 2010); Evan P. Donaldson Adoption Institute, *Finding Families for African-American Children: The Role of Race and Law in Adoption from Foster Care* (May 2008), www.adoptioninstitute.org/publications/MEPApaper20080527.pdf. (hereafter Finding Families); *see also* Sandra Patton, *Birth Marks: Transracial Adoption in Contemporary America*, (New York: New York University Press, 2000).

[55] MEPA-IEP, *supra* n. 4. As Solangel Maldonado notes, the total disregard for the concerns of the NABSW in drafting MEPA-IEP is even odder in light of Congress's express recognition of tribal rights and the interests of American Indian children in retaining communal ties so emphatically announced in the Indian Child Welfare Act. Solange Maldonado, "Race, Culture, and Adoption: Lessons from *Mississippi Band of Choctaws v. Holyfield*," *Columbia Journal of Gender and Law* 17 (2008): 1–43, 42.

placement is not available . . . [as] it is better for children to be adopted by parents of another race than not to be adopted at all."[56]

Because the original version of MEPA did not wholly prohibit the consideration of race and ethnicity in determining what placement would serve the best interests of a child, advocates of transracial adoption worried that placements would continue to be delayed or denied by child welfare professionals committed to the NABSW position and pushed to make MEPA less permissive. Amendments to the Act in 1996, the Interethnic Placement Provisions (IEP), revised MEPA to prohibit the consideration of race or ethnicity except in extraordinary circumstances.[57] As currently worded, MEPA-IEP allows child-care professionals to consider race or ethnicity only on a showing that there is a compelling need to consider such factors to meet the "distinctive and documented needs" of a particular child.[58] Interestingly, this more restrictive statute arguably conflicts with the Hague Convention on Intercountry Adoption, discussed in Chapter 5, which requires that countries of origin must determine that a child is eligible for adoption, giving, *inter alia*, "due consideration to the child's upbringing and to his or her ethnic, religious or cultural background."[59]

Further federal legislation affecting transracial placements appeared soon after the amendment of MEPA with the enactment of the recently renewed Adoption and Safe Families Act of 1997.[60] ASFA was intended to shift child welfare policy toward increasing permanent placements (permanency) for children in the child welfare system. Its policy goal is laudable: ASFA seeks to limit the number of children mired in foster care "drift," which refers to the all too common phenomenon of children who are repeatedly moved between their family homes and among foster homes, or from foster home to foster home. To avoid drift, ASFA requires states to work toward finding permanent placements for children – read: adoptive homes – when reunification with

---

[56] Statement of Senator Howard Metzenbaum, 140 Cong. Rec. S10281–01, S10303 (August 2, 1994), cited in Alice Bussiere and The ABA Center on Children and the Law, "A Guide to The Multiethnic Placement Act of 1994" (American Bar Association, 1995), www.acf.hhs.gov/programs/cb/laws_policies/policy/pi/1995/pi9523a5.htm.

[57] MEPA-IEP *supra* n. 4.

[58] Joan Heifetz Hollinger, "Overview of the Multiethnic Placement Act (MEPA)," 1997, updated 2007–2008, www.ct.gov/ccpa/lib/ccpa/MEPA_%28Multi-Ethnic_Placement_Act%29. pdf. MEPA-IEP applies to any state or private agency involved in placing children in foster care or adoption and receiving federal funding.

[59] *Convention on Protection of Children and Co-operation in Respect of Intercountry Adoption (Hague Convention)*, concluded May 29, 1993, 32 I.L.M. 1134, Article 16 (d), entered into force in the United States, April 2008, www.hcch.net/index_en.php?act=conventions. text&cid=69.

[60] ASFA, *supra* n. 12.

parents seems unlikely. Whereas child welfare agencies and family courts previously had been required to make demonstrable efforts to keep biological families together, ASFA requires state actors to suspend those efforts under certain circumstances, most notably where parents have allegedly abandoned their children or previously had their parental rights terminated. Although the Act includes several provisions intended to facilitate the adoption of children in foster care, providing incentives for the placement of special needs children for example, the most significant change wrought by ASFA turns on its termination of parental rights provisions: the Act requires states to initiate proceedings to terminate parental rights once a child has spent fifteen out of the prior twenty-two months in foster care and to identify and recruit an appropriate adoptive family for that child.[61]

This requirement to initiate proceedings to terminate parental rights based on the amount of time a child has spent in foster care limits the discretion of states to determine whether long-term foster care and family reunification is in a child's best interests. As Cynthia Godsoe has argued, ASFA reinforces the stereotype that children who enter the foster care system are there because their parents are wholly inadequate or irredeemable; it rests on the assumption that biological parents are likely to be perpetrators of harm – a term invoked by legislators when the Act was being debated – and places a priority on moving children to "good" families.[62] Godsoe points out that ASFA

> turns on its head the legal system's assumption that parents love their children and act in their best interests, [and therefore] the public family law parenthood framework embedded in ASFA allows for no gray area. These parents are bad so children would most likely benefit from the severance of ties and membership in a new and "better" family.[63]

Recent statistics show a decline in the number of children entering foster care between 2002 and 2010, as well as, since 2006, in the number of children awaiting adoption from the foster care, leading some observers to conclude that MEPA-IEP and ASFA have been successful.[64] The causal connections,

---

[61] ASFA *supra* n. 12 at sec. 103.

[62] Cynthia Godsoe, "Parsing Parenthood," Brooklyn Law School Legal Studies Paper No. 253 (October 27, 2011): 1–71, 11–16. Available at SSRN: http://ssrn.com/abstract=1950222 or http://dx.doi.org/10.2139/ssrn.1950222.

[63] *Id.* at. 14.

[64] It is still too early to fully assess the impact of ASFA. For an initial evaluation, *see* Emily Kernan and Jennifer E. Lansford, "Providing for the Best Interests of the Child?: The Adoption and Safe Families Act of 1997," *Journal of Applied Developmental Psychology* 25, no. 5 (Sept.-Oct. 1994): 523–539. Recent data from the Adoption and Foster Care Analysis and Reporting System (AFCARS) show relatively flat numbers. *Trends in Foster Care and Adoption – FY 2002-FY 2010* (Based on data submitted by states as of June 2011). Source:

however, are not entirely clear. Both before and after the passage of ASFA, the percentage of children awaiting adoption after parental rights have been terminated has consistently hovered around 60 percent, and the actual number of adoptions from the foster care system have remained "relatively stable."[65] A recent report for the National Council for Adoption reported that

> between 1998 and 2002, the absolute number of children adopted out of the foster care system rose from 38,000 to 51,000. During the same period, the percentage of all exiting children being adopted out of the system rose from 15 percent to 18 percent. Since 2002, these figures have remained relatively stable.[66]

In other words, the report notes, an initial surge in adoptions was predictable, but measuring ASFA's overall effectiveness in the long term remains difficult. The report also found that the probability that a child entering foster care would be adopted was higher overall at the end of the 1990s than it had been earlier; "this effect was not evenly distributed across whatever number of years a child might spend in foster care [and] the effects of ASFA accentuated, but did not initiate, the trend toward increasing numbers of adoption from the foster care system."[67]

The author of that report observed that

> while ASFA, in conjunction with state initiatives, moved a large number of children out of the foster care system via adoption, those children were disproportionately easy to place. This left a growing number of difficult-to-place children in the system waiting to be adopted, on whom ASFA has had much less of an effect.[68]

The report concluded that to move more children to adoptive homes, the next step had to focus on better recruitment of prospective foster and adoptive parents.

In 2008, the Evan P. Donaldson Adoption Institute issued a report on the problems of finding families for African American children in foster care, explicitly evaluating the impact of MEPA-IEP on that population.[69] The study,

---

AFCARS data, U.S. Children's Bureau, Administration for Children, Youth and Families, www.acf.hhs.gov/programs/cb/stats_research/afcars/trends_june2011.pdf .

[65] *Trends in Foster Care and Adoption, id.* at 3.

[66] Marc Zapala, "Parent Recruitment and Training: A Crucial, Neglected Child Welfare Strategy," *Adoption Advocate* 6, www.adoptioncouncil.org/publications/adoption-advocate-no6.html.

[67] *Id.*

[68] *Id.*

[69] Evan P. Donaldson Adoption Institute, Role of Race Report, supra n. 54.

hereafter referred to as "Finding Families," noted that while transracial adoptions of African American children had increased very slightly following the
enactment of MEPA-IEP, those children still faced proportionately greater
hurdles in moving from foster care to adoption, and found, in addition, that
MEPA-IEP's "color-blind" policies ultimately left adopting families without
adequate preparation for dealing with the issues faced by children adopted
from foster care. It also noted that few states or agencies had been notably
successful in recruiting foster and adoptive parents from within communities
of color. The report concluded that the assumptions about the wisdom of
color-blind placements for children in care required reassessment, noting that

> acknowledgement of race-related realities – not "color blindness" – must help
> to shape the development of sound adoption practices. Although color does
> not influence acceptance and opportunity in an ideal world, the reality of
> our society is still far from this ideal. Failure to address these social realities
> in practice is a disservice to children and their adoptive parents, and does not
> provide the best prospects for successful adoptions.[70]

The Finding Families report concluded that the original MEPA standard,
which prohibited the use of race alone to delay or deny placement, but allowed
race to be considered as one factor in foster care and adoptive placement,
should be reinstated. This recommendation was endorsed by a variety of child
welfare organizations, including, among others, the Child Welfare League of
America, the National Association of Black Social Workers, the Foster Care
Alumni of America, and the National Association of Social Workers.[71]

The report engendered immediate resistance. In a briefing before the Congressional Coalition on Adoption Institute, a lobby that works in Washington to
"raise awareness about the needs of children without families and to remove
policy barriers that hinder children from knowing the love and support a
family provides,"[72] noted adoption proponent Elizabeth Bartholet, speaking
for, *inter alia*, the National Counsel for Adoption and the American Association of Adoption Attorneys, urged Congress to have "the sense" to ignore
the report, arguing that amending MEPA would reinstate race-matching and
curtail adoptive placements.[73] She went on to argue that "[t]he Donaldson

---

[70] *Id.* at 8.
[71] *Id.* at 4–5.
[72] Congressional Coalition on Adoption Institute, "Who We Are," www.ccainstitute.org/
who-we-are/aboutus.html.
[73] Elizabeth Bartholet, "Response to Donaldson Institute Call for Amendment of the Multiethnic
Placement Act (MEPA) to Reinstate use of Race as a Placement Factor," Congressional Coalition on Adoption Institute Briefing (June 10, 2008): 2, www.law.harvard.edu/faculty/bartholet/
HsHearingRD2.pdf.

Institute is well-known in the adoption area as an advocacy organization committed to the idea that birth and racial heritage are of central importance, and this Report is an advocacy document, endorsed by organizations with well-known hostility to MEPA."[74]

As this continuing debate illustrates, the controversy over transracial adoption has not abated significantly since the passage of MEPA-IEP more than fifteen years ago, and the central disagreements have not changed as efforts to revise or amend MEPA-IEP have continued. Those who question the wisdom of transracial placements continue to argue that the practice harms children and perpetuates negative stereotypes of communities of color; deeply embedded in their position is a justifiable concern with securing dignity for groups who have endured, and continue to endure, oppression and marginalization. Proponents counter that any consideration of race, ethnicity, or culture inevitably leads to rigid race-matching, depriving children of the chance to connect speedily with loving families. They also argue that transracial placements, rather than denigrating historically disadvantaged communities, can play an important role in transcending racial differences.

These two sides, however, often talk past one another, in part because they fail to untangle several complicating factors, although scholars have discussed each of these issues at length. First, it is problematic to utilize concepts of race and culture interchangeably, particularly when they become the basis for asserting legal claims.[75] Arguments for creating mechanisms that allow children to be placed within or maintain ties to communities of origin are weighted differently depending on whether the problem is perceived as entailing race alone, culture alone, or racial culture. Second, arguments grounded in the idea of preserving children's ties to communities of origin often assume that a child "belongs" with one group more than another. But children move among and between groups naturally, whether they belong to a "single" race or define themselves as bi- or multiracial. The assertion that a child should be placed in the community with which that child will be identified because of racial characteristics is particularly troublesome when applied to multiracial children. Finally, the debate is frequently conducted as though the universe of adoptable children is homogeneous. It is not: arguments over connecting a child to his or her community of origin play out differently depending on the child's individual circumstances and the circumstances of the community that is asserting an interest in the child's welfare. Children whose ties to biological parents have been terminated because of alleged abuse or neglect and

---

[74] *Id.*

[75] The same problems occur in the context of transnational placements, but the regulatory scheme is significantly different. *See* Chapter 5.

have been placed for adoption through a state child welfare system may have substantially different needs for communal connections than a child whose biological mother has selected an adoptive family of her own accord and has placed the child at birth. At the same time, the resources available to care for vulnerable children may vary considerably from community to community, and that difficult fact must be clearly faced in making placement decisions.

RACE, CULTURE, AND RACIAL CULTURE

It is common for courts, agencies, and individuals to link race and culture when discussing adoption and foster care. For some commentators, that connection is deliberate because it is a self-evident truth. Others utilize race and culture interchangeably without any apparent self-consciousness.[76] Between those two positions, the transposition of race and culture seems to have been a rhetorical shift during the last two decades, as "culture" has become, at times, a contemporary code for race. Indeed, framing the dispute in terms of "culture" helps to avoid MEPA-IEP's strictures. As Joan Hollinger has pointed out, under the guidelines to interpreting the Act issued by the U.S. Department of Health and Human Services, "MEPA . . . do[es] not treat culture as a suspect category and do[es] not prohibit consideration of a child's cultural background and experience in making placement decisions. However, 'culture' needs to be defined carefully and cannot be used simply as a proxy for unlawful consideration of race, color, or national origin."[77]

The NABSW has long maintained that African American communities have unique cultures that proponents of transracial placement unfairly disregard. In its 1994 statement, for example, the NABSW took the position that MEPA-IEP "condemn[s] considerations of race, color, and national, origin and by extension, culture, in placement decisions."[78] Today, the organization continues to pointedly criticize how MEPA-IEP and ASFA affect the cultural identity of African American children:

---

[76] In other contexts, race and culture are conflated less self-consciously, but with the same complications. The North American Council on Adoptive Children, which is particularly focused on meeting the needs of children in foster care for permanent placement, takes the position that "every child should be placed with a family who recognizes preservation of the child's ethnic and cultural heritage as an inherent right. [Training and support for foster and adoptive families is essential to] ensure that children have ongoing opportunities to develop an understanding and appreciation of their racial and cultural identity." NCAC *Position Statement on Race and Ethnicity in Child Welfare*, www.nacac.org/policy/race.html.

[77] Hollinger, *supra* n. 58 at 3.

[78] Preserving Families of African Ancestry, *supra* n. 52.

The significance of culture in the life of a person is profound. "Culture" is the essence of being human. Culture is the bridge that links the present with the past and the past with the future. Culture provides a sense of historical continuity. It is a protective device structured to eliminate trial and error in the past and the future. Culture is second nature. It is a person's values, beliefs, learning, practices, and understandings that are passed on.... Children removed from their home, school, religious environment, physicians, friends, and families are disengaged from their cultural background. They are denied the opportunity for optimal development and functioning.[79]

This position builds on Carol Stack's argument, noted earlier, that extensive kinship and fictive kinship networks exist in those communities to provide care for dependent children. Those communities of care, initially developed in response to the exigencies of slavery, continued because African Americans were largely excluded from formal social welfare systems as they took shape during the beginning of the twentieth century, resulting in cultural patterns distinctly different than those found in mainstream white society.[80]

Dorothy Roberts also asserts a cultural difference argument in framing her objections to transracial adoptive placements:

A Black parent's essential contribution to his or her children is not passing down genetic information but sharing lessons needed to survive in a racist society. Black parents transmit to their children their own cultural identity and teach them to defy racist stereotypes and practices, teaching their children to live in two cultures, both Black and white.[81]

Roberts has further argued that "African American families are penalized by 'culturally biased definitions of child neglect'" that dismiss "cultural traditions of sharing parenting responsibilities among kin" and ignore its "rich tradition of women-centered, communal child care."[82] She notes that "most African Americans... identify themselves as part of a group whose members are tied together by a common heritage, culture, and social experience... [and hold] a race consciousness rooted in a sense of shared destiny."[83] Similarly, writer Jacinda Townsend argues that downplaying the racial identities of African

---

[79] *Id.* (citations omitted).

[80] Stack, *supra* n. 20. *See also,* Joyce E. Everett, Sandra S. Chipingu, and Bogart S. Leashore, eds., *Child Welfare Revisited: An Africentric Perspective* (New Brunswick, NJ: Rutgers University Press, 2004).

[81] Dorothy Roberts, "The Genetic Tie," *University of Chicago Law Review* 62 (1995): 209–273, 234.

[82] Dorothy Roberts, "The Child Welfare System's Racial Harm," in *Nomos XLIV: Child, Family and State,* eds. Stephen Macedo and Iris Marion Young (New York: New York University Press, 2003): 98–133, 102.

[83] *Id.* at 116.

American children "prioritizes assimilation over the preservation of a distinct Black culture.... [T]he Black community maintains its own set of family values, including collective responsibility, self-determination, and cooperative economics, [which define] a communitarian Black society."[84] At least one scholar who subscribes to the racial culture position suggested that African Americans should be accorded legal jurisdiction over the placement of African American children similar to that accorded to American Indian tribes under the Indian Child Welfare Act.[85] This position echoes the 1994 position of the NABSW, noted earlier, that children should not be placed transracially until efforts to secure same-race placements have been reviewed by appropriate community representatives.

Twila Perry likewise has been deeply concerned about how transracial adoption deprives African American children of the opportunity to interact with their "own" culture.[86] Like Townsend, Perry worries that distinctive characteristics in the African American community – its attention to community and extended kinship ties – are ignored as white parents claim the right to parent any child of their choosing.[87] For these writers and scholars, the damage to both children and communities inflicted by transracial adoption is widespread, even if the numbers of African American children adopted transracially are small in comparison to the African American community in the United States or in comparison to the number of children adopted overall.

The primary concern of these writers centers on how transracial adoption devalues parenting and families in the African American community. As Perry notes, African American families have long been presumed to be inadequate to the task of childrearing.[88] Arguments in favor of transracial adoption, these scholars argue, draw attention away from pervasive, ongoing injustices that systematically handicap African American communities and place African American children at risk. In addition, those arguments ignore the extent to which African American families are singled out for surveillance

---

[84] Jacinda T. Townsend, "Reclaiming Self-Determination: A Call for Intraracial Adoption," *Duke Journal of Gender, Law and Policy* 2 (1995): 173–187, 181.

[85] Cynthia L. Hawkins-Leon, "The Indian Child Welfare Act and the African American Tribe: Facing the Adoption Crisis," *Brandeis Journal of Family Law* 36 (Spring 1997–1998): 201–218, 211–215. Hawkins-Leon suggested that "tribe" should be redefined without reference to sovereignty in order to encompass African American extended kinship structures and that ethnicity should be viewed in cultural rather than racial terms. This assertion has drawn significant fire from American Indian scholars. *See* Christine M. Metteer, "A Law Unto Itself: The Indian Child Welfare Act as Inapplicable and Inappropriate to the Transracial/Race-Matching Adoption Controversy," *Brandeis Law Journal* 38 (Fall 1999): 47–87.

[86] Perry, "The Transracial Adoption Controversy," *supra* n. 6 at 72–73.

[87] *Id.* at 107.

[88] *Id.* at 89–92.

by child welfare professionals, resulting in disproportionate rates of removal of such children.[89] Perry observes that transracial adoption treats children like "commodities that can be bought and sold [while] the white families who adopt them are portrayed as humanitarian pioneers forging the path to a non-racist society."[90]

Other commentators are far less sanguine about conjoining race and culture, noting that racial and ethnic membership is often contestable and that categories of belonging bleed into one another. Indeed, a 2007 report from the Pew Research Center made national headlines when it reported that "blacks and whites agree that there has been a convergence in the past decade in the values held by blacks and whites," to the extent that nearly 40 percent of African Americans surveyed reported that "because of diversity within their community, blacks can no longer be thought of as a single race."[91] More than 60 percent of African Americans interviewed felt that higher-income African Americans have more in common with middle and upper middle-class whites than with lower income members of the same race.[92]

In the transracial adoption context, Randall Kennedy has been highly critical of race-matching arguments that appeal to racial culture, articulating that position in his early statements supporting the passage of MEPA in 1994:

> [Race-matching] strengthens the baleful notion that race is destiny. It buttresses the notion that people of different racial backgrounds really are different in some moral, unbridgeable, permanent sense. It affirms the notion that race should be a cage to which people are assigned at birth and from which people should not be allowed to wander.[93]

While arguing for a more race-sensitive approach to adoption than Kennedy, Fogg-Davis also notes that racial solidarity arguments "succumb[] to a static notion of racial self-understanding."[94] Richard Ford, in *Racial Culture*, similarly argues against confusing an ascriptive social identity based on race with an "intrinsic characteristic: culture."[95] Ford flatly challenges the contention

---

[89] *See generally* Roberts, *supra* n. 6.

[90] Perry *supra* n. 6 at 27.

[91] Pew Research Center Social and Demographic Trends Report, *Blacks See Growing Values Gap Between Poor and Middle Class* (Nov. 13, 2007): 4.

[92] *Id.* at 16.

[93] Kennedy, *supra* n. 8. Kennedy subsequently expanded these arguments in a book, Randall Kennedy, *Interracial Intimacies: Sex, Marriage, Identity, and Adoption* (New York: Vintage Books, 2004).

[94] Fogg-Davis, *supra* n. 11 at 20.

[95] Richard T. Ford, *Racial Culture: A Critique* (Princeton, NJ: Princeton University Press, 2005): 29.

that social practices among African American communities amount to "a 'culture' includ[ing] not only practices but distinctive norms, ideologies, cognitive maps, and epistemologies," and argues that such assertions manufacture, rather than reflect, objective differences.[96] He worries about conflating lifestyle with identity rather than understanding group identity as a "collective response to social prejudice," and concludes that efforts to ground legal rights centered on an idea of cultural difference "are likely to be quite bad at reflecting the dynamism and complexity of cultural struggle."[97]

These writers are convincing in their rejection of a distinct racial culture per se that should be recognized via cultural rights accorded in law. As Kennedy notes, reaching agreement about whose ideas represent an authentic African American culture would be virtually impossible: "Is an appropriate sense of blackness evidenced by celebrating Kwanza, listening to rap, and seeking admission to Morehouse College? What about celebrating Christmas, listening to Mahalia Jackson, and seeking admission to Harvard? . . . And who should do the grading on what constitutes racial appropriateness? Louis Farrakhan? Jesse Jackson? Clarence Thomas?"[98] Under this analysis, the NABSW position that placements should be reviewed by the African American community raises insurmountable problems in determining who the appropriate representatives might be. In addition, although there may be discernible parenting and kinship care norms among African American families that deserve recognition and deference, those patterns have emerged in significant part as what Ford notes has been "a collective response to social prejudice," albeit jointly experienced, rather than as a distinctive cultural practice.[99]

At the same time, the arguments of scholars such as Perry and Roberts that transracial adoption feeds the preconception that African American communities are deficient and, particularly, that African American parenting is inadequate, have considerable power. Thus, taking a child's race or ethnicity into account in the foster care or adoption regime – not as a deciding factor and regardless of whether that consideration is compelled by a concern for protecting culture per se or simply acknowledging that race matters for children and communities – seems appropriate.

[96] *Id.* at 31.
[97] *Id.* at 71. Ford also objects to recognizing legal rights that privilege the beliefs or practices of a particular family or community over beliefs and practices learned or acquired later in life. *Id.* at 87.
[98] Kennedy, *supra* n. 8.
[99] Ford, *supra* n. 95 at 39.

MULTIRACIAL CHILDREN AND NAVIGATING IDENTITY

The arguments for and against recognizing racial culture become even more complicated when applied to children who are bi- or multiracial, which, as previously noted, is now the fastest growing demographic in the United States.[100] In the adoption world, multiracial children were historically placed with families with whom they would presumably be identified by society at large as they aged; thus, biracial African American children would often be placed with African American families to preserve the idea of the "as if" family. However, as greater numbers of young people identify themselves as multiracial and children and their biological and adoptive families cross the boundaries among different communities with increasing frequency, the cultural argument becomes less coherent.

Courts have struggled to understand how to interpret culture and race in the adoption context, especially involving biracial children.[101] For example, a Massachusetts case decided in 2000, *In re Adoption of Vito*,[102] overturned a trial court's order requiring post-adoption contact with the African American biological mother of a child who had been removed from her custody as the result of child welfare proceedings. Vito had been in the custody of Latino foster parents to whom he was firmly attached and who sought to adopt him. Noting that although courts had authority to order such post-adoption contact when necessary to serve the best interest of a child, a general assumption that a child's continued contact with a biological parent is essential in placements across racial lines, the court opined, was ungrounded. According to the court, no showing that such contact was crucial to assuring Vito's "racial and cultural development" had been made: "Vito 'is a typical Latino child growing up in a Latino family [who] describes himself as Latino' ... [and is] fully integrated into his foster family both emotionally and ethnically."[103]

Cases like this place courts in the uncomfortable position of deciding where a child's roots lie and what factors they will utilize to determine what continuing degree of connection to a biological parent – and, by extension, typically a community of origin – should be made. The court noted that Vito's "physical appearance was not strikingly different from his foster parents," and that he spoke both Spanish and English in his foster parents' home.[104] This point

[100] Pew Report, *supra* n. 91.
[101] These issues arise primarily in cases involving children enmeshed in the child welfare system. The situation is distinctly different for children placed through private adoptions, to which ASFA does not apply.
[102] *In re Adoption of Vito*, 728 N.E.2d 292 (2000).
[103] *Id.* at 305.
[104] *Id.*

raises a question about whether the child's best interests might have been read differently by the court had Vito been less similar to the foster family in appearance or had not been bilingual. At the same time, the fact that courts in Massachusetts and most other states routinely hold the power to shape adoption orders in ways that facilitate a child's continuing connection to a biological family or extended kinship network means that deciding when a child's best interests will be served by such connections will always be dependent on an individual determination.

Recognizing that multiracial children can reshape the meaning of belonging does not mean that the arguments for preserving the African American family – or other families of color – become less persuasive, however. Nor does it mean that the current MEPA-IEP approach is satisfactory. In fact, as noted earlier, MEPA-IEP has primarily increased adoptions of bi- or multiracial children rather than the African American children overrepresented in the foster care system.[105] Rather, it means that arguments grounded in cultural and/or biological resemblance become particularly fraught when assessing the needs of bi-and multiracial children. At present, debates over transracial adoption and MEPA-IEP typically elide the fact of multiple belonging, but only by recognizing the ways in which race is configured and how it matters for children can the issue be fully addressed.

INNOCENCE, INCORRIGIBILITY, AND THE RHETORIC OF RESCUE

Another confusion in the public discourse around transracial adoption turns on the child imagined at its center. The scenarios typically envisioned in discussions of adoption involve an infant surrendered at birth by a mother sacrificing her claims to motherhood in order to bestow a better life on a child. In the wake of that sacrifice or abandonment, a new family is constructed: the child is emotionally and legally separated from his former life, however brief, and repositioned with loving parents to create a "forever family."

This picture of adoption appeals to most families seeking to adopt, who overwhelmingly seek very young children or infants. That preference is perfectly understandable: parents seeking to raise a child as their own prefer children whose lives they can shape and with whom they can bond as early as possible. Moreover, they want to undergo, to the extent possible, the full range of parental experiences from birth forward. Like biological parents, they hope to parent children who are, in essence, a blank slate, and are reluctant to take on children whose lives have been difficult or traumatic and who may have, as

---

[105] *See* Jennings, *supra* n. 12.

a result, sometimes overwhelming special needs. Of course, adopted children are never a tabula rasa; as both Shanley and Yngvesson have noted, these "found" children always have histories, and are rooted both in and between the families and communities from which they originate and the new families and communities to which they migrate.[106]

Images of young children as vulnerable or abandoned innocents in need of loving families at the earliest possible moment were foremost in the minds of legislators during the passage of both MEPA-IEP and ASFA, who accepted the idea that the overriding principle in providing care for needy children should always be placing them into permanent adoptive homes as quickly as possible. The assumption that children need permanency is not in itself invalid, but it does not account for the fact that for many children, ties to kin and to a community may be significant, even if they have been removed from the custody of biological parents for reasons of abuse and neglect. As noted earlier, children often feel strong ties to families, regardless of the circumstances of their removal, and they want to maintain contact with what is familiar.[107] When contact with those parents is not possible, maintaining some kind of open door by facilitating contact with the community in which they and their parents have lived may be helpful and provide needed structure, stability, and continuity.

Given that minority children are overrepresented in state child welfare systems, placements coming out of the foster care system are more likely to be transracial than those in private adoptive placements. Adoption advocates, particularly those who pushed for the adoption of MEPA-IEP and ASFA, have frequently argued that it is primarily reluctance to endorse transracial placements that results in large numbers of children "languishing" in foster care – that is, because more children in the foster care system are children of color, those children are the most at risk of being stuck in foster care drift.[108] But populations of adoptable children are hugely variable. While children in foster care are often the poster children for arguments about making adoption faster and easier by eliminating consideration of race or ethnicity, many of them are distinctly difficult to place. The face of a battered or neglected two year old moves families to reach out, but by the time that same child has

---

[106] Mary Lyndon Shanley, "Toward New Understandings of Adoption: Individuals and Relationships in Transracial and Open Adoption," in *Nomos XLIV: Child, Family, and State*, eds. Stephen Macedo and Iris Marion Young (New York: New York University Press, 2003): 17, 26–30; Barbara Yngvesson, *Belonging in an Adopted World* (Chicago: University of Chicago Press, 2010).

[107] Godsoe, *supra* n. 62 at 10–11 et seq.

[108] Bartholet, *Nobody's Children, supra* n. 8.

become the problem child of the classroom in second grade or the acting-out adolescent at fourteen, the incentive to adopt drops dramatically. Indeed, the focus on adoption under MEPA-IEP draws attention away from the area where it arguably has the greatest impact – the placement of children in foster care.

The youngest children available for adoption are those voluntarily surrendered for adoption at or shortly after birth, many of whom are placed through private agencies or private arrangements.[109] Children who become available for adoption through a state's child welfare system following the voluntary or involuntary termination of parental rights, however, are likely to be older. Although some very young children and infants do become eligible for adoption through state systems, even those children will typically spend at least some time in foster care while determinations about their status are made; often those children have been returned to parents for some period and many have spent time in more than one foster home.[110]

The primary effects of MEPA-IEP and ASFA have been to increase the adoption of the youngest children in public welfare systems by freeing them for adoption at the earliest possible moment with less time spent trying to reunite the birth family. In part, this responds to the common belief that children who have spent time in foster care are by definition damaged.[111] It is true, of course, that such children have often been traumatized by neglect or abuse. Moreover, any child who has been moved through foster care is likely to have suffered a cognizable loss and may be dealing with the consequences of that loss. At the same time, the moral panic over such damaged children is due in part to constructing parents of color and other parents living in poverty as bad parents.[112] Ortiz and Briggs argue that the delineation of a "culture of poverty" in the 1950s and 1960s, the "crack baby" crisis of the 1980s – which increased the numbers of children in foster care by approximately 25 percent – and welfare changes during the mid-1990s created "a biologically suspect

---

[109] *See* Pamela Anne Quiroz, "From Race Matching to Transracial Adoption: Race and the Changing Discourse of U.S. Adoption," *Critical Discourse Studies* 5, no. 3 (August 2008): 249–264, 249.

[110] *See generally* "Adopting a Child through a Public Agency (Foster Care)," Child Welfare Information Gateway, U.S. Department of Health and Human Services, www.childwelfare. gov/adoption/adoptive/foster_care.cfm.

[111] Christine Ward Gailey, *Blue Ribbon Babies and Labors of Love: Race, Class, and Gender in U.S. Adoption Practice* (Austin: University of Texas Press, 2010): 101; Ana Teresa Ortiz and Laura Briggs, "The Culture of Poverty, Crack Babies, and Welfare Cheats: The Making of the 'Healthy White Baby Crisis,'" *Social Text*, no. 76 (2003): 39–57.

[112] *See generally* Godsoe, *supra* n. 62.

and racialized underclass . . . that rendered its members – and particularly its children – intrinsically pathological and completely irredeemable."[113]

As domestic welfare policy during the 1990s in particular shifted away from addressing the structural roots of poverty – which is the primary reason that children find themselves in state child-protection systems – the focus of child welfare programs reflected in MEPA-IEP and ASFA moved from family rehabilitation to removing children from the allegedly damaging influence of dysfunctional families and communities. Framed in that manner, adoption became an appealing answer to the problem of child dependency, particularly if it could be effected at the earliest possible moment in a child's life.

These policy changes are deeply reminiscent of child-saving ideologies during the second half of the nineteenth century. Those ideologies, noted earlier, blamed child dependency on the moral failure and inherent criminality of biological parents and the communities in which they were located. Just as in the 1880s, the push behind MEPA-IEP and ASFA lay in delivering children from such circumstances, providing a clean slate where the newly freed child could be reconstituted. This undercurrent of rescue and redemption has not been lost on minority communities, who then come to view transracial placements as exercises of white privilege.

It is not surprising, then, that adoption is viewed by marginalized communities as an act of social engineering, with the public care system providing a conduit for the transfer of its youngest children from underclass communities of color to white communities. (In an interesting aside traced by Kim Pearson, the movement of children from minority communities to white gay and lesbian parents has set up a tension between two disfavored communities, as gay men in particular have come to be viewed as rivals to African American families, especially fathers.[114]) The feeling that transracial adoption is a barb directed at the heart of minority communities persists even though adoptive parents themselves may not conceive of their actions in such terms. As Bergquist notes, (white) parents adopting transracially "tend to be publicly acknowledged for the selflessness and courage in taking on the challenge

[113] Ortiz and Briggs, *supra* n. 111 at 40. Ortiz and Briggs explore how adopters decided that children from overseas were more adoptable than children in the United States. Those children, they argued, were seen as redeemable through medicine and education; they were not "characterologically tainted" in the way that children in the foster care system were viewed.

[114] Kim H. Pearson, "Absent and Unnatural Fathers: The False Competition Between Black Dads and Gay Dads," paper presented at the annual meeting of the Law and Society Association, Westin St. Francis Hotel, San Francisco, CA, May 30, 2012. *See generally* Kim H. Pearson, "Displaced Mothers, Absent and Unnatural Fathers: LGBT Transracial Adoption," *Michigan Journal of Gender and Law* 19 (2012): 149–215.

of raising children of color,"[115] while minority parents and communities continue to be portrayed as antithetical to children's well-being.

It is, of course, true that providing permanent placements for children is infinitely preferable to allowing them to waste away in inadequate foster care placements until they age out of the system. (Of course, not all foster care is inadequate; many foster parents do heroic work with children who have little reason to trust the system.) In 2010, an estimated 408,000 children were in foster care in the United States; of that number some 53,000 were adopted.[116] For children whose parents' rights have been terminated but are not adopted, the outlook is grim as they move through the system. With no safety net of family or community as they reach majority, these children are likely to find themselves without job skills or homes and/or find themselves involved with the criminal justice or mental health care systems, and, in general, suffer negative outcomes across virtually all dimensions of well-being.[117]

At the same time, the rush to move children to adoptive homes from foster care ignores the broader reasons for the inadequacy of foster care in the United States and the multiplicity of circumstances that lead to children's foster care placement. Some are in foster care only temporarily before being reunited with family, some are in foster care with relatives who cannot adopt, and others are older or have special needs that make adoptive placement difficult. The foster care system is quite rightly blamed for harming children; no state in the nation can lay claim to operating a wholly successful program. In her 1999 book, *Nobody's Children*, Elizabeth Bartholet levied a series of attacks on the welfare system for its inadequate treatment of children in public care, correctly chronicling the many ways in which state care falls short of its promise.[118]

Her conclusion, however – that removing barriers to adoption holds the best, and virtually the only, promise for protecting the future of vulnerable children – has been convincingly critiqued. Her assertions, for example, that all children in foster care are there because their homes are unsafe, that foster parents are manifestly unfit to care for children and that all kinship care is

---

[115] Kathleen Ja Sook Bergquist, "International Asian Adoption: In the Best Interest of the Child?," *Tex. Wesleyan Law Rev.* 10 (Spring, 2004): 343–349, 347.

[116] Trends in Foster Care and Adoption – FY 2002-FY 2010, www.acf.hhs.gov/programs/cb/stats_research/index.htm#afcars.

[117] *See generally,* D. Wayne Osgood, E. Michael Foster, Constance Flanagan, and Gretchen R. Ruth, *On Your Own without a Net: The Transition to Adulthood for Vulnerable Populations* (Chicago: University of Chicago Press, 2005).

[118] Bartholet, *Nobody's Children, supra* n. 8.

worse, simply do not withstand scrutiny.[119] The inability and unwillingness of states and the federal government to provide adequate social and economic support to families at risk, as well as kin and nonkinship networks, means that the system is riddled with problems, but endorsing Bartholet's conclusion – that adoption is the best and only answer – is a simplistic approach that disregards the interests of communities and families and misconstrues the dynamics of children's attachments.

The assumption, moreover, that there is a ready supply of families willing to adopt transracially from the foster care system and that racial and/or cultural matching policies have been responsible for the majority of children remaining in that system are not supported by the facts.[120] Although it is a popular and appealing trope to argue that social workers in state systems are foot-dragging in order to secure same-race placements in both foster care and adoptive placements, most state systems are chronically short of quality foster homes for all children.[121] As a result, matching for race or ethnicity is often the last concern of juvenile courts and welfare professionals, who are often clutching at straws to find *any* suitable placements for children in need of either short- or long-term foster care. Compensation for acting as a foster parent is inadequate and both children and foster parents often find that needed counseling and other support is absent.[122]

Kinship care tends to be the most immediately available foster care placement option, but in public rhetoric, that option is often disdained based on the assumption that if a biological parent is inadequate, the entire family system must be deficient and the community in which the family is located must invariably be inadequate.[123] It is true that the statistics for the success of kinship care can be as depressing as those for foster care in general; kinship caretakers

---

[119] Martin Guggenheim, "Somebody's Children: Sustaining the Family's Place in Child Welfare Policy," *Harvard Law Review* 113, no. 7 (May 2000); *see also* Godsoe, *supra* n. 62 at 17–18 *et seq.*

[120] Madelyn Freundlich, *The Role of Race, Culture, and National Origin in Adoption* (Washington, DC: Child Welfare League of America, Evan B. Donaldson Adoption Institute, 2000).

[121] *See, e.g.*, Lisa W. Foderaro, "For Separated Families, City Never Seemed Bigger," *New York Times* (Nov. 28, 2008), www.nytimes.com/2008/11/29/nyregion/29foster.html; Leslie Kaufman and Richard Lezin Jones, "Misplaced Trust: Child Welfare in Crisis; Cradle to Grave in Flawed New Jersey Foster Care," *New York Times* (April 6, 2003), www.nytimes.com/2003/04/06/nyregion/misplaced-trust-child-welfare-crisis-cradle-grave-flawed-new-jersey-foster-care.html; Erik Eckholm, "Bleak Stories Follow a Lawsuit on Oklahoma Foster Care," *New York Times* (April 16, 2008), www.nytimes.com/2008/04/16/us/16foster.html.

[122] *Id.* A compelling account of the children in foster care and the challenges faced by foster parents is contained in Kathy Harrison, *Another Place at the Table* (New York: Jeremy P. Tarcher/Penguin, 2004).

[123] *See generally* Godsoe, *supra* n. 62.

tend to be older and poorer than the general population of foster families, and may have more difficulty accessing needed services for children.[124] At the same time, kinship care can provide ongoing ties with family and community, which in many cases may be less traumatic for the child. Moreover, with adequate support, the prospects for success tend to be higher, as kinship care-givers tend to be more invested in children and willing to "stick it out" when difficulties arise. In fact, in 2008, Congress enacted the Fostering Connections to Success and Increasing Adoptions Act, which provides increased support for kinship care in a variety of ways.[125] Because the Act has only recently gone into effect, it is too early to assess its impact, but clearly child welfare professionals are emphasizing the need to provide better support for extended families in dealing with children in foster care.

The focus on adoption for all children who find themselves in state child welfare systems suggests a quick fix for the problem of providing care for children whose parents are permanently – or even temporarily – unable to meet their needs. That solution buries a complicated set of issues and tends to sideline efforts to preserve families and/or provide connections for children that might provide better outcomes in the long run. It also reinforces stereo-types about who is and is not qualified to parent children, reminiscent of the child-saving movement of the late nineteenth century. Although facilitating adoption in these circumstances may be important for some children, it is not the best option for all, and providing a full range of care opportunities is critical.

TRANSRACIAL ADOPTION AND COMMUNAL CONNECTIONS

For the last two decades, debates over multiculturalism have made it clear that communities have interests in maintaining their integrity that deserve consideration. Ignoring the voices of communities, at least those that have been historically marginalized, undercuts the implicit promises made by liberal democracies to guarantee substantive equality and allow individuals to develop their capacities to the full. Attending to those interests is essential to creating a cohesive national community, one in which all members can feel valued and view themselves as having a stake in the future of that larger society. Because

---

[124] Jennifer Ehrle, Rob Geen, and Regan Main, "Kinship Foster Care: Custody, Hardships, and Services," 14 *Snapshots of America's Families* 14 (2003); Jill Duerr Berrick, "When Children Cannot Remain Home: Foster Family Care and Kinship Care," *The Future of Children* 8 (1998).

[125] *Fostering Connections to Success and Increasing Adoptions Act of* 2008, P.L.110–357, 122 Stat. 3949 (codified as amended in scattered sections of 42 U.S.C.).

those debates have not considered the position of children, however, they provide little guidance for resolving questions when children are at the center. The controversy around domestic transracial adoption provides a lens through which to examine what multiculturalism means when children are added to the discussion. Placing communal interests, as well as the interests of children themselves in maintaining or creating communal ties, at the center of the discussion over transracial placements is essential to redressing the injuries that marginalized communities feel when their integrity is placed in issue, even obliquely, by the removal of their children.

The public debate over this issue tends to be conducted on the broadest possible plane, in which one side frames the issue as "vulnerable children v. selfish communities" whereas the other frames it as "greedy adoptive parents v. children, families, and communities." At one end of the spectrum, some groups have argued that placements of children of color, whether placed privately or through a state child welfare system, should be determined within their communities of origin. Taken to its logical extreme, such a change would entail recognizing specific jurisdictional rights for such communities with formal authority over the placement of children.[126] At the other (politically successful) end of the spectrum, supporters of MEPA-IEP and ASFA are quick to assume that poor minority communities will provide only harmful environments for children as they lobby for measures that would hasten the termination of parental rights to free those children for adoption.

However, a more community-conscious middle ground can be imagined, and flexibility is the key. It is important to provide a broader range of options, as Barbara Woodhouse, among others, has observed. Citing Twila Perry, Woodhouse notes that "[p]rotecting the child's community ... protects the child, because the child's life-chances will inevitably be connected to the status of the racial and ethnic community of which she is visibly a part, even if she is placed outside that community during her childhood years."[127]

Considering the interests of communities and children in maintaining ties does not mean reverting to race-matching policies that unduly limit the speedy placement of children. At the same time, the focus on adoptive placements should not hijack a broader conversation about all of the care options available for children. Nor, in the domestic context, does recognizing the importance of

---

[126] Under that position, the argument is that the community's interest is uniform whether the child is placed privately or through the mechanisms of a child welfare system based on an assumption that the child's need to develop within his or her community is similar whether the child is adopted at birth or at a later date in the child's life.

[127] Barbara Bennett Woodhouse, "'Are You My Mother?': Conceptualizing Children's Identity Rights in Transracial Adoptions," *Duke Journal of Gender Law and Policy* 2 (1995): 123.

facilitating ties mean that historically disadvantaged communities should be granted legal authority to control the placement of "their" children, because, at least in this context, it is clear that the boundaries of such communities are too mutable to allow the creation of any bright-line distinctions among groups.

In addition to the myriad problems associated with determining the boundaries of any particular community, recognizing a multiplicity of semi-sovereign communities in the adoption context, which would be the result of according such communities legal jurisdiction in such matters, has the potential for overriding the wishes of biological parents to place children with families they have selected, which has been problematic under the Indian Child Welfare Act, addressed in Chapter 4. That issue has been discussed in detail by Shanley and Sanger, both of whom argue that deference to parental wishes for placement is appropriate and, indeed, required as a matter of parental rights guaranteed by the U.S. Constitution.[128] Although parental rights may be terminated by a state when a child has been subject to abuse or neglect, parents/mothers outside of child welfare systems should maintain the authority to place a child with a family of his or her choosing. This position is consistent with virtually all formulations of parental rights: it is uncontested that biological parents have the authority to remove children to any community of their choosing, even if others may believe that such changes are not in a child's best interests. In the absence of concerns about abuse or neglect, parents can and should be able to move unhindered, from community to community or from nation to nation. Indeed, even when parents have been adjudged abusive or neglectful, there is much to be said for deferring to a parent's wishes for placing a child with a particular caregiver or within a particular community, absent a compelling reason to avoid such a placement.[129] As noted earlier, such deference may also

---

[128] Mary Lyndon Shanley, "Toward New Understandings of Adoption: Individuals and Relationships in Transracial and Open Adoption," in *Nomos XLIV: Child, Family, and State*, eds. Stephen Macedo and Iris Marion Young (New York: New York University Press, 2003); Carol Sanger, "Placing the Adoptive Self," in *Nomos XLIV: Child, Family, and State*, eds. Stephen Macedo and Iris Marion Young (New York: New York University Press, 2003). Respecting the wishes of parents – typically mothers – to place children with particular caregivers outside of the context of abuse and neglect proceedings is entirely appropriate, and may be appropriate, as well, even when a parent's rights have been terminated involuntarily. Although fully cognizant of the fact that many "voluntary" adoptions outside of child welfare systems are not voluntary in the sense that there can be overwhelming pressure on single mothers to surrender their infants for adoption, *see* Rickie Solinger, *Wake Up Little Susie* (New York: Routledge, 2000) and Fessler, *supra* n. 42, in today's world, it is a mistake to assume that parents should never be accorded the agency to make such a decision.

[129] Many "voluntary" relinquishments of children in child welfare systems are voluntary in name only, as parents may be faced with the prospect of involuntary terminations unless they agree to voluntarily relinquish custody.

provide continuity in a child's life by placing the child with extended kin or established relationships with nonkin members in a community.

To shy away from granting disadvantaged communities in domestic adoptions jurisdictional rights to control the placement of children is not to say that these interests should not be taken seriously. Moreover, it is not to say that children, in their turn, should not have some kind of cognizable interest in connecting to a community of origin that can and should be considered by courts entering adoption decrees. Parents, of course, significantly affect the development of children's identities, and because of the privacy granted to the family under the U.S. Constitution, the state may not typically intervene in how parents shape that identity, absent concerns about abuse or neglect. The transracial adoption context, however, is distinct. As Fogg-Davis notes, race matters: "We don't choose our racial starting point in life, others choose it for us" and, as a result, children have to "make sense of themselves by understanding this external gaze."[130] Fogg-Davis continues: "Race has a unique social salience, such that "parents should encourage children to develop their own racial self-understanding."[131] That fact, in turn, suggests that children should have some form of access to their families and communities of origin as they negotiate and revise their understandings of their own identity.

Of course, families adopting transracially today typically are acutely aware of the need to provide children with an understanding of their origins, and numerous options are now becoming available to assist children and parents in transracial families to do so.[132] Social service agencies, as well, are being pushed to adopt culturally competent practices as one avenue for ensuring that families can cope with the challenges of adopting or fostering transracially, just as the trend toward open adoption has opened more avenues for connection among communities, families, and the child.

Arguments for more community-sensitive approaches are most compelling when dealing with children whose placements have resulted from the actions of child welfare systems. It is children in state systems who often have the greatest need to be connected to families and communities of origin, especially if they are older and have established ties to families and other communal relationships. Adoption in these cases may not always be the best solution for meeting a particular child's need. Federal laws that mandate rapid adoptive

---

[130] Fogg-Davis, *supra* n. 11 at 31.

[131] *Id.* at 61.

[132] It is today an expected aspect of good practice to provide parents who are considering adopting or fostering transracially with counseling to ensure that such parents are prepared for concerns that may arise. *See, e.g.,* www.childwelfare.gov/pubs/f_trans.cfm.

placement without regard to a child's racial or ethnic origin thus ignore both community interests and the interests of children themselves. Older children are likely to have had significant ties to communities and families of origin, and may suffer when adoption severs those ties completely. Children who are part of a sibling group, even if removed from parents when they are young, often benefit from the maintenance of the ties that adoption severs.[133]

The answer, in part, then, is moving away from the current fixation on adoption-or-nothing for needy children reflected in MEPA-IEP and ASFA. At the very least, MEPA-IEP should be amended to return to its original language, which simply forbade racial or ethnic concerns from being the *sole* determinant in placement decisions rather than requiring that they be considered only in compelling circumstances, as the 2008 Donaldson study noted earlier has recommended. And although ASFA has been successful in moving the most adoptable children out of the foster care system, its requirements for absolutely terminating parental rights after a child has been in foster care for fourteen of twenty-two months can leave many children legally parentless but without other options. ASFA's mandates making children available for stranger adoption may take children away from satisfactory kinship or other relationships. "Adoption" is the sound bite that makes permanency seem neatly tied up for a child, but it does not always fully meet a child's needs.

The policy focus on adoption under MEPA-IEP and ASFA often pushes other options off the table. Constructive conversations about those options, such as group homes, long-term foster care, and permanent guardianship, are discounted as they immediately trigger images of impersonal institutional care and children drifting forever through inadequate foster homes. The fact that foster care systems are inadequate, however, means that foster care itself should be improved, not that every child in foster care should be moved out of the system as rapidly as possible. For the reasons noted, kinship care can often be the best alternative where parental rights are terminated, as maintaining kinship and communal ties are often less traumatic for children in the long run.

---

[133] Of course, there will be situations in which continuing connections to abusive parents run counter to the best interests of the child; case law is replete with termination proceedings in which courts note that a parent's issues with substance abuse, violence, or neglect warrant the total severance of ties to parents and often to kinship systems that are largely dysfunctional. However, the assumption that any child who has ever suffered from any form of abuse or neglect should never have contact with a biological parent or a kinship or community network is insufficiently attentive to the dynamics of each individual situation.

ASFA has also made it more difficult to think about long-term guardianships for some children, which can be as successful for placing a child in a family as adoption. In *CASA v. Department of Services for Children*,[134] the Supreme Court of Delaware found that permanent guardianship was consistent with ASFA and could be extended if the best interest of a child would be served by continuing efforts to return the child to parental custody. The court noted that

> when committed non-relative foster parents wish a child to be a permanent part of their lives, but also wish the child to have continued interaction with its natural parents, termination of parental rights and adoption is not an option that is in the child's best interest. In these cases, a child is not in 'limbo,' and a standard guardianship can provide the kind of safe and stable environment that 'rises to the level of permanency. . . . [While guardianship] is less legally secure than adoption, [it] is more permanent than foster care and contains all the indicia of parental rights.[135]

The Washington Court of Appeals subsequently cited the Delaware decision in a case requiring it to determine whether placing a child in a guardianship or terminating parental rights in order to free the child for adoption was preferable in a particular case. While deciding on the facts in that case that termination was appropriate, the court nonetheless noted that guardianships can be consistent with permanency concerns, and that such arrangements "reflect the increasing interest in providing children with continuing connections to their extended families, culture, traditions and history."[136] Such arrangements would not be appropriate for all – or even many – children. Nonetheless, it is important to keep such options available (and this is part of the approach utilized in the Fostering Connections to Success Act noted earlier) rather than bypassing them in the interests of adoption and rapid – and final – termination of family and communal ties.

There are other options as well. Although no one would assert that large-scale institutional care for children as it has been practiced in the United States and elsewhere is the best option, there are promising alternatives. The Treehouse Foundation, for example, is providing new options, bringing together elders, foster families, and others in an environment specifically geared to provide foster children with a supportive community.[137] The Family-to-Family initiative of the Annie E. Casey Foundation also provides

---

[134] *CASA v. Department of Services for Children*, 834 A.2d 63 (Del. 2003).
[135] *Id.* at 66–67.
[136] *In the Matter of the Dependency of A.C. and S.Y. v. Chaffin*, 98 P.3d 89 (Washington C.A., 2004).
[137] "About the Treehouse Foundation," www.treehousecommunities.org/easthampton_tem.htm.

a model of neighborhood-based, culturally sensitive care for children that emphasizes communal connections.[138] These options are not without problems; for some children in particularly impoverished communities, neighborhood care may not be optimal.[139] Instituting truly workable neighborhood care systems requires a substantial investment in both child welfare services and in communities. But these options should nonetheless be fully examined if building trust with marginalized communities, an idea at the heart of the multiculturalism debate, is to be realized.[140]

---

[138] The Annie E. Casey Foundation Family to Family Initiative, www.aecf.org/majorinitiatives/family%20to%20family.aspx.

[139] *See generally* Berrick, *supra* n. 124.

[140] Woodhouse, *supra* n. 127 at 128, has also urged the recognition of a wide range of options: "These options should include not only traditional adoption, with its nuclear family model, but also open adoption, which allows creation of new ties without necessarily severing the old, and kinship adoption, which also maintains children's ties with families of origin. Ideas like long-term kinship foster care, group homes for teens, and foster care with tenure need not be dismissed simply because they fail to reflect the nuclear family model. Laws should respect children's rights to visitation with biological siblings and extended family. We should encourage exploration of novel concepts like 'community visitation,' which can provide a context in which children are able to explore their kinship with racial and cultural communities of origin."

4

Reclaiming the Diaspora and American Indian Children

If the debate over domestic transracial adoption illustrates the difficulties of attempting to be cognizant of communal belonging in the absence of clearly defined group boundaries, the complications that ensue when political boundaries are constructed for a subnational community become apparent when looking at the adoptive and foster care placement of American Indian children.[1] In an approach diametrically opposed to that of MEPA-IEP, adoption and foster care proceedings involving Indian children require explicit recognition of the child's ties to a tribal community. The Indian Child Welfare Act (ICWA)[2] reflects an attempt to create culturally sensitive adoption and foster care practices, and speaks directly to concerns about both the Indian identity of individual children and tribal interests in maintaining cohesive political and cultural communities. ICWA, enacted in 1978, assigns authority for the foster and adoptive placement of Indian children to the tribes of which those children are, or are eligible to become, members. Under the Act, tribes have exclusive jurisdiction to determine the placement of children domiciled on reservations, and presumptive jurisdiction over other classes of Indian children. Moreover, when cases involving Indian children are not transferred to tribal courts, ICWA seeks to sensitize non-Indians to the distinct needs of Indian children and to educate them about the nature of tribal kinship systems and community life.

---

[1] The Indian Child Welfare Act uses the term *Indian* or *American Indian*, defined as members of recognized tribes and individuals defined as Alaska Natives. Because that is the language contained in the Act, this chapter will utilize that term rather than any other term such as Native American.

[2] Indian Child Welfare Act of 1978, Pub. L. No. 95–608 (codified at 25 U.S.C. secs. 1901–1963 (2006)). ICWA's provisions were not modified by the passage of the 1998 Adoption and Safe Families Act, discussed in the preceding chapter.

In the decades preceding the enactment of ICWA, the welfare of Indian children was typically overseen by state social service systems because many tribes did not have the resources to run their own social welfare and court systems and instead contracted with states for the provision of services. Cases of alleged abuse or neglect were therefore evaluated by state social service workers and adjudicated in state courts, whose views of tribal life ranged from benign misunderstanding to active hostility toward Indian values. The shift of jurisdiction imposed by the Act reflected a concrete attempt by Congress to secure Indian self-determination by returning power to tribes over internal matters.

By strengthening the ability of tribes to maintain their communities as distinct entities, and engendering respect and protection for Indian nations, ICWA represents a significant step toward securing the deeply pluralist society envisioned by theorists of multiculturalism. Indeed, the Act underscores the understanding that the survival of diverse communities requires attention to the intergenerational transmission of cultural norms and traditions. Its approach in some respects represents precisely the kind of multicultural accommodation that scholars such as Shachar and Kymlicka have urged, in which authority over certain spheres of life is allocated among different governmental authorities.

Putting ICWA fully into effect has not been easy, however; states, tribes, and the federal government continue to struggle over the meaning of the Act and determine the proper divisions of authority. Part of the problem in deciphering the hard cases under ICWA lies in the fact that Indian children – all Indians, in fact – typically hold overlapping categories of citizenship: they are citizens of the United States and the state in which they reside at the same time that they are tribal citizens, and efforts to provide bright-line distinctions between these classes of citizenship have been difficult. Moreover, there is both a mobility and an opacity to tribal citizenship that is not ordinarily present when considering, for example, transnational citizenship: some Indians may be enrolled tribal members but live outside reservation boundaries, whereas others may belong to tribes that have no defined geographic base. Some Indians may belong to tribes that were once federally recognized but have lost that recognition and are now trying to reinstate it; others may belong to tribes that were never formally recognized. The resulting patchwork makes determining the boundaries of belonging difficult, to say the least.

Although there is much to be lauded in ICWA's communally responsive approach, the Act is not a panacea, and its shortcomings point up the difficulty in drawing distinctions between the claims that a group may assert so that its members may function in the present and the claims it may assert to try to assure its long-term survival.[3] Because it deals with issues of *children's* identity, ICWA essentially tries to speak to both those present and future claims without distinguishing between them – that is, it protects a tribe's present interest in children in order to secure the tribe's own long-term survival. The Act generates innumerable contests over deciding who is an "authentic" Indian, as the situations of individual children – and of tribes – varies widely. As Kevin Maillard has observed, "The question, 'Who is Indian?' marks a standard subject of academic inquiry, but to ask 'who decides and how' is much more interesting."[4]

These problematic cases generally emerge in association with two assumptions firmly embedded in ICWA's text. The first assumption is that the children subject to its provisions have fixed and singular identities as "Indians," while the second is that the Act's placement directives secure the needs of any and all such Indian children, regardless of their age or the context in which an adoption or foster care proceeding takes place.[5] Furthermore, the Act's solution to the dilemmas of protecting tribes and Indian children is one-dimensional: it simply shifts either exclusive or permissive jurisdiction over these cases between tribes and state courts.[6]

Assigning jurisdictional authority in such a fashion means a child must be classified as *either* an Indian *or* a non-Indian child; there is no recognition that a child's identity may fall into more than one category. This approach sets up a binary that is bound to be over- or underinclusive. As Barbara Atwood and Kevin Maillard have observed, state courts have balked at compliance on

---

[3] *See generally* Charles Taylor, "The Politics of Recognition," in *Multiculturalism: Examining the Politics of Recognition*, ed. Amy Gutmann (Princeton, NJ: Princeton University Press, 1994); Michael Walzer, "The New Tribalism: Notes on a Difficult Problem," in *Theorizing Nationalism*, ed. Ronald Beiner (Albany: State University of New York Press, 1999).

[4] *See* Kevin Noble Maillard, "Parental Ratification: Legal Manifestations of Cultural Authenticity in Cross-Racial Adoption, *American Indian Law Review* 28, no. 1 (2003–2004): 107–140, 107.

[5] Alice Hearst, "Reclaiming the Diaspora: Law and the Problems of Cultural Identity," (October 1999), http://ssrn.com/abstract=189608 or http://dx.doi.org/10.2139/ssrn.1896081999; Barbara Ann Atwood, "Flashpoints under the Indian Child Welfare Act: Toward a New Understanding of State Court Resistance," *Emory Law Journal* 51 (2002): 587–676; Barbara Ann Atwood, *Children, Tribes and States: Adoption and Custody Conflicts over American Indian Children* (Durham, NC: Carolina Academic Press, 2010) (hereafter *Children, Tribes and States*).

[6] The BIA Guidelines for the Act try to help states and tribes accommodate each other's needs. Bureau of Indian Affairs, "Guidelines for State Courts; Indian Child Custody Proceedings," *Federal Register No.* 228, p. 67584 (Nov. 26, 1979). Moreover, many states have developed agreements with tribes to facilitate enforcement of the Act, although complying with the agreements continues to be difficult.

both of these accounts, invoking a variety of judge-made doctrines, such as the "existing Indian family" concept discussed *infra*, to limit the scope of the Act.[7] These state court actions have, in turn, prompted repeated efforts to amend the statute and write those exceptions into law. Tribes have also sought to amend the Act to clarify and strengthen their jurisdictional authority, especially in light of an emerging international discourse recognizing the distinctive claims of indigenous peoples.[8]

The previous chapter argued that a legal regime mandating the wholesale disregard of children's racial and communal roots in adoptive and foster care placement may end up harming both individual children and the communities to which they belong because such an approach fails to consider the myriad contexts within which such placements occur. By the same token, a policy that makes ethnicity (or, more accurately, eligibility for tribal membership) its linchpin may err in the other direction by unduly privileging only a single dimension of belonging. Examining a number of contested cases arising under the ICWA reveals the difficulties created in trying to frame a policy around shifting identity categories, especially with communities that are dispersed or where ties to a culture of origin have faded over time.

At the same time, these cases poignantly illustrate why tribes are anxious to maintain ties with their children. Claims for protecting the links between children and tribes are compelling precisely because those connections are fragile – and they are fragile because they were deliberately attenuated by a series of federal and state policies that openly undermined Indian families and communities. As a result, distrust of the motives of state child welfare workers in dealing with Indian children is a constant theme when considering the placement of Indian children, and overcoming that distrust is critical to promoting cooperation and understanding between tribes and white society.[9] As Slaughter has argued, there are no clear resolutions, and the conflict thus "repeats itself endlessly in Indian-American legal relations and will not, like the buffalo, simply disappear."[10]

---

[7] Atwood, *Children, Tribes and States, supra* n. 5 at 202–217; Maillard, *supra* n. 4 at 124–129.
[8] That international rights movement and the Declaration on the Rights of Indigenous Peoples are discussed in Chapter 5. For clarity, this chapter focuses solely on cases arising in U.S. state and federal courts dealing with ICWA. Ultimately, issues arising under ICWA will need to take these international declarations and developments into account.
[9] *See generally* Kelly Halverson, Maria Elena Puig, and Steven R. Byers, "Culture Loss: American Indian Family Disruption, Urbanization, and the Indian Child Welfare Act," *Child Welfare* 81, no. 2 (March/April 2002): 319–336 (discussing the results of a study inquiring into Indian attitudes toward foster care).
[10] M. M. Slaughter, "Contested Identities: The Adoption of American Indian Children and the Liberal State," *Social & Legal Studies* 9 (June 2000): 227–248, 242.

More than thirty years after the passage of ICWA, the situation for Indian children continues to be dire. National Public Radio recently ran a several-part series looking at the situation of Indian children in South Dakota, and turned up several findings that reveal how cases involving Indian children continue to be mishandled by state welfare workers. In that state, Indian children make up 15 percent of the population of children, but account for 60 percent of children in foster care; they are often removed from their families by inexperienced social workers who have no sense of the Indian community and no tolerance for Indian values. Although ICWA mandates that Indian children should be placed with Indian foster care providers, several licensed Indian foster care providers interviewed for the story had never been asked to take Indian children.[11]

Debates over the scope of ICWA underscore how deeply belonging matters, and nowhere does it matter more profoundly than for peoples whose cultures were targeted for extinction through the very bodies of their children. Under-standing the treatment of Indian children raises questions about how liberal societies should provide security for distinct cultural communities and redress for deliberate wrongs, on the one hand, and the arguments advanced by cos-mopolitan theorists who argue that historical wrongs must, at some point, be consigned to the past.[12] These discussions also bring into sharp relief the ways in which belonging reaches both backward and forward in time to give shape to the understandings of belonging that both communities and individuals have articulated. Debates over who should direct the placement of Indian children are replete with references to the "constructed primordiality" dis-cussed in Chapter 2, where tribal identity is understood to flow from ancient origins that continue to bind the community as a people.[13]

Constructed primordiality may sound like an oxymoron, but it is certainly true that in most, if not all, American Indian cultures – and certainly within the pan-Indian diaspora in the United States – ancestors hold a revered place, which means that ties across generations are of great import.[14] At the same time, to "be" Indian raises difficult definitional problems, as membership

[11] Laura Sullivan and Amy Walters, "Native Foster Care: Lost Children, Shattered Fam-ilies," National Public Radio, October 25, 2011, www.npr.org/2011/10/25/141672992/native-foster-care-lost-children-shattered-families (hereafter "Lost Children, Shattered Families").

[12] *See, e.g.*, Jeremy Waldron, "Superseding Historic Injustice," *Ethics* 103 (October 1992): 4–28; cf. Will Kymlicka, *Multicultural Citizenship: A Liberal Theory of Minority Rights* (New York: Oxford University Press, 1996) and *Politics in the Vernacular: Nationalism, Multiculturalism and Citizenship* (New York: Oxford University Press, 2001).

[13] Sheila L. Croucher, *Globalization and Belonging: The Politics of Identity in a Changing World* (New York: Rowman and Littlefield, 2003): 38.

[14] Atwood, *Children, Tribes and States, supra* n. 5 at 31.

standards vary from tribe to tribe and within federal law. In many federal statutes, membership eligibility turns on a blood quantum, but as many tribes note, that means of defining membership was largely imposed on tribes from the outside. Historically, in many tribes, one could acquire status as a member even if one had no "Indian" blood.[15]

By the same token, however, some children with Indian ancestry today come from biological families that have few extant ties to a tribe, which has led many state courts to raise questions about a child's status as an Indian. A number of those courts have used the absence of apparent social ties to defeat application of the Act, finding that the child is not part of an existing Indian family, which is defined loosely as a family that has current ties to an Indian community or lives an Indian "lifestyle."[16] The existing Indian family doctrine is certainly problematic: it is precisely because so many Indian families and communities have been systematically decimated that requiring that a child comes from an existing Indian family in order to find that the Act covers that child undercuts ICWA's aims. Under that judicially created exception to ICWA, state courts end up defining "Indianness," often relying on historical stereotypes of Indian identity. That practice contravenes the very notion of tribal self-determination.[17]

Under ICWA, the membership – and thus the jurisdictional – issue is not easily resolved. There are a number of cases, discussed in greater detail later, in which a child has more than one identity. Determining which cultural and political identity should take precedence makes resolving these issues difficult.

FEDERAL POLICIES FROM ERADICATION TO SELF-DETERMINATION

The politics of belonging for American Indians and their children entails a stark confrontation with history. The history of U.S. actions toward indigenous

---

[15] *Id.* at 34–46.

[16] *See, e.g., In re Bridget R.*, discussed *infra.*

[17] Maillard, *supra* n. 4 at 124. The hardest cases have arisen when a biological parent – typically a mother – tries to invoke ICWA to set aside an adoption decree on "discovering" her Indian ancestry, as discussed *infra*, because state courts dislike what appears to be an instrumental invocation of Indian ancestry to overturn an adoption when a woman regrets her decision. There is considerable debate, however, over whether, given the history of U.S. treatment of tribes, such an invocation is truly, or even frequently, instrumental; many Indians have fallen out of touch with their tribal origins because of policies that undercut tribal existence. *See* Slaughter, *supra* n. 10 at 240, n. 29, discussing formal and informal membership. More frequently, however, the exception is utilized to defeat tribal jurisdiction simply because a state court does not want to credit an Indian family with being "Indian" enough.

peoples displaced by the arrival and westward movement of the Anglo population illustrates why the debate over the ICWA is so politically and emotionally
charged: shifting legal definitions of tribal sovereignty, a lack of clarity about
the nature of tribal membership, with its distinct racial, ethnic, political, and
cultural dimensions, and the tortuous history of federal policy toward Indians
and tribes converge to create a perfect storm of complexity. Only a brief history
is possible here, but this explanation should point out the various factors that
comprise the background to the dispute over ICWA today.

Although tribes are sovereign political entities, the legal history of fed-
eral/tribal relations in the United States has shaped that sovereignty in distinctive ways. In *Cherokee Nation v. Georgia* in 1831, the U.S. Supreme Court
distinguished tribes from foreign states in the U.S. Constitution, characteriz-
ing them instead as "domestic dependent nations."[18] Those nations, according
to Chief Justice John Marshall, were "in a state of pupilage," relating to the
United States as "a ward to his guardian."[19] As a result, there is a fiduciary relationship between the United States and tribes that affects the ways in which
tribal sovereignty is exercised. The Marshall court also established in *Worcester
v. Georgia*[20] that Congress has exclusive authority to deal with tribes and that
individual states are barred from exercising authority over Indian matters and
in Indian country.

Today, the federal government engages with tribes as sovereign governments,[21] but tribal sovereignty is deeply inflected by a history that allows its
scope to be defined and circumscribed by Congress. Although tribes have with
increasing success broadened the reach of their self-governing powers, their
sovereignty continues to be generally limited to authority over matters arising within reservation boundaries and over Indians rather than non-Indians.[22]
As a general rule, states have no authority to act in most matters pertaining
to Indian affairs and may not interfere with tribal sovereignty, but the tangled history of tribal relations with state social welfare systems, which has

[18] *Cherokee Nation v. Georgia*, 30 U.S. 1 (1831). The concept of a domestic dependent nation
is endlessly problematic, although beyond the scope of the discussion here: in international
relations, a nation is either sovereign and subject to no other power or it is not.
[19] *Id.* at 17.
[20] *Worcester v. Georgia*, 31 U.S. (6 Pet.) (1832).
[21] "Department of Justice Policy on Indian Sovereignty and Government-to-Government Relations with Indian Tribes," June 1, 1995, www.justice.gov/ag/readingroom/sovereignty.htm.
[22] This area of the law is quite complicated. Tribes may regulate non-Indians in Indian country
as necessary to protect general health and welfare, or to protect tribal political integrity, for
example, but generally have no criminal authority over non-Indians. Tribes have some authority
to prosecute non-member Indians for crimes arising within reservation boundaries, but the
scope of authority over non-Indians continues to be subject to considerable dispute.

waxed and waned over several decades, has complicated the picture; understanding that history is critical to comprehending both the impetus behind
the passage of the ICWA and the complications that have emerged in the
wake of its enactment. As noted earlier, for many decades, social services for
children were provided (if at all) by state authorities, both inside and outside of
reservation boundaries. Although many tribes today operate their own social
service and court systems, others lack the resources to do so, with the result
that some states continue to provide child protection services and are often
deeply enmeshed with tribal families and communities.

Moreover, although tribes are sovereign nations, Indians and their children
hold multiple citizenships, as noted earlier. That fact creates further confusion
for sorting out who has jurisdiction over the placement of Indian children.
In jurisdictional disputes between U.S. states, disputes are resolved under the
aegis of the Uniform Child Custody Jurisdiction and Enforcement Act, which
uses a "home state" and "significant connection" standard to determine which
state court has authority. The same statute, along with the provisions of the
Hague Convention on the Civil Aspects of International Child Abduction,
applies to the majority of international custody disputes.[23] ICWA, however,
contains no such "significant connection" standard: the grant of jurisdiction
is absolute and wholly dependent on whether the child is an Indian child as
defined in the Act.

The historical relationship between Indians and non-Indian colonizers in
North America constitutes a long narrative of sustained and deliberate efforts
to eliminate tribal cultures. Incursion into Indian life took many forms. Some
involved direct efforts to annihilate Indian populations; some involved the dis-
placement and isolation of Indian peoples on segregated reservation enclaves,
while more recent efforts aimed at assimilation and "Americanization."
Indeed, at various times in this nation's history, all of these efforts were deployed
simultaneously.

The century following the founding of the American Republic was witness
to a long period of forced removals of tribes; by 1830, Congress had passed
the Indian Removal Act,[24] and the process of moving Indians to the west
of the Mississippi River accelerated. The process was frequently violent, and
federal and state governments often reneged on their promises to respect treaty
rights and to provide relocation or other assistance as tribes were moved out of

[23] Uniform Child Custody Jurisdiction and Enforcement Act, 9(1A) U.L.A. 657 (1997), www.law.
upenn.edu/bll/archives/ulc/uccjea/final1997act.htm. The home state generally has priority,
with the significant connection test applying when there is no home state. As presently worded,
ICWA takes precedence over the provisions of the UCCJA.
[24] Indian Removal Act, ch. 148, 4 Stat. 411 (1830).

traditional homelands. The most infamous of these removals was the forced expulsion of some 20,000 Cherokee from Georgia under the New Echota Treaty of 1835. The Trail of Tears, as that march was later called, resulted in some 4,000 Indian deaths, leading historian Helen Hunt Jackson to label that time period as "a century of dishonor."[25]

The removal period in American Indian history was followed by what is commonly known as the allotment period, running from roughly the last quarter of the nineteenth century through the first quarter of the twentieth century. In what is arguably the most critical piece of legislation affecting the cohesion of tribal peoples, the General Allotment or Dawes Act stripped tribes of their communal authority over lands, placing title in the hands of individual tribal members and disposing of "excess" lands to white settlers and others.[26] Congress insisted that under the Dawes Act, Indians would be assimilated and "civilized" by the act of becoming individual landowners. In fact, by eliminating the communal ownership that was central to many tribal belief systems, tribes were often destabilized and communities utterly disrupted.[27] More importantly for the discussion here, however, it was during this time that efforts to separate Indian tribes and families from their children and to erase those children's Indian identities became a central precept of federal Indian policy, as discussed later.

By 1934, the allotment policy was deemed a failure – poverty among Indians was the highest among any minority group in the nation, with all of its attendant problems, and many communities were in wholesale disarray. Congress then enacted the Tribal Self-Government and Indian Reorganization Act (IRA), [28] which was intended to give Indian communities the ability to organize themselves into independent governing entities. The IRA was passed at the urging of John Collier, an advocate of Indian self-governance who was appointed the United States Commissioner for Indian Affairs in 1933. He

[25] New Echota Treaty of 1835, 7 Stat. 478 (Dec. 29, 1835). *See generally* Helen Hunt Jackson, *A Century of Dishonor* (New York: Harper and Row, 1881) reprinted by Dover Publications (2003).

[26] General Allotment (Dawes) Act of 1887, ch. 199, 24 Stat. 119 (codified as amended at 25 U.S.C. various sections). The Act authorized the president to survey tribal land and divide it into sections allotted to individual Indians, granting families 160 acres if they agreed to farm, 80 acres if they raised cattle, and 40 acres for other living purposes. Lands left over after families were allotted their shares were then sold to non-Indians; by the end of the Allotment period, tribes had lost almost two-thirds of the land base that they had possessed in 1887 when the Dawes Act was passed.

[27] Ralph W. Johnson, "Fragile Gains: Two Centuries of Canadian and United States Policy Toward Indians," *Washington Law Review* 66 (July, 1991): 643–718, 659–660.

[28] Indian Reorganization Act of 1934, P.L. 73–383 (June 18, 1934).

argued that self-government was essential to freeing Indians from the "despo-
tism" and mismanagement of the Bureau of Indian Affairs.[29] The IRA halted
the disposal of tribal lands and granted powers of self-government to individual
tribes, with its object being to prepare Indians "either to merge into the social
and economic life of the prevailing civilization as developed by the whites or to
live in the presence of that civilization at least in accordance with a minimum
standard of health and decency."[30]

As might be expected, the IRA was only minimally successful in fostering
Indian self-government, as it provided little concrete support for rebuilding
tribal communities. Indeed, it has been widely criticized as undercutting
traditional tribal governance and imposing institutions designed by and for
whites on tribes.[31] What is critical for understanding the position of tribes,
Indian children, and belonging, however, is that the IRA took the position,
for the first time in U.S. federal policy, that tribes should be self-governing,
and charged tribes with articulating their criteria for membership – a problem
intricately bound up in interpreting ICWA today. The IRA also empowered
tribes to contract for the provision of various services from state governments
if they lacked their own resources to provide such services, as they often did.[32]
Under that authority, social service agencies in a number of states acquired
authority over the welfare of Indian children, with significant consequences
for tribes and Indian families.

In response to a Senate report detailing the social chaos and poverty prevailing on many Indian reservations, in the 1940s Congress began to move
away from the goals articulated in the IRA toward a new policy of "complete integration" of Indians so that Indians would move "into the mass of
the population as full, taxpaying citizens."[33] That complete integration was to
be effected by terminating Congressional recognition of various tribes in an
effort intended to hasten the demise of Indians *qua* Indians and convert them
into American citizens shorn of tribal connections. During this "termination era," the federal government argued that tribes (and Indians) no longer

[29] *See,* Lawrence C. Kelly, *The Assault on Assimilation: John Collier and the Origins of Indian Policy Reform* (Albuquerque: University of New Mexico Press, 1983).
[30] Institute for Gov. Research (Brookings Institute), "The Problem of Indian Administration (Meriam Report)," (1928) reprinted in Lawrence Armand French, *Legislating Indian Country: Milestones in Transforming Tribalism* (New York: Peter Lang Publishing, Inc., 2007): 88.
[31] Vine Deloria, Jr. and Clifford M. Lytle, *The Nations Within: The Past and Future of American Indian Sovereignty* (Austin: University of Texas Press, 1998): 5, 194–195.
[32] Indian Reorganization Act, *supra* n. 28.
[33] John Leiper Freeman, Jr., "A Program for Indian Affairs: Summary of the Report of the Hoover Commission Task Force on Indian Affairs," *American Indian* 7 (Spring 1954): 48–62. The IRA has not been repealed – in fact, its provisions (as amended) continue to form the basis for Indian self-governance.

needed the "protection" they had been accorded by virtue of their independent political status. Of course, as mentioned earlier, termination entailed its own complications. Many tribes had never been recognized by federal law: today, Indians may belong to recognized tribes, tribes whose recognition was terminated, or tribes whose status was never recognized, which further muddies the water in determining who is an Indian child.

Terminating tribal recognition rendered Indians "subject to the same laws and entitled to the same privileges and responsibilities as are applicable to other citizens of the United States."[34] In consequence, numerous tribes were de-recognized and jurisdiction over tribal lands was accorded to state governments. These changes were coupled with an exodus from reservations following World War II, as Indians sought to escape the grinding poverty endemic in Indian Country. By the 1950s, almost two-thirds of Indians had moved outside of reservation boundaries. Indian families both on and off reservations found themselves under the direct jurisdiction of state social welfare bureaucracies, who were quick to respond to any perceived family dysfunction by removing children and placing them in non-Indian homes.

As Stephen Cornell and Douglas Hartman have noted, "[by the 1950s], many Indians became fully aware of the 'diametrical opposition between Indian and non-Indian objectives,' of the essentially ideological confrontation between assimilation on the one hand and the commitment many Indians still felt to preservation of nation and community on the other."[35] But the social disruption and endemic poverty on reservations and among American Indians in general made immediate action difficult. As part of his announcement of a war on poverty, President Johnson took special cognizance of the situation on reservations and for Indians in general,[36] and as the civil rights movement began to echo beyond the black/white divide, an Indian renaissance began to take shape. That renaissance ushered in the current period of self-determination as Indian leaders fought to retain tribal status and to infuse tribal sovereignty with content. But the situation in the early 1970s was grave: by every social indicator, American Indians were deeply disadvantaged. More than a third of Indian families lived in poverty and conditions on many reservations and among nonreservation American Indian communities were desperate. The prospect of rebuilding vital tribal communities was daunting, but for many tribes, a first step lay in reclaiming its children.

[34] Public Law 83–280, August 15, 1953, codified at 18, 28, and 25 U.S.C., various sections.
[35] Stephen Cornell and Douglas Hartmann, *Ethnicity and Race: Making Identities in a Changing World*, 2nd ed. (Thousand Oaks, CA: Pine Forge Press, 2007): 124.
[36] President Lyndon B. Johnson, "Special Message to the Congress on the Problems of the American Indian: 'The Forgotten American'" (March 6, 1968), www.presidency.ucsb.edu/ws/index.php?pid=28709#axzz1mCJypGEO.

"KILL THE INDIAN . . . AND SAVE THE MAN"

Contemporary conversations about the adoption and foster care placement of Indian children play out in the shadow of this history, which generated considerable confusion about the nature and scope of tribal sovereignty and, indeed, about what it meant to be an American Indian. More importantly, however, efforts to assimilate – indeed, erase – Indians and Indian communities that lay at the heart of U.S. policies uniquely victimized Indian children. These children were viewed by white society as the means through which tribal cultures could be domesticated and ultimately extinguished. Critically, too, the policies that sought to separate Indian children from their families and tribes were not simply benighted policies reflecting misguided values of eons past. Far from being shrouded in the mists of time, the wrongs inflicted on tribes and families through the removal of their children are part of recent memory, and the consequences of those policies are daily visible in Indian communities.[37]

Non-Indians have sought to "civilize" Indians through their children since conquest began; tribes have resisted for the same period of time. In the mid-1700s, for example, non-Indian settlers trying to convince Iroquois parents to send their children to non-Indian schools were rebuffed with the answer that the children "learned nothing of value" in the colonizer's schools; they returned home without the skills necessary to live in their communities. (When the Iroquois made a reciprocal offer to rear English children to "make men of them," the offer was declined.)[38]

The pressure to assimilate Indian children, then, began early, and did not diminish even after many Indians were banished to reservations. In 1819, for example, Congress established a "Civilization Fund" to provide funding for reform and missionary societies to educate Indian children. The Act empowered the president to "employ capable persons of good moral character, to instruct [Indians] in the mode of agriculture suited to their situation; and teach their children in writing, reading and arithmetic" in order to "provide against the further decline and final extinction of the Indian tribes, adjoining the frontier settlements of the United States, and for introducing among them the habits and arts of civilization."[39]

Within twenty years of passage of the Civilization Fund act, thousands of Indian children found themselves living in boarding schools operated by missionary and other reform groups. Attendance was voluntary, but only in a

---

[37] *See generally* "Lost Children, Shattered Families," *supra* n. 11.

[38] Peter Nabokov, *Native American Testimony: A Chronicle of Indian-White Relations from Prophecy to the Present, 1492–1992* (New York: Penguin Books, 1992): 214.

[39] Civilization Fund Act, 3 Stat. 516 (March 3, 1819).

limited sense: many Indian parents felt that they had no option but to send children to these white-run schools, and many did not understand that children would be asked to surrender their Indian identities. Initially, many of these schools were located within reservation boundaries – in the 1860s, forty-eight day schools were operating. Reformers became disenchanted with that model, however, as it became clear that the day school was not transforming Indians into whites; children, reformers complained, too easily retained their Indian ways when they returned to their families at the end of the school day.[40] Enter the reservation boarding school and the separation of the child from his or her family and tribe – children lived at the school, usually located near the Indian Office headquarters for the region, returning home only for school vacations. Soon, however, even these programs came under fire: critics argued that children who had the opportunity to visit with family and tribal members on a regular basis simply clung to their "savage" traditions.[41]

The response to these concerns came in the form of the off-reservation boarding school, exemplified by the U.S. Training and Industrial School in Carlisle, Pennsylvania, run by Colonel Richard Pratt. Pratt viewed his mission as one of severing children's ties to their families and cultures: "[A]ll the Indian there is in the race should be dead. Kill the Indian in him, and save the man."[42] Carlisle's philosophy and approach were simple; Indian children had to be completely isolated from any contact with their cultural community. They had to "feel the touch [of American civilization] day after day, until they become saturated with the spirit of it and thus become equal to it."[43]

The Carlisle school soon became a model for other institutions as Pratt's philosophy struck a chord with white populations. Indian children soon found themselves boarding trains that would take them long miles from their homes; on arrival, they were subjected to a number of rituals intended to effectuate their discarding of Indian ways. Boys' hair was cut – long hair being seen as a mark of savagery – and children had to discard Indian dress. They were renamed and prohibited from speaking their own languages; they had to learn to live under strict regimens borrowed from military academies, with severe punishment meted out for infractions. Although conditions varied from school

[40] *See generally* David Wallace Adams, *Education for Extinction: American Indians and the Boarding School Experience, 1875–1928* (Lawrence: University Press of Kansas, 1995).

[41] *Id.*

[42] *Official Report of the Nineteenth Annual Conference of Charities and Correction* (1892), 46–59. Reprinted in Richard H. Pratt, "The Advantages of Mingling Indians with Whites," *Americanizing the American Indians: Writings by the "Friends of the Indian" 1880–1900* (Cambridge, MA: Harvard University Press, 1973): 270–271.

[43] Pratt, *in* Adams, *supra* n. 40 at 53.

to school, children were often underfed and otherwise mistreated. Trained to take up positions as domestic or agricultural laborers, their futures were mapped out in a way designed to place them at the bottom of the American economic order.[44]

When children returned to their homes and families, they often lacked the resources to fit back into tribal life. They lived in a shadow world, rejected by white society and often unable to function in their communities of origin. In some tribal communities, children were ostracized, and many of the skills they had learned made little sense in the context of tribal life. Tribal values were often at odds with the values of the white community, leaving children bereft.[45]

The situation for Indian children eventually attracted the attention of policy makers, and in 1926, the Secretary of the Interior commissioned a report on Indian affairs from the Institute for Government Research in response to a growing chorus of criticism. The resulting Meriam Report condemned the philosophy behind the off-reservation boarding schools. The report observed that the boarding school system, which "take[s] Indian children, even very young children, as completely as possible away from their home and family life, is at variance with modern views of education and social work, which regard the home and family as essential social institutions from which it is generally undesirable to uproot children."[46]

With the publicity that attended the disclosure of abuses at boarding schools, many closed. The Bureau of Indian Affairs (BIA) reinstated both day and local boarding schools on many reservations, but did little to change the approach that had developed at the off-reservation schools: children continued to be subjected to the control of non-Indians, many of whom saw little to no value in Indian ways of life. BIA boarding schools continued to enroll some 60,000 students through the 1970s.[47] Most boarding schools were closed in the 1980s and 1990s, although in 2007, nearly 10,000 American Indian children continued to attend on- and off-reservation schools.[48] The closure of the boarding schools, however, did not necessarily remedy many of the social problems that Indian children faced, as most found themselves attending

[44] Adams, *supra* n. 40.
[45] Nabokov, *supra* n. 38 at 217.
[46] Meriam Report, *supra* n. 30 at 99.
[47] S. A. Colmant, "U.S. and Canadian Boarding Schools: A Review, Past and Present," *Native Americas Journal* 17, no. 4 (2000): 24–30.
[48] Bureau of Indian Affairs (2008). 2006–2007 School Year Education Directory. Office of Indian Education Programs, U.S. Department of the Interior, Washington, D.C. www.oiep.bia.edu/bie/about_bie/our_programs/pre_kind_op.cfm.

public schools in state school districts, where Indian ways of life were ignored and racism and exclusion were routine.[49]

The long-term negative consequences of the boarding school experience cannot be underestimated. Many of the social problems that plague tribal groups today are directly traceable to the abuse and neglect inflicted on Indian children through that educational system; children lost their moorings and communities fell apart. As Kevin Gover, former Assistant Secretary for Indian Affairs in the Department of the Interior, stated in 2000, "[T]he Bureau of Indian Affairs committed these acts against the children entrusted to its boarding schools, brutalizing them emotionally, psychologically, physically, and spiritually. . . . [T]he legacy of these misdeeds haunts us. The trauma of shame, fear and anger has passed from one generation to the next."[50]

The problems facing Indian children and their families were exacerbated by the complicated relationships developing between tribal and state social service programs. As noted, states had gained considerable authority over Indians and Indian Country under the policies enacted during the termination period. To the extent that children's welfare services were provided, states became wholly entangled with tribes and Indian families.[51] Those systems were administered with little attention to the cultural or ethnic differences between Indian and non-Indian children. To be sure, given the poverty and social problems many Indians faced, many Indian children lived in difficult circumstances. But social workers routinely mistook poverty for neglect, and were quick to remove children from their families, making few efforts to provide the kind of support that would normally be offered to families in distress. Family courts frequently assumed that children in Indian homes had been abandoned because they misunderstood the practice of placing of children with extended families, or assumed that children were neglected by "permissive" disciplinary practices. Reports of these abuses and misunderstandings permeated the hearings on the Indian Child Welfare Act during its consideration in the 1970s.

Before moving to that story, however, one last historical piece must be threaded in. In the late 1950s, the Child Welfare League of America, under

---

[49] Jon Reyhner and Jeanne Eder, *American Indian Education: A History* (Norman: University of Oklahoma Press, 2004).

[50] Kevin Gover, "Remarks at the Ceremony Acknowledging the 175th Anniversary of the Establishment of the Bureau of Indian Affairs," (Sept. 8, 2000) reprinted in *American Indian Law Review* 25 (2000/2001): 161–163.

[51] *See, e.g., Mescalero Apache Tribe v. Jones*, 411 U.S. 145 (1973) (Indians outside of reservation boundaries subject to general state laws); *Decoteau v. District County Court*, 420 U.S. 425, *reh'g den.*, 421 U.S. 939 (1975) (state jurisdiction over children outside of Indian country unchallenged by parties).

a contract with the BIA, was charged with administering the Indian Adoption Project.[52] The project, which ran from 1958 to 1967, was specifically aimed at increasing the adoption of Indian children by non-Indians and placed almost 400 Indian children with non-Indian families. The program operated under a directive running directly counter to the dominant policy of race-matching in adoptions at the time. As Ellen Herman has noted, the director of the Indian Adoption Project, Arnold Lyslo, viewed this deliberate effort to separate Indian children from Indian parents as an "enlightened" policy that provided homes for difficult-to-place children while eliminating racial prejudice against Indians as a whole.[53] Indeed, the arguments asserted by supporters of the Project tracked almost word for word the arguments that have been repeatedly used by contemporary supporters of MEPA-IEP: those who endorsed the Indian Adoption Project deplored the plight of "forgotten" Indian children, and felt that the adoption of Indian children by non-Indians represented a step toward a more tolerant and integrated society. Not all of the motives, however, were malign: child welfare workers were also responding to the significant consequences of poverty among Indian families.

The Indian Adoption Project expired in 1967, but was succeeded with a project entitled the Adoption Resource Exchange of North America (ARENA). ARENA placed approximately 250 additional Indian children into adoptive homes, as part of an effort to "rescue" Indian children from their families and cultures, a project that continued through the early 1970s.[54] The ARENA project prompted other actors, many of them private child welfare organizations, to increase their efforts to have Indian children adopted by non-Indian families and to sunder the ties between those children and tribes; the Church of Jesus Christ of the Latter Day Saints, for example, sponsored an Indian Placement Program aimed at moving children into foster care with Mormon families that lasted through the mid-1990s.[55]

The cumulative effect of these programs was that between the 1950s and the early 1970s, at least one-quarter of all Indian children were removed from their parents at some point and placed in foster or adoptive care; some estimates are

---

[52] *See generally* Kristen Kreisher, "Coming Home: The Lingering Effects of the Indian Adoption Project," *Children's Voice* (Child Welfare League of America, March 2002).

[53] Remarks of Arnold Lyslo, *cited in* Ellen Herman, *Kinship by Design: A History of Adoption in the United States* (Chicago: University of Chicago Press, 2008): 239.

[54] *Id.*

[55] James B. Allen, "The Rise and Decline of the LDS Indian Student Placement Program, 1947–1996," in *Mormons, Scripture, and the Ancient World: Studies in Honor of John L. Sorenson,* ed. Davis Bitton (Provo, UT: Foundation for Mormon Studies, 1998): 85–119.

far higher.[56] Most were placed with non-Indian families who had little conception of tribal life or values. Sometimes Indian children found themselves placed with families who actively disdained their Indian heritage, urging children to be grateful that they had been rescued. One adoptee reported that "I was told that what I came from was horrible, savage, pagan, and that I was so lucky to be taken away from all of that.... When I became a teenager and went through normal teenage difficulties, my mother told me, 'Don't grow up to be a good for nothing Indian.'"[57] The erosion of self-confidence produced by these practices was reinforced by patent racial and cultural discrimination in the outside world. Caught in this system, many Indians today argue that generations of Indian children and their tribes were deeply and permanently traumatized.

That point was also made by psychologists testifying before Congress in hearings preceding the passage of ICWA. In *Mississippi Band of Choctaws v. Holyfield*,[58] the Supreme Court cited the testimony of Dr. Joseph Westermeyer, a University of Minnesota social psychiatrist, concerning his research with Indian adolescents who had been adopted by white families:

> T]hey were raised with a white cultural and social identity... and really came to understand very little about Indian culture, Indian behavior, and had virtually no viable Indian identity. They can recall such things as seeing cowboys and Indians on TV and feeling that Indians were a historical figure but were not a viable contemporary social group.... Then during adolescence, they found that society was not to grant them the white identity that they had.... For example, a universal experience was that when they began to date white children, the parents of the white youngsters were against this, and there were pressures among white children from the parents not to date these Indian children.... The other experience was derogatory name calling in relation to their racial identity.... [T]hey were finding that society was putting on them an identity which they didn't possess and taking from them an identity that they did possess.[59]

Adoptive placements under the Indian Adoption Project were not considered problematic by standard social welfare measurements. In 1972, an outcome study evaluating the Indian Adoption Project mentioned earlier followed up

---

[56] A 1976 study by the Association on American Indian Affairs found that 25 to 35 percent of all Indian children were placed in out-of-home care. Eighty-five percent of those children were placed in non-Indian homes or institutions. Steven Unger, ed., *The Destruction of American Indian Families* (New York: Association on American Indian Affairs, 1977).

[57] Kreisher, *supra* n. 52.

[58] *Mississippi Band of Choctaws v. Holyfield*, 490 U.S. 30 (1989).

[59] *Id.* at 46.

on ninety-seven Indian children adopted by non-Indian families, all of whom had been determined by child welfare workers to be at significant risk of being raised in foster care or boarding schools. David Fanshel, a child welfare scholar, reported that most of the families were "remarkably successful," with children meeting or exceeding professional developmental guidelines. At the same time, he noted, the study was not designed to evaluate the impact on the children of leaving their cultures of origin – the issue addressed by Dr. Westermayer. Moreover, given that the children were still relatively young when the follow-up study was conducted, Fanshel observed that it would take longer to determine the impact of their removal as they came to terms with their Indian identity. He observed that "even with the benign outcomes reported . . . [i]t may be that Indian leaders would rather see their children share the fate of their fellow Indians than lose them in the white world. It is for the Indian people to decide."[60]

Nor did the study evaluate the impact of the loss of these children to their communities, which has as much relevance for understanding the politics of belonging as the impact on children themselves. Testimony from Indian families and tribes during hearings on the Indian Child Welfare Act painted a distressing picture. In 2001, the CEO of the Child Welfare League of America apologized to members of the National Indian Child Welfare Association for its actions under the Indian Adoption project. In rendering that apology, Shay Bilchik observed that

> One ethnic group [in American society] – American Indians and Alaskan Natives –. . . was singled out for treatment that ranged over the decades from outright massacre to arrogant and paternalistic "improvement." CWLA played a role in that attempt. We must face this truth. . . . While adoption was not as wholesale as the infamous Indian schools, in terms of lost heritage, it was even more absolute. I deeply regret the fact that CWLA's active participation gave credibility to such a hurtful, biased, and disgraceful course of action.[61]

---

[60] David Fanshel, *Far from the Reservation: The Transracial Adoption of American Indian Children* (Metuchen, NJ: Scarecrow Press, 1972): 341–342.

[61] Shay Bilchik, "Working Together to Strengthen Supports for Indian Children and Families: A National Perspective," NICWA Conference, Anchorage, Alaska (April 24, 2001), www.cwla. org/execdir/edremarks010424.htm. Harvard Law professor Randall Kennedy has been deeply critical of Congress's acceptance of the claims about trauma to Indian children and the impact of the removal of children on Indian communities, arguing that very little of the testimony presented at the hearings was backed by scholarly evidence. Randall Kennedy, *Interracial Intimacies: Sex, Marriage, Identity, and Adoption* (New York: Vintage Books, 2004): 489–499.

RESURRECTING TRIBAL IDENTITY

By the early 1970s, a movement to restore tribal identities and sovereignty had taken hold among Indian communities. A new generation of urban Indians began asserting Red Power; the American Indian Movement (AIM) was founded in 1968. The reform movement gained momentum with AIM's occupation of Alcatraz Island off the coast of San Francisco by nearly 5,600 Indians between 1969 and 1971, demanding rights and recognition of Indian concerns.[62]

One substantial step came in 1970 when President Nixon declared his intent to strengthen tribal sovereignty and transfer authority over a variety of programs from the federal government back to tribes. Nixon stated that the federal government needed to "recognize and build upon the capacities of the Indian people. The time has come to break decisively with the past and create the conditions for a new era in which the Indian future is determined by Indian acts and Indian decisions."[63] In the same year, AIM convened its first conference, fomenting a grassroots movement to reclaim Indian identity and to secure sovereignty for tribal peoples; its mission was to "fight White Man's injustice to Indians, his oppression, persecution, discrimination and malfeasance in the handling of Indian Affairs."[64] A 1973 declaration by Birgil Kills Straight, of the Oglala Lakota Nation, stated:

> From the inside AIM people are cleansing themselves; many have returned to the old traditional religions of their tribes, away from the confused notions of a society that has made them slaves of their own unguided lives. . . . AIM is first, a spiritual movement, a religious re-birth, and then the re-birth of dignity and pride in a people.[65]

The effort to reclaim sovereignty and reinvigorate Indian identity took place on a number of fronts. A number of important Supreme Court cases expanded tribal rights, significantly curtailing the authority of states to regulate matters within Indian country, increasing the obligation of states and the federal government to respect treaty rights, and granting tribal businesses immunity from a number of state taxes, among other things. Nearly forty years later, the situation for many tribes has rebounded, although the problems of poverty

---

[62] *See generally* Troy R. Johnson and Donald Fixico, *The American Indian Occupation of Alcatraz Island: Red Power and Self-Determination* (Lincoln: University of Nebraska Press, 2008).

[63] Richard M. Nixon, "Message from the President of the United States Transmitting Recommendations for Indian Policy," (July 8, 1970) *House Rep. Doc. No. 363,* 91st Cong., 2nd sess.

[64] Statement of Louis Hall, Mohawk Elder, 1973, describing AIM's purposes on AIM Web site, www.aimovement.org/ggc/index.html.

[65] *Id.*

among many Indian populations have by no means disappeared, and American Indians continue to be located at the bottom of the American economic hierarchy.

The question of tribal sovereignty breathes through every dispute over ICWA. In general political parlance, sovereignty entails the power to exercise exclusive authority over a people or a territory. In contemporary democracies, sovereign power must be exercised legitimately. In other words, the exercise of power must be carried out with the consent of those being governed – who must, in turn, be identifiable. Thus, the politics of belonging are critical to tribal sovereignty: to be sovereign, tribes must be empowered to determine who belongs and outsiders must be willing to defer to that determination and respect the exercise of sovereignty. Determining which children are subject to the provisions of ICWA, then, raises questions critical to both these internal and external aspects of sovereignty: how is an Indian child defined by a tribe and will that definition bind outsiders to respect that determination?

Before turning to that specific question, however, it is important to take note of an important Supreme Court ruling on the issue of tribal authority to set membership standards for its own community. The case, *Santa Clara Pueblo v. Martinez*,[66] was decided by the Supreme Court in 1978, wending its way through the federal courts at the same time that ICWA was being debated in Congress. Julia Martinez, a member of the Santa Clara Pueblo, married a Navajo man in 1941, and the couple had several children. The family had lived wholly within the Santa Clara Pueblo. Just prior to her marriage, the Pueblo had adopted a rule conferring tribal membership on the children of male Pueblo members who married outside the tribe but denying that same privilege to the children of female Pueblo members who did so. After unsuccessfully attempting to persuade the Pueblo that the rule should be changed to enable her children to become members, Ms. Martinez filed suit in federal court. She argued that the membership rule violated the equal protection clause of the Indian Civil Rights Act by discriminating on the basis of race and ancestry. The question before the Court was whether the tribe could be sued in federal court under the Indian Civil Rights Act for allegedly violating Martinez's equal protection rights.

The Court held that the Pueblo was not subject to suit: "As separate sovereigns pre-existing the Constitution, tribes have historically been regarded as unconstrained by those constitutional provisions framed specifically as limitations on federal or state authority."[67] The Court was particularly wary of

---

[66] *Santa Clara Pueblo v. Martinez*, 436 U.S. 49 (1978).
[67] *Id.* at 56.

interfering with internal tribal rules defining membership, agreeing with the lower court's determination that membership rules are a tool of "social . . . self-definition" and "basic to the tribe's survival as an economic and cultural entity."[68] The Court went on to cite with approval the language of the district court:

> [T]he equal protection guarantee of the Indian Civil Rights Act should not be construed in a manner which would require or authorize this Court to determine which traditional values will promote cultural survival and should therefore be preserved. . . . Such a determination should be made by the people of Santa Clara; not only because they can best decide what values are important, but also because they must live with the decision every day. . . . To abrogate tribal decisions, particularly in the delicate area of membership, for whatever "good" reasons, is to destroy cultural identity under the guise of saving it.[69]

The crux of the case, then, was that sovereignty critically entails the ability to define membership in the community, in the same way that every sovereign may – indeed, must – determine its own membership standards. However, although *Santa Clara* underlines the proposition that tribes have authority to determine their own standards for membership, that decision is only the starting point for a complex series of questions, as defining membership is complicated on many levels. Part of that complexity is attributable to the labyrinthine path traced by federal/tribal relations, which, although not determinative of how a *tribe* may recognize a member, nonetheless affects how an Indian child is subsequently defined in the ICWA.

Determining membership has also been affected by varying standards articulated in federal law, as noted earlier. Although there is considerable debate over how "blood quantum" standards emerged and how those standards were utilized by both tribes and the federal government, blood quantum was frequently used by the federal government to define who was and who was not Indian in treaties, in statutes and in other directives, and often in contradictory ways – one-quarter Indian blood in one case, one-eighth or one-half in another.[70] The Indian Reorganization Act of 1934, although it ceded authority to tribes to determine their membership requirements, applied to "all persons of Indian descent who are members of any recognized Indian tribe now under Federal jurisdiction, and all persons who are descendants of such members

---

[68] *Id.* at 54.

[69] *Id.*

[70] Paul Spruhan, "A Legal History of Blood Quantum in Federal Indian Law to 1935," *South Dakota Law Review* 51, No. 1 (2006): 1–50.

who were, on June 1, 1934, residing within the present boundaries of any Indian reservation, and . . . persons of one-half or more Indian blood."[71] As Spruhan points out, the Bureau of Indian Affairs interpreted the IRA to allow tribes to set their own membership standards as a critical aspect of sovereignty, and "the question of tribal membership, and whether to use blood quantum to define it, generally became the choice of tribes themselves. However, definitions of Indian eligibility for federal programs, and the choice to use blood quantum or not, would remain within the authority of the federal government."[72]

Today, there is considerable variation in the standards for membership from tribe to tribe: some tribes utilize a blood quantum, while others define a member as an individual descended from a member enrolled at a particular time in the past (1906 for the Choctaw Nation of Oklahoma; 1937 for the Sac and Fox Tribes of Oklahoma); some, like the Mescalero Apache, combine the requirements, so that membership extends to "persons on the official roll of 1936 and children born to at least one enrolled member who are at least one-fourth degree Mescalero Apache blood."[73] Other tribes, especially those whose status was never recognized by Congress or was recognized but later terminated, may have open-ended standards, fitting none of the indicia traditionally relied on by federal courts to determine a tribe's status. As Atwood has noted in her thoughtful book extensively exploring conflicts over ICWA, "Tribal membership criteria are not frozen but, instead, are dynamic and can respond to social or political pressure."[74] Because the application of ICWA hinges on defining who is an Indian child, the potential for dispute is substantial.

RECLAIMING INDIAN CHILDREN

As Indian activism grew through the 1960s, disputes between tribes and states escalated as tribes objected to the "Indian genocide" brought on by the removal of their children via the boarding school system as well as the Indian Adoption Project and its progeny. Tribes decried the removal of children, and spoke movingly of the damage inflicted on their communities and cultures by that history. In congressional hearings on ICWA, a representative of the National Tribal Chairmen's Association, for example, testified that "the chances of Indian survival are significantly reduced if our children, the only real means for the transmission of the tribal heritage, are to be raised in non-Indian homes and denied exposure to the way of their People. . . . Probably in no area is it

---

[71] Indian Reorganization Act, *supra* n. 28, sec. 19.
[72] Spruhan, *supra* n. 70 at 47.
[73] *See Rice v. Cayetano*, 528 U.S. 495 (2000) (Justice Breyer, *concurring*, at 526).
[74] Atwood, *Children, Tribes and States, supra* n. 5 at 39.

more important that tribal sovereignty be respected than in an area as socially and culturally determinative as family relationships."[75]

The depth of that injustice began to be recognized in the early 1970s, as state and federal courts began responding to tribal concerns. In 1973, a U.S. District Court in Michigan, for example, recognized the right of the Potawatomie tribe to assume jurisdiction over the adoptive placement of three children who had been orphaned by the murder/suicide of their mother and father, respectively. The children, whose mother was white and whose father was a member of the Potawatomie tribe, were enrolled members of the tribe and had lived on the reservation until shortly before the tragedy that left them orphaned. Because the shooting occurred while the family was living outside of reservation boundaries – the children's mother had moved off the reservation shortly before the incident but traveled back frequently – the children were taken into custody by the Michigan Department of Social Services. Within a day, the children's paternal relatives tried to locate the children, but were denied access by Michigan child welfare authorities, who argued that allowing the children to see their paternal relatives was difficult given the tensions surrounding the circumstances of their mother's death. At a subsequent placement hearing, the state court directed that the children be placed with a maternal aunt and uncle living in Florida.

After efforts by a paternal uncle and his wife, both licensed foster parents, failed to secure the children's placement with their father's family, the tribe brought suit in federal court, seeking a ruling that the custody determination should have been confided to the tribe and the ruling made in accordance with tribal custom. The federal court agreed, noting that "[i]f tribal sovereignty is to have any meaning at all at this juncture of history, it must necessarily include the right, within its own boundaries and membership, to provide for the care and upbringing of its young, a *sine qua non* to the preservation of its identity."[76] Similarly, a Maryland state court refused to exercise jurisdiction over a custody dispute in a guardianship case involving a Crow Indian child, observing that "child-rearing is an 'essential tribal relation'" within the authority of the Crow Tribe.[77] Both of these cases turned on jurisdictional questions, embroiling the parties and the courts in a determination of who should hear the cases. It should come as no surprise that when such cases were heard in state courts,

---

[75] *Holyfield, supra* n. 58 at 34.

[76] *Wisconsin Potowatomies v. Houston*, 393 F. Supp. 719, 731 (W.D. Mich., 1973). The children were placed in Florida, and in the following year, the Florida court refused to rule on the tribe's petition for a writ of habeas corpus.

[77] *Wakefield v. Little Light*, 347 A.2d 228, 237–238 (Md. App. 1975).

tribes and tribal members felt that their claims were discounted by state judges and state welfare workers.

Continuing disputes of this sort eventually focused congressional attention and led to the proposal that ultimately became the Indian Child Welfare Act of 1978. Hearings on the proposed bill were replete with stories of children lost from Indian families. In its findings, Congress concluded that Indian children served by state welfare systems were affected by striking cultural biases. It found that between 25 percent and 30 percent of all Indian children were removed from their parents' custody – a rate five times higher than the rate for non-Indian children – and 85 percent of those children were placed in non-Indian homes. The tribes urged Congress to return their children, arguing persuasively that Indian children needed access to their unique cultures of origin both for their own and the tribes' well-being.[78]

As eventually passed, ICWA reflected a clear sensitivity to tribal concerns about the transmission of tribal cultures; it recognized the special importance of children for the survival of American Indians both as a political and a cultural group. The Act begins by proclaiming that "it is the policy of this Nation to protect the best interests of Indian children and to promote the stability and security of Indian tribes and families by the establishment of minimum Federal standards for the removal of Indian children and the placement of such children in foster and adoptive homes which will reflect the unique values of Indian culture."[79] Congress explicitly acknowledged that "there is no resource that is more vital to the continued existence and integrity of Indian tribes than their children [and] that the United States has a direct interest, as trustee, in protecting Indian children who are members of or are eligible for membership in an Indian tribe," particularly where "the states have often failed to recognize the essential tribal relations of Indian people and the cultural and social standards prevailing in Indian communities and families."[80]

As noted, the heart of the Act is jurisdictional. Given the fact that tribal sovereignty is deeply implicated in matters relating to children, on first glance this appears to be the most straightforward means of resolving many of the dilemmas involving Indian children. (With very few exceptions, international law endorses the proposition that a sovereign has complete authority over its citizens, and that foreign states may not interfere in such a sovereign state's

---

[78] The full text of the hearings on the Indian Child Welfare Act is available at the Web site of the Native American Rights Fund, http://narf.org/icwa/federal/lh.htm.

[79] ICWA, *supra* n. 2, sec. 1902.

[80] *Id.* at sec. 1901.

domestic affairs.) ICWA endows tribes with jurisdiction to adjudicate both voluntary and involuntary adoptive and foster care placements of Indian children using a two-tiered system. First, tribes have exclusive jurisdiction to determine the placement of children who reside or are domiciled on a reservation.[81] With respect to Indian children domiciled outside of a reservation, the initial jurisdictional grant is concurrent between state and tribal systems. Tribes must be notified of any proceedings for foster care placement of or termination of parental rights to Indian children, and have the right to intervene and/or request transfer of the case to a tribal forum.[82] In voluntary adoptive placements, an Indian parent may revoke his or her consent to the adoption at any time prior to the finalization of the decree, and the child must be returned to that parent.[83] Transfer requests by tribes must be granted unless the state finds "good cause" not to do so.[84] If the case remains in a state court, that is, if a tribal court declines to exercise jurisdiction, the state court must follow the placement preferences outlined in the Act to ensure that the child will be placed in an environment sensitive to his or her Indian heritage.[85] The placement preferences require that in adoption proceedings the child be placed first with members of the child's family, then with tribal members, then with other Indian families. In foster care proceedings, the child is to be placed with his or her extended family, with a foster home licensed by the tribe, with an Indian family licensed by another entity, or in an institution approved by the tribe.

The silences in the Act are as important as its language for understanding the relationship between tribal and state child welfare systems and courts. Nothing in the Act precludes non-Indian petitioners or state and private welfare agencies from initiating adoption or foster care proceedings in tribal systems; the reluctance of non-Indian parties to utilize those forums has much to do with assumptions that tribes will not fairly consider non-Indian claims, just as Indians are wary of their reception in state courts. Of course, given the interest that tribes have in keeping children connected to their cultures of origin, it is to be expected that tribes will give preference to parties who have a tribal

---

[81] *Id.* at sec. 1911(a).
[82] *Id.* at sec. 1911(b). This section of ICWA speaks to foster care placement rather than adoption, which has led one court recently to find that transfer from a state to a tribal forum was not required in an adoption proceeding. Because other provisions in the Act talk about transfers of proceedings when a parent's rights have been relinquished or terminated, that narrow reading appears to contravene the purposes of the Act. See *In re Child of R.S.*, 793 N.W. 2d 752 (2011).
[83] *Id.* at sec. 1913.
[84] *Id.* at sec. 1915.
[85] *Id.* at sec. 1915(b).

connection, but the Act only governs the forum in which claims for children may be advanced; it does not limit tribes to hearing only Indian petitioners.

The placement preferences just noted, however, do not bind tribes: tribes may place a child into any situation that they deem best for that child. This point is critically important because the unwillingness of many state courts to transfer cases appears to stem from the assumptions that non-Indian petitioners will be treated unfairly in Indian forums. State courts often intimate that tribes will be so eager to place Indian children with their extended families or others in the tribe that they will not fully evaluate children's needs in developmentally appropriate ways, although in the few cases where the issue has arisen, there is little evidence to substantiate the claim, as discussed next.

Although there is no evidence that tribes will run roughshod over children's needs, there is reason to think that tribes and Indian petitioners have rarely been accorded full deference by state courts. Prior to the passage of ICWA, Indians seeking to be appointed as guardians or foster parents, as well as those who sought to adopt children, frequently faced discrimination in state courts – a factor that was important in prompting the legislation. This experience reverberated from the philosophy underlying the Indian Adoption Project: state courts simply assumed that, given the depth of poverty on reservations and the attendant problems, any Indian child would be better off if adopted outside of that community. More than thirty years later, as the cases discussed in the next section illustrate, some state courts continue to hold those beliefs.

Litigation followed quickly on ICWA's passage, beginning with its most straightforward provisions granting tribes exclusive jurisdiction over Indian children domiciled on reservations. In these high-profile cases, the parties lined up roughly in two ideological camps. Tribes, Indian families, and their allies argued that the Act provided the only means for recognizing even a minimal degree of tribal sovereignty and for protecting the fragile bonds that communities and families often had with their children, whose well-being depended in part on understanding their Indian identity.[86] Others accused tribes of needlessly severing children's psychological bonds with caretakers to make a political point.[87]

---

[86] *See, e.g.*, Lorie M. Graham, "The Past Never Vanishes: A Contextual Critique of the Existing Indian Family Doctrine," *American Indian Law Rev.* 23 (1999): 1–54 (hereafter, "The Past Never Vanishes") and "Reparations, Self-Determination, and the Seventh Generation," *Harvard Human Rights Journal* 21 (Winter 2008): 47–103 (hereafter "Reparations").

[87] Christine D. Bakeis, "The Indian Child Welfare Act of 1978: Violating Personal Rights for the Sake of the Tribe," *North Dakota Journal of Law, Ethics and Public Policy* 10 (1996): 543–586 (arguing that the Act improperly overrides parents' constitutional rights); Elizabeth Bartholet, "International Adoption: The Child's Story," *Georgia State University Law Review* 24 (Winter

The Supreme Court clarified the operation of the exclusive jurisdictional dictates of the Act in the 1989 case of *Mississippi Band of Choctaws v. Holyfield*.[88] Although the case did not raise many of the questions about Indian children's identity that are today proving most problematic, the Court did speak directly to the importance of preserving tribal cultures. Indeed, the Court made a finding unprecedented in child custody and adoption cases by holding that tribal interests in maintaining its community could trump the interests of other parties, including parents.

In *Holyfield*, the Court had to determine whether twin babies, whose biological parents were enrolled members of the Choctaw Nation and living on the reservation, were subject to the exclusive jurisdictional provisions of the Act. The twins had been surrendered for adoption at birth in a hospital located outside of the reservation's boundaries; there was no hospital located within the reservation. Having decided to give up her children for adoption and having selected the Holyfields as the adoptive family, the twins' biological mother had moved off the reservation during the latter part of her pregnancy and lived with the adoptive parents.[89] The adoption was finalized by a state court, which ruled that the children were not subject to the provisions of ICWA as they had never resided on the reservation. In something of a sleight of hand, the court held that when the children were relinquished by their mother and father at the hospital and outside of reservation boundaries, the Act did not apply. The twins were, rather, considered to be abandoned – and thus domiciled – at the hospital in which they were born and therefore subject to state court jurisdiction.

The Choctaw Nation initiated proceedings to set aside the decree when the children were approximately three months old. In accordance with settled U.S. legal doctrines, the Supreme Court found that the children took the domicile of their mother immediately on birth; because their mother had never intended to move permanently off the reservation, her domicile had not changed even though she had lived briefly outside of reservation boundaries. The Supreme Court therefore found that the children were subject to the exclusive jurisdiction provisions of Section 1911(a), vacated the adoption decree, and remanded the case for transfer to the tribal court.

2007): 333–379, 357–363 (arguing generally against the concept that communities have any interest in a child's placement).

[88] *Holyfield, supra* n. 58.

[89] Solange Maldonado, "Race, Culture, and Adoption: Lessons from *Mississippi Band of Choctaws v. Holyfield*," *Columbia Journal of Gender and Law* 17 (2008): 1–43. The article chronicles the history of the *Holyfield* case.

The essential point in the case was the Court's recognition of the importance of allowing tribes *qua* tribes to create and maintain ties to Indian children. The Holyfields argued that the Act should not be construed to defeat the intent of the biological parents who had voluntarily selected them as the adoptive parents – they argued that the parents' actions should trump tribal authority.[90] The Supreme Court, however, held that the birth mother's wishes had no bearing on the jurisdictional issue;[91] ICWA reflected congressional concerns with "not only the interests of individual Indian children and families, but also of the tribes themselves."[92] The fact that the mother attempted to alter the reach of ICWA by selecting a non-Indian couple to adopt their children did not alter the jurisdictional directives in the Act: "[P]ermitting individual members of the tribe to avoid exclusive tribal jurisdiction by the simple expedient of giving birth off the reservation would, to a large extent, nullify the purpose the ICWA was intended to accomplish."[93] The Court then cited an earlier decision by the Utah Supreme Court, which had upheld the interest of the Navajo tribe under similar facts. That decision, *In re Halloway*, had declared that "the protection of this tribal interest [in children] is at the core of the ICWA, which recognizes that the tribe has an interest in the child which is distinct from but on a parity with the interests of the parents."[94]

In both the *Halloway* and the *Holyfield* cases, the children in issue were indisputably Indian. What made the cases difficult was the fact that the children had been voluntarily surrendered for adoption; their adoptive parents argued that the children had been abandoned off-reservation with the intent that they be placed with non-Indian families. Many of the egregious cases involving the removal of Indian children from their families that had prompted passage of the ICWA had involved families being supervised by state social services bureaucracies for alleged neglect, and neither *Halloway* nor *Holyfield* fit into those categories: they involved adoptions in which the birth mother had selected adoptive parents. Testimony at hearings on the Act, however, revealed that Congress was also responding to a deep-seated concern that many Indian families were improperly pressured into "voluntarily"

---

[90] This position is consistent with the arguments of Carol Sanger and Mary Lyndon Shanley, discussed in Chapter 2, as well as Bakeis, *supra* n. 87, who argue that parental preferences should supersede the interests of the tribe, recognizing the authority of parents to determine where to place a child.

[91] According to Maldonado, *supra* n. 89, the biological father was not particularly involved in the selection of the adoptive parents.

[92] *Holyfield*, *supra* n. 58 at 37.

[93] *Id.*

[94] *Id.* at 52, citing *In re Adoption of Halloway*, 732 P.2d 962 (Utah, 1986).

surrendering children for adoption by non-Indian families, especially through the influence of church groups and other charitable organizations. The Supreme Court thus found that the situation in *Holyfield* raised precisely the kind of problem that the Act was intended to remedy. The Act was intended to stem the removal of children from Indian homes and to grant tribes control over the placement of such children in all cases; even the voluntary placement of children by parents fell directly into that rubric, especially because the voluntariness of such surrenders was likely to be suspect.[95]

Halloway and *Holyfield* garnered significant public attention because both involved Indian children who had spent significant periods of time with their adoptive parents, although that lapse of time was attributable in both cases, in significant part, to state court delays: the twins in *Holyfield* were three years old by the time the case was resolved by the Supreme Court, and the child in *Halloway* had lived with his non-Indian parents for the preceding seven of his nine years. Assumptions about the reception of non-Indian petitioners in the tribal systems were revealed in both opinions. In *Halloway*, the Utah Supreme Court, recounting the history of the case, presumed that the original parties to the adoption proceeding had deliberately evaded the Navajo court, noting that "quite frankly [the Utah Court] might be expected to be more receptive than a tribal court to [the child's] placement with non-Indian adoptive parents."[96]

Both the U.S. Supreme Court and the Utah Supreme Court returned the cases to the tribes with some apparent reluctance, underscoring the fact that even decisions favorable to tribes in this area can be threaded with distrust. It is worth noting, of course, that distrust between competing sovereigns is common in child custody cases – whether the cases are between parties in Iowa and Michigan, as in the Baby Jessica case,[97] or between states in the international arena, as in the Elian Gonzales case.[98] Courts are simply chary

---

[95] In *Halloway*, for example, the child had been surrendered by his mother, who had a substance abuse problem, when he was two. The placement had been arranged by the mother's sister, who had joined the Mormon Church and assured her sister that the child would be best cared for by a Mormon family. *Halloway, id* at 964.

[96] *Id.* at 968–969.

[97] Both the Baby Jessica and Baby Richard cases, which garnered considerable media attention in the early 1990s, involved jurisdictional disputes between American states, both of which claimed authority to decide in adoption disputes, and both involved successful efforts to set aside adoptions in which a putative father had not been informed of the child's birth. *See, e.g.,* "Court Upholds Divisive Ruling on Custody," *New York Times*, January 26, 1995; Isabel Wilkerson, "Michigan Couple is Ordered to Return Girl, 2, to Biological Parents," *New York Times*, March 31, 1993.

[98] Elian Gonzales was returned to Cuba to live with his biological father after his mother died while attempting to emigrate to the United States from Cuba. His mother's family sought to keep the child in Florida, and sought to institute asylum proceedings in the U.S. courts; their

about ceding jurisdiction in such cases, as each presumes that it is in a superior position to decide what is best for a child.

In both *Holyfield* and *Halloway*, the courts signaled an alarm to the tribes even as they acknowledged tribal authority, being careful to draw the tribes' attention to the long-established bonds between the children and their adoptive parents and urging the tribes to look carefully at the impact that the transfer would have on the children. The *Holyfield* court, quoting *Halloway*, observed that

> a separation [from the adoptive family] at this point will doubtless cause considerable pain . . . It is not ours to say whether the trauma that might result from removing these children from their adoptive family should outweigh the interest of the Tribe – and perhaps the children themselves – in having them raised as part of the Choctaw community. Rather, "we must defer to the experience, wisdom and compassion of the [Choctaw] tribal courts to fashion an appropriate remedy."[99]

The Court went on to observe, in a footnote, that it had been assured by counsel for the tribe that the tribe had authority to allow the children to stay with their white adoptive parents.[100]

While tribes lauded the Holyfield decision, some commentators observed that with such language, the Court had nonetheless betrayed some skepticism about the ability of tribal courts to render a correct decision.[101] Given the suspicion with which Indian culture is viewed even when tribes succeed, then, it should come as no surprise that tribes have continued to seek to mark the broadest possible boundaries of authority. There was no suggestion in the record of either case to suggest that tribal courts would dismiss the importance of the children's bonds to the parents with whom they had been placed, although it was certainly possible that the tribal courts could weigh the importance of those bonds and the children's ties to the tribe differently. Likewise, there was no reason to presume that the adoptive parents in either

claims were supported by the Cuban community in Florida. Although the Justice Department did not contest the authority of Elian's father to secure return of the child, the event garnered significant publicity, with President Fidel Castro at one point offering to come to the United States to secure custody of the child. Richard Bragg, "The Elian Gonzales Case: The Overview; Cuban Boy Seized by U.S. Agents and Reunited with His Father," *New York Times*, April 23, 2000.

[99] *Holyfield* at 54, citing *Halloway*.

[100] *Id.*

[101] Carole Goldberg-Ambrose, "Heeding the 'Voice' of Tribal Law in Indian Child Welfare Proceedings," in *Law and Anthropology* 7, eds. Rene Kuppe and Richard Potz (1994): 1–26 (arguing that tribal courts should be trusted to make decisions that meet the best interests of Indian children).

case would be treated unfairly in the tribal systems. In point of fact, both the Choctaw and Navajo courts ultimately fashioned decrees that left the children in the custody of their Anglo adoptive parents in *Holyfield* and *Holloway*, while fashioning decrees that would allow the children to become familiar with their Indian heritage as they grew older.[102]

More than thirty years after the passage of ICWA and twenty years since the Supreme Court decisively upheld tribal authority over Indian children, however, courts continue to parse the language of the Act. A recent Minnesota case, for example, *In re Child of R.S.*,[103] found that ICWA did not require, and in fact did not permit, the transfer of a case involving preadoptive proceedings for an Indian child domiciled outside of a reservation whose parent's rights had been involuntarily terminated in state court. The court held that the Act grants presumptive jurisdiction only in termination of parental rights proceedings and foster care placement proceedings, but not in preadoptive or adoptive proceedings. In reaching that conclusion, the Minnesota case acknowledged that it was reaching a decision at odds with what other states have done. This narrow reading of ICWA seems to contravene the clear intent of the Act, because it limits the authority of tribes to determine the adoptive placement of Indian children.

DEFINING THE INDIAN CHILD AND "INDIANNESS"

Not only is there continuing debate over how to read the jurisdictional provisions of ICWA – when good cause not to transfer cases exists, for example, and what kind of proceedings require transfer; more fundamental ambiguities exist in determining who is an Indian child in the first place. Determining who is an Indian is controversial in the United States for all of the reasons noted earlier – issues around recognizing and terminating tribes, historically high rates of intermarriage between Indians and non-Indians, and conflicts among shifting definitions in federal law and in tribal constitutions. Those problems increase exponentially when applied to children subject to the Act and the difficulty of resolving whether a child is "Indian" should not be underestimated. Deciphering who is an Indian child takes place in a world where cultural identity is notoriously fragmented, and where it may be difficult to rely on a single factor to determine belonging and membership.

Of the 1.4 million children who were identified in the 2000 census as Alaska Native or American Indian, more than a third were identified as

---

[102] Maldonado, *supra* n. 89.
[103] *In re Child of R.S.*, *supra* n. 82.

multiracial.[104] The Act, however, has a singular definition of Indian identity, defining an "Indian child" as "any unmarried person who is under age
eighteen and is either (a) a member of an Indian tribe or (b) is eligible for
membership in an Indian tribe and is the biological child of a member of an
Indian tribe."[105] The decision in *Holyfield*, while recognizing the importance
of maintaining ties between tribes and their children, provides little guidance
in these problematic cases, as the parents in that case were indisputably Indian
parents, both of whom lived on the reservation. Cases involving children who
have mixed heritage and/or whose connections with tribal life are attenuated,
either because their families of origin have had few connections to an Indian
community or the children have been living for a considerable period of time
with non-Indian caregivers, illustrate how difficult untangling this Gordian
knot can become.

The power accorded to tribes under Sections 1911(b) and (c) of the Act is
unprecedented in domestic and international law to the extent that it grants
authority to tribes over children located in a diasporic community. Those
sections require that state courts transfer custody proceedings involving "Indian
children domiciled or residing outside of a reservation" to tribes on request
by the tribe, an Indian custodian, or a parent. That obligation to transfer is
mandatory, unless a state court finds "good cause" not to transfer. The good
cause provision, as might be expected, has been the source of considerable
dispute. In cases where the transfer is not requested or it is declined by the
tribe, as allowed by the Act, tribes or Indian custodians have a continuing and
unlimited right to intervene at any point in the state court proceedings. Tribes,
of course, under the *Santa Clara* case discussed earlier, and as an accepted
aspect of their status as sovereign nations, have authority to determine who is
an Indian child for purposes of the Act.[106]

On one reading, this extension of authority over a diasporic population
represents a sensitive response to both the interests of tribes in maintaining
connections and the needs of Indian children who may find themselves adrift
in an environment that not only fails to recognize their Indian origins, but may
actively deride them. Tribes can bring children back to their communities and

[104] As Matthew Snipp points out in a report prepared for the Casey Family Foundation, changes
in the way the census is constructed have made it easier for *individuals* to identify themselves
as Indian. One significant factor may be that the census in 2000 "allowed respondents to
select as many categories as they wish[ed] to express their racial heritage." Matthew C.
Snipp, "American Indian and Alaska Native Children in the 2000 Census," The Annie E.
Casey Foundation and the Population Reference Bureau (2000) http://www.aecf.org/upload/
publicationfiles/american%20indian%20and%20alaska.pdf.
[105] ICWA, *supra* n. 2, Sec. 1903 (4).
[106] *See, e.g., In re J.W.*, 498 N.W. 2d 417 (Ia. App. 1993).

connect them to broad kinship circles: the aim of ICWA is to enhance tribal efforts to create that cultural link. The fact that the political, social, and cultural cohesion of tribes was deliberately undermined provides a strong argument for viewing the ICWA as a reparations statute with redress importantly hinged on the transfer of power to tribes, as Lorie Graham has noted.[107] Under the Act and the Bureau of Indian Affairs Guidelines interpreting the Act, state courts have discretion to appoint counsel for a child; the Guidelines also suggest that older children may object to preclude a transfer from state to tribal courts.[108] This approach suggests that children have a legally cognizable interest in asserting a particular, historically contingent identity. At the same time, the Act and the Guidelines recognize that tribes have authority to enforce and protect the identity of Indian children, at least while they are too young to take a position themselves.

On another reading, however – and in less cut-and-dried cases – the Act simply applies a Band-Aid® to a very complicated identity issue. It approaches identity as an either/or proposition, parsing jurisdiction between tribal and state courts to resolve the dilemma: either a child is or is not Indian. Under this interpretation, ICWA simply elides fraught issues of identity, culture, and belonging, making no provision for compromise when legitimate disputes arise.

Many state courts have strenuously resisted transferring cases to tribes, result-ing in a body of law that is uneven, not just from state to state, but from court to court within states. As Atwood has pointed out, state courts have balked most frequently in two classes of cases: when the child's heritage is mixed Indian and non-Indian, or when an Indian child has spent significant time in a non-Indian family and is assumed to have developed long-term bonds with non-Indian caretakers.[109] These state courts have typically stepped around ICWA's requirements by determining that the child either does not come from an "existing Indian family" or by determining that even if a child is arguably Indian, good cause nonetheless exists to refuse to transfer the case.

The "existing Indian family" doctrine derives from the assertion that a child who has never lived in a "functioning Indian family" cannot, and should not, be subject to the Act. The logic of that reasoning is that since ICWA was intended to protect "Indian" families and cultures, Indian families must be demonstrably different from other families; if no such demonstrable difference

[107] *See generally* Graham, "Reparations," *supra* n. 86.
[108] Atwood, *Children, Tribes and States, supra* n. 5 at 201 *et seq.* As a point of comparison, in custody cases involving divorcing parents, virtually all states grant older children a right to indicate a preference for living with one or another parent.
[109] Atwood, *supra* n. 5 at 203.

exists, no "Indian" family exists. In the case in which the exception originated almost twenty-five years ago, *Matter of Baby Boy L.*, a non-Indian mother sought to have her child adopted by a non-Indian couple. The child's father, who was 5/16ths Kiowa Indian, objected to the adoption and initially sought sole custody of the baby, later amending his request to ask that the child be placed with his extended family or another Kiowa family. Dismissing the efforts of the Kiowa tribe to have the case transferred to a tribal forum, the state court declared that ICWA simply did not apply when there was no extant Indian family being broken up by the adoption proceeding. The court declared that

> the underlying thread that runs throughout the entire Act . . . [is] that the Act is concerned with the removal of Indian children from an existing Indian family unit and the resultant breakup of the Indian family. In this case Baby Boy L. is only 5/16th Kiowa Indian, has never been removed from an Indian family and so long as the mother is alive to object, would probably never become a part of the [father's] or any other Indian family. . . . [W]e are of the opinion that to apply the Act to a factual situation such as the one before us would be to violate the policy and intent of Congress rather than uphold them.[110]

This invocation of the "existing Indian family" doctrine is distinctly at odds with the Act. While ICWA was passed in part to respond to the tragedy of Indian children being removed from their families without sufficient cause – those cases where child welfare workers simply misunderstood tribal values and kinship systems – the facts of the *Baby Boy L.* case also suggested that the case was to be covered by the Act, although the Act does not speak to a child's "dominant" heritage. It seems specious to say that because an infant has been surrendered at birth before any "family" developed, there was no "Indian family" affected by the child's placement. Where, as in that case, one of the child's parents was an enrolled member of a tribe and engaged in life in that community, and the child was clearly eligible for membership, the conclusion that no Indian family existed because the child was surrendered as an infant and the parents were unmarried seems clearly premature.

[110] *Matter of Adoption of Baby Boy L.*, 643 P.2d 168 (1982). As is often the case, the facts were complicated. According to the state court's recitation of the facts, at the time of the child's birth, the father, who was apparently actively connected to the Kiowa tribe, was in prison, and had a long and sometimes violent criminal record. In addition, the father had not supported the mother during her pregnancy, although he had indicated at one point that he had pulled together money for an abortion. What the state court decision does not elaborate on is the fact that the father, in his amended answers to the petition to terminate his parental rights, asked "among other things, that the child be placed with a member of its extended family, or other members of the Kiowa Tribe, or with other Indian families as defined by the [ICWA]." He was joined in this action by his parents, the child's paternal grandparents.

From the standpoint of understanding the meaning of belonging, however, the *Baby Boy L.* case raises difficult questions about what aspects of a child's identity matter. The court was anxious to defer to the biological mother's characterization of the child's "dominant" cultural heritage – apparently based on the notion that the child was 11/16 non-Indian. The court emphasized that the purpose of ICWA "was not to dictate that an illegitimate infant who has never been a member of an Indian home or culture, and probably never would be, should be removed from its *primary* cultural heritage and placed in an Indian environment over the express objections of its non-Indian mother."[111]

One of the most widely discussed cases in which "Indianness" became an issue, and that extended the existing Indian family exception, was *In re Bridget R.*, decided in California in 1996.[112] A young unmarried couple, already raising two small children, surrendered custody of their newborn twin daughters to an Ohio couple. The children were 3/32 Pomo Indian through their father, who was recognized under tribal custom as a member of the Dry Creek Pomo tribe, although he was not formally enrolled prior to the onset of the custody litigation. Prior to the adoption, the father had had no contact with the tribe and lived several hundred miles from the reservation.

The twins were placed for adoption without the knowledge of their paternal grandmother. Distraught when she subsequently learned that she had grandchildren who had been placed for adoption, she contacted the Pomo tribe and enrolled herself; her son followed suit. The tribe then initiated proceedings to set aside the adoption; the children's paternal grandmother sought to have the twins placed with their aunt, her daughter.

The California court rejected the *Baby Boy L.* framing of the existing Indian family doctrine for the reasons just noted – that it would be premature to determine that a child did not come from an existing Indian family because he or she was surrendered at birth. However, it reworked the exception, as had some courts before it, to hold that ICWA did not apply where neither the child nor the child's biological parents had "significant connections" to an Indian community, similar to the standard used in the UCCJEA discussed earlier. The court held that

there are significant constitutional impediments to applying ICWA, rather than state law, in proceedings affecting the family relationships of persons who are not residents or domiciliaries of an Indian reservation, are not socially or culturally connected with an Indian community, and, in all respects except genetic heritage, are indistinguishable from other residents of the

[111] *Id.* at 175, *emphasis added.*
[112] 49 Cal. Rptr. 2d 507 (Cal. App. 1996).

state. These impediments arise from the due process and equal protection guarantees of the Fifth and Fourteenth Amendments and from the Tenth Amendment's reservation to the states of all powers not delegated to the federal government.[113]

Even after the *Holyfield* case had declared that a tribe's interest was co-equal to that of parents, the California court held that construing ICWA to rescind a parent's voluntary surrender of a child violated the due process rights of the parent under the Fifth and Fourteenth Amendments to the U.S. Constitution when the parent was not closely tied to tribal life.

More critically, the Court focused on the due process right of children "to remain through their developing years in one stable and loving home."[114] Although the U.S. Supreme Court has never found such a due process right for children – and, indeed, the recognition of such a constitutionally grounded right would significantly alter the panoply of family and parental rights currently articulated in U.S. constitutional doctrine – the California court drew from its own prior decisions and from dicta in several Supreme Court opinions to conclude that "the twins . . . have a presently existing fundamental and constitutionally protected interest in their relationship with the only family they have ever known," and refused to apply the ICWA.[115] The court went on to note that

> [w]e have no quarrel with the proposition that preserving American Indian culture is a legitimate, even compelling, governmental interest. At the same time, however, we agree with those courts which have held that this purpose will not be served by applying the provisions of ICWA . . . to children whose biological parents do not have a significant social, cultural or political relationship with an Indian community. It is almost too obvious to require articulation that "the unique values of Indian culture" . . . will not be preserved in the homes of parents who have become fully assimilated into non-Indian culture.[116]

---

[113] *Id.* at 526–527.
[114] *Id.* at 522.
[115] *Id.* at 526.
[116] *Id.* The court also found the application of ICWA to violate equal protection rights. While ordinarily, it is permissible under the Equal Protection Clause to treat Indian children differently from non-Indian children (as Indian status is a political, rather than a racial, classification), the court held that "where such social, cultural or political relationships do not exist or are very attenuated, the only remaining basis for applying ICWA rather than state law in proceedings affecting an Indian child's custody is the child's genetic heritage – in other words, race," and that under those circumstances, the classification was not permissible. The court also found that under the Tenth Amendment, ICWA could not apply, as application under these circumstances interfered with traditional state authority over family matters. *Id.*

The case raised issues difficult to resolve. Arguably, the court was reacting to the instrumental use of ICWA by a parent and grandmother who simply regretted the decision. The decision drew significant public attention in both Ohio and California as the case was developing, especially as the non-Indian media fueled fears that resolving the case in favor of the tribe would generate widespread instability in adoptive proceedings, and the result generated an immediate outcry from both tribes and non-Indians. Its ultimate resolution, leaving the case in the state courts, provoked strident objections from tribes and Indian advocates, who argued that the state court's decision reflected a misunderstanding of Indian culture, although it was not clear how the decision flew in the face of distinctly Indian values. More importantly, those advocates noted that ICWA does not protect tribal interests in children because those tribes promote a romantic, sentimentalized Indian lifestyle, but because the tribe has legitimate interests in securing its survival. Supporters of the decision, however, argued that imposing this sort of "significant connection" test protected "real" Indian families and discouraged unhappy biological parents from reneging on decisions by searching for a tenuous Indian connection. As Atwood has argued, the doctrine is clearly at odds with the ICWA, noting that some courts have recognized that "allowing state courts to assess the sufficiency of an individual's ties with his or Indian heritage, the [existing Indian family] doctrine invites precisely the kind of state court interference that ICWA was intended to eliminate."[117]

Following *Bridget R.*, legislation backed by the American Association of Adoption Attorneys, among others, was introduced in Congress to amend ICWA and enable state courts to deny transfer of cases where the child's parents lacked "significant social, cultural, or political ties with the tribe of which they are a member."[118] That legislative effort was defeated, but would have done little to resolve the basic issue in any event as it would simply have bounced the jurisdictional power to determine who would decide on a child's "Indianness" back to state courts, without working toward any kind of compromise in difficult cases.

As *Bridget R.* illustrates, troubling cases arise when state courts fear that ICWA is being invoked simply to evade the consequences of state adoption-laws, especially when a biological parent has little acquaintance with her Indian heritage. In *In re Adoption of Crews*,[119] which the *Bridget R.* court cited, a biological mother sought to revoke her consent to an adoption and regain custody of her child within days after the child was placed with adoptive

[117] Atwood, *Children, Tribes and States, supra* n. 5 at 216.
[118] S. 1448, 104th Cong. 1995.
[119] *In re Adoption of Crews*, 825 P.2d 305 (Wash. 1992).

parents. The mother had informed the placement agency prior to the adoption that she was part Indian, but did not know much about her background; the social worker testified at a hearing on the matter that the mother did not know what tribe she might be affiliated with nor did she provide any information that would allow her Indian membership to be verified. After the proceedings to secure the return of the child were begun, it was determined Crews and her child were eligible for tribal membership in the Oklahoma Choctaw Nation. In finding that ICWA nonetheless did not apply, the court stated:

> Neither Crews nor her family has ever lived on the Choctaw reservation in Oklahoma and there are no plans to relocate the family from Seattle to Oklahoma. Bertiaux, B.'s father, has no ties to any Indian tribe or community and opposes B.'s removal from his adoptive parents. Moreover, there is no allegation by Crews or the Choctaw Nation that, if custody were returned to Crews, B. would grow up in an Indian environment. To the contrary, Crews has shown no substantive interest in her Indian heritage in the past and has given no indication this will change in the future.[120]

Similarly, in *Alexandria Y. v. Renea Y.*[121] a dispute arose over whether a California court should comply with the placement preferences stated in ICWA.[122] The case involved a child whose father was Hispanic, and whose mother, Renea, was eligible for membership in the Seminole tribe, although Renea had been adopted into a non-Indian family as an infant (a not uncommon scenario for many Indian parents, especially during the 1970s and 1980s). Their child had been placed in foster care with a Latino family at the age of seven months and that family eventually sought to adopt her. The court examined the "existing Indian family" doctrine, holding that "whether there is an existing Indian family is dependent on the unique facts of each situation," and that "*Holyfield* did not reject any form of the existing Indian family doctrine."[123] The court then went on to hold that

> [n]either Alexandria nor Renea has any relationship with the [Seminole Nation], let alone a significant one. Renea was raised by a non-Indian family, and her extended family is non-Indian. . . . [N]o evidence was presented to

---

[120] *Id.* at 310.

[121] *Alexandria Y. v. Renea Y.*, 53 Cal. Rptr. 2d 679 (Cal. 1996).

[122] The facts were complicated, as is typical in family law cases. The Seminole tribe initially chose not to assert jurisdiction, but asked the California court to comply with the ICWA preferences. Later, Renea appeared in the case and filed a request to transfer the case, which the Seminole court accepted. At that point, however, the state court found that there was good cause not to apply the placement preferences, finding that the child, Alexandria, had bonded with her foster family – who was seeking her adoption – and disruption was likely to be harmful to her.

[123] *Id.* at 687.

suggest Renea had ever been exposed to her Indian heritage as a child or pursued such an interest as an adult. The father is Hispanic, and Alexandria is placed in a preadoptive Hispanic home where Spanish is spoken. Under these circumstances, it would be anomalous to allow . . . ICWA to govern the termination proceedings. It was clearly not the intent of the Congress to do so.[124]

Contention over the scope – indeed, the validity of – the "existing Indian family" doctrine has not abated significantly, although some state courts have been willing to limit its use. In *In re CLJ*, for example, the Alabama Court of Civil Appeals recently refused to extend the "existing Indian family" exception to a case where "the child's mother is an Indian but the child is alleged to have had little to no contact with an Indian tribe"; the court noted that the exception had previously only been applied in cases where a non-Indian mother had relinquished her child, usually at birth.[125] In that case, the child had been removed from her mother's care at age three and placed in foster care. In fact, the Chickasaw Nation contended that the only reason the child had not been in an "Indian family environment" was because the child had been removed from her mother's custody by the state child welfare agency and placed in a non-Indian foster home.[126] Thus, the court decided that ICWA applied, but refused to grant the lower court's order transferring the case to the Chickasaw Nation pending a determination of whether there was "good cause" not to transfer the case. Later in the opinion, the court noted that the state-court appointed guardian for the child contested the degree to which the great-aunt who was seeking transfer (along with the mother and the Chickasaw Nation) had connections to the child, and suggested that the state's juvenile court might have authority to determine whether the great-aunt was a member of the child's "extended family" under the Act.[127]

Similarly, the Colorado Court of Appeals refused to extend the existing Indian family doctrine to bar the application of ICWA in a case involving a stepparent adoption, *In re N.B.*, where the stepmother sought to terminate

---

[124] *Id.*
[125] *Ex parte CLJ*, 946 So. 2d 880 (Ala. Civ. App., 2006).
[126] The court then observed: "The Chickasaw Nation alleges that DHR took that action in spite of its knowledge of the child's heritage as an Indian. The allegations contained in the guardian ad litem's . . . motion dispute those allegations. Among other things, the guardian ad litem has alleged that the great aunt and the mother had only recently joined the Chickasaw Nation, that the mother's family has not participated in any Indian culture, and that the mother did not advocate placing the child with the great aunt until the filing of the termination petition was imminent." *Id.* at 889, n. 7.
[127] *Id.* at 893 et seq.

an Indian mother's rights and adopt a child who had been in the custody of the child's father and herself for the majority of the child's life.[128] The court upheld the lower court's decision, which had applied ICWA, finding beyond a reasonable doubt that while "continued custody of the child by mother would likely result in serious emotional damage to him, . . . the stepmother had not shown that active efforts were made to provide remedial services or rehabilitative programs to prevent the breakup of the Indian family." Thus, the court refused to grant the stepmother's petition, noting that before terminating the mother's rights, active efforts to reunify the child's Indian family would have to be undertaken.

Cases such as the one just noted provide the occasion for much handwringing. In *In re N.B.*, the child's father had been the child's primary caretaker since birth, and the child had had only sporadic contact with his mother. When the child was three, the mother left the state and visited only three times in the ensuing three years. She provided no child support payments. The stepmother's petition for termination of the mother's rights and adoption alleged that the child had been abandoned. But the difficult facts were not insurmountable: given the reluctance of the biological mother to reach out to the child, it should not have been particularly difficult to establish that efforts to reunite the family would be futile.

If states do not balk at applying ICWA by invoking the existing Indian family doctrine, they may step around the requirements of the Act by finding "good cause" not to transfer a case under Section 1911(b) of the Act. Under the BIA Guidelines, good cause not to transfer a case may exist in several instances: if there is no judicial forum in the tribe to handle the case; if the child is over twelve and objects to the transfer; if the proceeding is at an advanced stage and the tribe did not promptly seek intervention when notified of that proceeding; if a transfer would impose an undue hardship on the parties because of the distance involved; or, finally, if the child is over five years of age, the parents are not available, and the child has had "minimal contact" with the tribe.[129] The latter provision, of course, has provoked some concern, particularly in cases where an Indian child has been placed in foster care with non-Indians for several years which has made contact difficult.

Many state courts, in addition, utilize the good cause standard interchangeably with a "best interest of the child" standard to preclude transfer of cases to tribes. The difficulty with that approach is that a state court's determination

---

[128] *In re N.B.*, 199 P.3d 16 (Colo. App. 2007).
[129] *Guidelines, supra* n. 6 at C.3.b.

of what a child's best interest might be is likely to be inflected with cultural biases.[130] Even if such a bias could be eliminated or minimized, nothing in the Act suggests that the good cause standard should be collapsed into a best interests standard as the purpose of ICWA was precisely to enable tribes to determine what the best interests of Indian children are.

SINKING INTO A JURISDICTIONAL BOG

Disputes over the scope of ICWA have been relatively constant since the Act's passage in 1978. The *Bridget R.* case, for example, led California Representative Cynthia Price to attempt to write the "existing Indian family" exception into law: the proposed legislation would have redefined an Indian child as one who had "at least one . . . parent[] of Indian descent and at least one of the Indian child's parents maintains a significant social, cultural or political affiliation with the Indian tribe of which either parent is a member."[131] That amendment was defeated. Tribes and Indian advocates, at the same time, have tried to amend the Act to entirely eliminate the existing Indian family provision and to narrow the discretion of state courts to find good cause not to transfer cases, although those efforts have been equally unsuccessful. In 2003, tribes unsuccessfully sought to amend ICWA on a variety of fronts to strengthen tribal interests.[132]

Enhancing the ties among Indian children, their families, and their communities dovetails directly into efforts to secure self-determination for tribes. The Act manifests an honest recognition that U.S. policy systematically injured tribes by removing their children and that Indian communities cannot rebuild themselves unless specific actions that facilitate the regeneration of those connections can be made. Because Indian children were removed from their families at such high rates and over so many generations, the ties between Indian children and tribes are often faint; many, many Indian children live in circumstances that are distant from tribal life and tribal communities. Many of those same children and their families, however, also live extremely precarious lives, as those families continue to be disproportionately socially and economically disadvantaged. Reading the facts in these cases confirms how fragile the circumstances often are. In fact, the cases discussed in the previous section are not anomalous, but reveal what is too

---

[130] *E.g., In re N.B., supra* n. 128; Atwood, *Children, Tribes and States, supra* n. 5, 219–229.

[131] H.R. 3286, *An Act to Help Families Defray Adoption Costs and Promote the Adoption of Minority Children,* 104th Congress (1996).

[132] H.R. 2750, *Indian Child Welfare Act Amendments of* 2003, 108th Congress (2003–2004).

often commonplace in a community that has been ravaged by neglect for generations. These facts do not often generate sympathy among non-Indians for protecting the integrity of tribes, but many Indian parents' lives are in disarray precisely because white society was so quick to break up families: the mother of the child in *In re CLJ* had herself been removed from her home as a toddler; the Indian father in *In re Crews* had grown up in foster care; and the father in *Baby Boy L.* was in prison at the time the case was heard. Reclaiming children may be a first step in breaking that cycle of dislocation and despair.[133]

At the same time, tribal communities may be hard-pressed to provide services, and individual children, depending on their circumstances, may find it difficult to move into tribal culture if they have spent long periods outside of it. In addition, non-Indians often find it hard to accept that a child whose Indian ancestry is faint should be classified as Indian, contending that such children, at the very least, belong to more than one cultural group and that neither should be deemed dominant, an argument that closely resembles the arguments advanced by Fogg-Davis that children's in-betweenness must be recognized. These very real problems cannot be ignored, and must inform the general debate over multiculturalism: while assisting historically marginalized communities to maintain and perpetuate themselves is compelled as a matter of justice and fairness, policies must also respond to the immediate needs of children whose lives may be disrupted by the exigencies of living in fragile environments. As discussed in Chapter 3, meeting the needs of both the group and the child surely must not preclude any consideration of the child's origins. Neither, however, should it make that connection the sole determinative factor in the child's placement.

The jurisdictional resolution contained in ICWA, although granting the maximum degree of authority to tribes, represents an all-or-nothing approach that can be problematic at a number of levels. Of course, ICWA does not make "Indianness" the sole factor in the ultimate custody determination; there is every reason to believe that tribes will be attentive to children's needs and make developmentally appropriate determinations.[134] At the same time, litigation over a child's status as Indian or non-Indian is often protracted while children's attachments and needs may change over time. More critically, ICWA's failure to provide any guidelines for dealing with children whose heritage and/or lived experience crosses more than one cultural group is problematic. As has been

[133] *See generally* Graham, "Reparations," *supra* n. 86.
[134] Goldberg-Ambrose, *supra* n. 101.

noted, cultural and communal membership can be ambiguous at its very core, and both states and tribes must face up to that ambiguity.

ICWA provides one example of how the multicultural accommodation urged by Shachar might operate.[135] However, it also illustrates the pitfalls of trying to create accommodations by drawing strict jurisdictional boundaries. As Atwood has noted, flexibility is essential on both sides – both states and tribes have to work together to fashion solutions for particular children.[136] Tribes should have considerable leeway to determine who is an Indian child and place such children appropriately, but should also be wary of sweeping every eligible child into its ambit – especially those who have established ties with non-Indian caretakers. Furthermore, tribes must be sensitive, as well, to the decisions that individual parents have made in deciding to place children with particular caretakers. Although, as noted earlier, there may be reason to doubt the voluntariness of some surrenders of children, the voices of parents – most typically mothers – should be accorded some degree of deference as well, pulling back from the language in *Holyfield* that allows tribes to discount those voices at will. At the same time, state courts need to trust that tribes are as adept at evaluating the needs of individual children as they presume themselves to be.

Indian children across the nation continue to be removed from Indian homes and communities and placed in non-Indian foster and adoptive homes, increasing the likelihood that children will lose their connections with tribal communities. Thus, disputes about ICWA require a more global response than a push and pull between sovereigns over jurisdiction: there must be better efforts to recruit and facilitate the placement of Indian children with Indian foster and adoptive families, and there must be more efforts to remedy the inequality that places Indian children and families at risk.[137] In the meantime, however, both tribes and states must look at the life a particular child has lived in order to use the Act in a way that benefits both tribes and children.

In the future, implementing ICWA may require a greater understanding of the international human rights regime respecting indigenous populations. When the Declaration of the Rights of Indigenous Peoples was adopted by the United Nations in 2007, the United States was one of four nations to vote

---

[135] Ayelet Shachar, *Multicultural Jurisdictions: Cultural Differences and Women's Rights* (New York: Cambridge University Press, 2001)

[136] Atwood, *Children, Tribes and States, supra* n. 5 at 248–249.

[137] The recently enacted *Fostering Connections to Success Act*, allocates resources to assist tribes in foster care and adoption programs. *Fostering Connections to Success and Increasing Adoptions Act of 2008*, P.L.110–357, 122 Stat. 3949 (codified as amended in scattered sections of 42 U.S.C.).

against it, but has since revised that position and stated that it endorses the principles contained in that human rights document. As new international human rights regimes develop – not only with respect to indigenous persons but with regard to other groups – they are likely to affect the ways in which the placement of children without parental care. Those issues are explored in Chapter 5.

5

Transnational Adoption in a Shifting World

A host of new concerns for understanding cultural and communal belonging arises when adoption reaches across national boundaries. The regulatory environment in which transnational adoption takes place draws on international human rights covenants and declarations, the provisions of the Hague Convention on Protection of Children and Cooperation in Respect of Intercountry Adoption, and the rules imposed domestically by individual nation-states. It is an area rife with tension: many actors in the international community, concerned about child trafficking and the general vulnerability of families in sending nations – those from which children originate – increasingly object to transnational transfers of children at the very time that families and adoption advocates in receiving nations – those to which children are moved – articulate an accelerating interest in such placements.

Nowhere did that tension emerge more clearly than after the catastrophic earthquake in Haiti in 2010. Despite clear, early directives from the U.S. Department of State and a variety of international aid agencies emphasizing the need to move deliberately to ensure the reunification of children and families where possible – an effort to avoid the confusion caused when well-meaning adults in developed nations rushed to provide homes for children affected by the devastating tsunami in Indonesia in 2004 – scandal nonetheless erupted when on January 29, 2010, a group of individuals from the New Life Children's Refuge, an Idaho-based religious group led by Laura Silsby, were apprehended moving thirty-three children across the border to an "orphanage" in the Dominican Republic. As that story unfolded, it became clear that many of the children were not orphans and that the self-styled missionaries had little sense of the rules and regulations governing transnational placement. To cap

An earlier version of Chapter 5 appeared as Alice Hearst, "Between Restavek and Relocation," *Journal of the History of Childhood and Youth* 3 (2010): (2): 267–292.

it off, one of the group's putative legal advisors, Jorge Puello, was wanted on child sex-trafficking charges in four countries.[1] The story only gave tangible form to the concerns often expressed about corruption and coercion in the international adoption arena.

The Haiti scandal was not an isolated incident. Newspapers frequently report concerns about the origins of children adopted internationally. On August 11, 2011, the *New York Times*, for example, reported on claims by parents that Chinese officials in at least one province had confiscated children, mostly girls, who were subsequently placed for adoption, suggesting that some children in Chinese orphanages might not have been legitimately available for adoption.[2] Within four months, the *Times* again reported that at least 600 persons had been arrested on child-selling charges in Hunan Province alone, and that several of the children sold ended up being adopted by foreigners.[3] These stories have been particularly troubling because, in the transnational adoption universe, China has been one country with enough bureaucratic infrastructure that adoptive parents have felt relatively confident about the status of adoptive children as abandoned or orphaned, especially as China's one-child policy, coupled with a cultural preference for boys, made the adoption of Chinese girls almost a feminist mission beginning in the mid-1990s.

Problems determining which children are legitimately available for adoption reach far beyond China, and the consequences can be wrenching for all concerned. Just two days before the first *New York Times* story on China, *Slate* magazine reported on a child whose adoptive parents realized that the malnourished child they had adopted sixteen years earlier from an orphanage under siege during the civil war in Sierra Leone – a child, the adoptive family firmly believed, who would have died had they not adopted him – had parents who were looking for him among "the children who were sold to these white people."[4] The *Slate* story suggested a frenzied situation in Sierra Leone in which mistakes were made, but the annals of transnational adoption are replete with stories of corrupt and haphazard practices: In 2002,

[1] Marc Lacey and Ian Urbina, "Adviser to Jailed Americans in Haiti is Accused of Trafficking," *New York Times*, Feb. 16, 2010.
[2] Sharon LaFraniere, "Chinese Officials Seized and Sold Babies, Parents Say," *New York Times*, Aug. 4, 2011.
[3] Edward Wong, "China: Hundreds Arrested on Child-Selling Charges," *New York Times*, Dec. 7, 2011. The BBC, reporting on the same story, noted that many of the trafficked children are sold as laborers and domestic servants, but two years earlier had reported that dozens of baby girls had been confiscated and placed for adoption by corrupt officials when parents could not pay exorbitant fines for violating China's policies limiting the number of children couples may have. "China Babies Sold for Adoption," *BBC News*, July 2, 2009.
[4] E. J. Graff, "In 1998, Americans Adopted 29 Children from a Town in Sierra Leone: Their Birth Families Say They Were Stolen," *Slate*, Aug. 9, 2011.

Lauren Galindo, who ran an adoption agency out of Cambodia, was investigated by agents from the U.S. Customs and Immigration Service. She was subsequently charged with several felonies in connection with trafficking more than 800 children who were placed with adoptive families, primarily in the United States. Galindo, who was convicted in 2005, allegedly made more than $8 million during the time she operated her agency.[5]

Concerns about the provenance of children available for adoption transnationally have continually floated in the background over the last two decades as transnational adoption has increased in appeal for adoptive parents. (Foster care across national boundaries is rare, although it is implicated by the practice of transnational adoption, which often shifts focus away from providing local care.) What was meant to be a humane response to the plight of children living in dire straits has become big business with the most important transactions – securing children for adoption – taking place in the shadows. Sometimes, as in the Galindo case, the agencies have been complicit. However, even legitimate agencies often have little control over how children come into care and how their status as orphans is determined.[6] And while scandals continue to erupt, more and more children continue to live in poverty and despair around the globe.

To understand the concerns about transnational adoption and how international laws and conventions are now shaping the practice requires an initial understanding of relatively recent changes in international paradigms for meeting children's needs. For many decades, both governmental and nongovernmental actors designed their aid programs and policies with a focus on children's dependency and vulnerability. In 1989, with the adoption of the UN Convention on the Rights of the Child (CRC),[7] the conversation shifted into the register of rights. Although relief efforts for children still respond to children's needs, many of the claims are now pressed as rights, arguably commanding greater attention than pleas based solely on need. As noted in

---

[5] The Galindo case and a number of other cases are discussed in detail by Johanna Oreskovic and Trish Maskew, "Red Thread or Slender Reed: Deconstructing Prof. Bartholet's Mythology of International Adoption," *Buffalo Human Rights Law Review* 14 (2008): 71–128.

[6] *Id.* at 82–88; *see also* Katie Rasor, Richard M. Rothblatt, Elizabeth A. Russo and Julie A. Turner, "Imperfect Remedies: The Arsenal of Criminal Statutes Available to Prosecute International Adoption Fraud in the United States," *New York Law School Law Review* 55 (2010/2011): 801–822, exploring the various U.S. statutes that can be invoked to prosecute adoption fraud, with particular attention to the *Intercountry Adoption Act of 2000*, 42 U.S.C. sec. 14901 (2006), which went into full effect in 2008, after the United States had ratified the Hague Convention in December 2007.

[7] Convention on the Rights of the Child, G.A. res. 44/25, annex, 44 U.N GAOR Supp. (No. 49) at 167, U.N. Doc. A/44/49 (1989), entered into force Sept. 2, 1990, www2.ohchr.org/english/law/crc.htm (herein CRC).

Chapters 1 and 2, however, this rights language is both highly ambiguous and hard to put into operation given children's dependency and immaturity.

The move to a rights orientation for children was mirrored across the international community as international groups pushed for the need to recognize a variety of "third-generation" rights. Demands for the protection of individual rights were joined by the assertion of rights for particularly vulnerable groups, as human rights advocates recognized that claims for individual rights may come to naught when the individual is a member of a community whose status has been historically degraded. This recognition spurred the creation of a variety of conventions and declarations on behalf of women, members of ethnic, racial, religious, and linguistic minorities, and indigenous groups, among others.[8]

As a result, international rights regimes today envelop children in complicated ways, shaping their connections with families, communities, and nations of origin, as well as their relationships with both their biological and adoptive families. Belonging itself is increasingly viewed today in terms of rights for both children and their communities of origin. In light of this reorientation, it is not surprising that the existence of a global children's diaspora through transnational adoption raises sensitive issues, and the unprecedented transfer of children from poor families in the developing world to wealthier families in the West generates bitterness. Advocates of transnational adoption argue that providing stable, loving homes for children is simply one part of a compassionate response to global dislocation and poverty; opponents label the practice as a virulent new form of colonialism that drapes the exploitation of children, families, and communities in the soothing imagery of global understanding and cooperation.

Today, some thirty to forty thousand children are adopted transnationally every year, with approximately half of those into families in the United States. The number of children adopted transnationally into the United States has dropped significantly in recent years, from a high of almost 23,000 in 2004 to a little more than 9,000 in 2011.[9] Although it is not yet fully clear what accounts for that drop, it is likely due to both increasing disclosures about trafficking and the emergence of more stringent regimes governing the practice.[10]

---

[8] *See, e.g., Declaration on the Rights of Indigenous Peoples*, G.A. Res. 61/295, U.N. Doc. A/RES/47/1 (2007); *Declaration on the Rights of Persons Belonging to National or Ethnic, Religious or Linguistic Minorities*, G.A. res. 47/135, annex, 47 U.N. GAOR Supp. (No. 49), U.N. Doc. a/47/49 (1993).

[9] Elisa A. Rosman, Charles E. Johnson, and Nicole M. Callahan, *Adoption Factbook V* (Baltimore, MD: National Council for Adoption, 2011) at 82.

[10] Intercountry Adoption, Bureau of Consular Affairs, *Fiscal Year 2011 Annual Report*, U.S. Department of State. http://adoption.state.gov/about_us/statistics.php.

As the demand for adopting children across national borders has grown over the last two decades, so, too, has opposition: the issue is now a high priority on the political agendas in many sending nations. In 1998, for example, former South Korean President Kim Dae-Jung issued a formal apology to a group of South Korean adoptees for having sent them out of the country for adoption.[11] The concern has not just been that sending nations have used transnational adoption to "dump" unwanted children – a charge levied at South Korea – but that in poor countries, biological families have been manipulated into surrendering children. In recent years, numerous nations have imposed temporary moratoria on adoptions in response to concerns about trafficking and corruption, often leaving adoptive families in limbo and throwing transnational adoption into sharp relief.

The high demand for adoptable infants has generated a market in which unscrupulous practices have thrived.[12] The Hague Convention, now widely adopted internationally and adopted in the United States in 2008,[13] has the laudable aim of reducing trafficking in children by creating stringent guidelines for overseeing the adoption process in both sending and receiving countries. Although the Convention goes far in its efforts to ensure that children are legitimately eligible for adoption, it does not (and, in fairness, cannot) address the deeper structural issues that leave children abandoned or in need of care in the first place. Its provisions are intended to ensure that biological parents are not coerced into surrendering children for adoption, although its effectiveness is wholly dependent on the ability of officials in sending countries to enforce its provisions. Nor does the Convention contain provisions to enhance options for care at the local level; because the business of adoptions is quite lucrative, local adoptive families are often priced out of the market. Compliance with

---

[11] In a letter to a Korean adoptee after this meeting, Kim Dae-Jung wrote: "Globalization does not mean to live together with other countries and nations, but in the first place to reconnect to our own blood line, amicably and tenderly. That may function as the bridge which will make globalization possible." Letter from President Kim Dae-Jung to Lena-Kim Arctaedius-Svenungsson, January 11, 2001, in Tobias Hübinette, "The Adopted Koreans of Sweden and the Korean Adoption Issue," *Review of Korean Studies* 6(1) (Spring 2003): 251–266.

[12] See Oreskovic and Maskew, *supra* n. 5; David M. Smolin, "Child Laundering: How the Intercountry Adoption System Legitimizes and Incentivizes the Practice of Buying, Trafficking, Kidnapping and Stealing Children," *Wayne Law Review* 52 (2006): 113–200.

[13] *Hague Convention on the Protection of Children and Co-operation in Respect of Intercountry Adoption*, May 29, 1993, Miscellaneous No. 40 (1994) (hereafter Hague Convention). Not all nations have ratified the Hague Convention, which applies only among signatories. Status Table, Convention of 29 May 1993 on Protection of Children and Co-operation in Respect of Intercountry Adoption, www.hcch.net/index_en.php?act=conventions.status&cid=69. Adoptions from nonsignatory states are governed only by the Immigration and Naturalization Act; only a very few states have regulations specific to intercountry adoptions, and none regulate the actions of overseas agents of domestic agencies. Oreskovic and Maskew, *supra* n. 5, 93–103.

the Convention thus may give adoptive parents some assurance that the child they adopted was genuinely available for adoption, but does nothing to staunch the losses felt by communities whose children are sent around the globe.[14]

Transnational adoption informs the debate over multiculturalism in a number of ways. The need for recognition felt by many subnational groups in the domestic context – as discussed in Chapters 3 and 4 – exists in the international context as well. Communities marginalized on a global stage are likely to be particularly sensitive when it appears that their children are targeted for removal. In addition to the impact of adoption practices on communities of origin, all of the complicated issues of belonging for children are magnified in the global context. Children moved through adoption and foster care are always subject to some sort of forced exit, even when that exit is necessary to secure their well-being, and many feel the loss strongly as they mature.[15] Hammering out resolutions to these concerns at an international level – engaging in the intercultural or intercommunal dialogue advised by Parekh – is integral to providing the respect for children and communities that is at the center of debates over belonging and communal identity.[16]

Increasingly, sending nations are advocating community-based solutions to the problem of children without families, reflecting what, on some readings, seems to be suggested by the Convention on the Rights of the Child; other international human rights documents clearly view transnational placements only as a last resort, as discussed later. But as the ensuing discussion points out, many of the documents are ambiguous and may thus be interpreted by adoption advocates and receiving nations as placing transnational adoption as a priority in meeting children's human rights. The lack of clarity in the documents is further complicated because the depth of historical disadvantage

[14] It is, of course, true that the total number of children transferred through adoption around the world is vanishingly small compared to the number of children in need, so that communities should celebrate the fact that at least some children find homes through adoption, a position that Bartholet, for example, has voiced with frequency. *See, e.g.,* Elizabeth Bartholet, "International Adoption: Thoughts on the Human Rights Issue," *Buffalo Human Rights Law Review* 13 (2007): 151–203. Although the absolute numbers may be small (and adoption advocates tend to overstate the numbers of "orphans" actually available for adoption) transnational adoption remains an explosive issue, as it becomes a vector through which race, class, and gender inequalities are illuminated on a global scale. Just as with transracial adoption domestically, the "rescue" of children via transnational adoption invites resentment, particularly among the marginalized groups whose children are most likely to find their way into the adoption market.

[15] *See, e.g.,* Eleana Kim, "Remembering Loss: The Koreanness of Overseas Adopted Koreans," in *International Korean Adoption: A Fifty-Year History of Policy and Practice*, eds. Kathleen Ja Sook Bergquist, M. Elizabeth Vonk, Dong Soo Kim, and Marvin D. Feit (New York: The Haworth Press, 2007).

[16] Bhikhu Parekh, *Rethinking Multiculturalism: Cultural Diversity and Political Theory* (New York: Palgrave Macmillan, 2000).

encountered in many communities may make it impossible to provide effective and immediate community solutions to the problem of children without parents. The reality is that the scope of the economic and social problems many nations face – sometimes coupled with the sheer number of children in need – can transcend their ability to respond, even if that nation or subcommunities located within it want to keep their children within the fold.[17]

Regardless of where children are found globally, their identity is typically described by nationality: a child adopted from the Ukraine may be raised with the understanding that she is Ukrainian by birth, rather than Byelorussian or Crimean Tatar. This articulation of identity complicates the issue of belonging for adopted children and their communities of origin, as there may be conflicts between national and subnational communities. In other words, the problems that exist for children adopted domestically exist transnationally as well: the movement of children affects groups *within* nation-states differently, sometimes visiting unique harms on minority or aboriginal communities. These communities, often situated at the bottom of the social and economic hierarchies of the respective nation-states in which they are located, are far more likely than dominant groups in those same countries to find their children subject to adoption, and may therefore find it doubly difficult to assert an interest, much less a legal claim, for attachment to children. As with domestic adoption, then, it may be difficult to determine the community to which a specific child "belongs."

Last, but not least, the issues must be considered in light of concerns for the child's own agency in determining where he or she belongs. Identity issues can be particularly fraught for transnational adoptees. Although a transracially adopted child in the domestic context may long for connections to her own racial, ethnic, or cultural group, that group typically has numerous

---

[17] In some sending nations like South Korea and China, the issue has been less that the nation lacks the financial resources to deal with children, but that the stigma of single motherhood or other cultural values, such as the preference for male children in China,has been crippling. As discussed *infra*, transnational adoption in South Korea was initiated primarily to deal with children left homeless or orphaned during the chaos of the Korean War; it has continued in large part because of the continuing stigma attached to unmarried motherhood in Korean culture and an emphasis on biological family relationships that has discouraged in-country adoption. Dong Soo Kim, "A Country Divided: Contextualizing Adoption from a Korean Perspective," and Catherine Ceniza Choy, "Institutionalizing International Adoption: The Historical Origins of Korean Adoption in the United States," in *International Korean Adoption: A Fifty-Year History of Policy and Practice, supra* n. 15, 3–23 and 25–42. The *New York Times* reports that attitudes toward both unmarried parenthood and adoption in Korea, at least, have begun to change. Choe Sang-Hun, "Group Resists Korean Stigma for Unwed Mothers," *New York Times*, Oct. 7, 2009; Norimitsu Onishi, "Korea Aims to End Stigma Attached to Adoption and Stop 'Exporting' Babies," *New York Times*, Oct. 8, 2008.

connections to the dominant culture in which it is located, so that the distance between cultural groups can be spanned, albeit with some difficulty. A transnationally adopted child, however, may be dealing with a culture that differs dramatically from any to which she has been exposed growing up, and may find it particularly trying to bridge the gap. In addition, the child's desires to learn about or connect to a culture of origin may manifest in different ways as the child matures. Any assertion of a need or right to belong on behalf of the child or the group from which she originates must be attuned to the needs of the child him or herself.

This chapter briefly traces the history of transnational adoption, and looks broadly at the arguments for and against the practice. It then considers how the argument for cultural belonging has evolved in the transnational adoption community, particularly as adoptive parents and agencies have become educated about the importance of such questions for children, and events such as "roots trips" have become commonplace; it also asks about the extent to which such changes are perceived to meet the needs of adopted children and/or the concerns and objections of the groups or nations from which they originate. Next, the chapter delves into how various human rights documents are now shaping the debate, exploring the extent to which those documents articulate either children's "rights" to cultural identity or a group-based "right" to maintain connections to those children. Finally, it investigates how the Hague Convention deals with questions of cultural and communal belonging and how the Convention is likely to affect the transnational adoption regime in the future.

THE GLOBAL MIGRATION OF CHILDREN

Among Western nations, large-scale transnational adoption first emerged in the mid-1940s in response to the substantial numbers of children who found themselves homeless or orphaned during World War II. In the United States, under the Displaced Persons Act of 1948, some three thousand orphans from Europe entered the United States under sponsorship, with the sponsor agreeing to "properly care" for the child.[18] The practice accelerated during the 1950s, as the plight of Korean War orphans was highlighted in the media. Although Congress initially passed legislation admitting five hundred children for transnational adoption per year, adoptions soared after 1955 when an Oregon couple, Harry and Bertha Holt, adopted six Korean children and founded Holt International Adoption Agency, which was instrumental in accelerating

[18] S. 224; Pub. L. 80–774; 62 Stat. 1009, 80th Congress; June 25, 1948.

transnational adoptions, particularly from Korea.[19] By the early 1960s, Congress had amended the Immigration and Nationality Act to lift numerical restrictions on the number of children who could be adopted across national borders.

Transnational adoption became more highly visible when the domestic demographics of the adoption universe shifted in the 1960s and 1970s, as noted earlier, and the adoption conversation expanded from one centered on finding parents for needy children to include finding children for loving parents. As the number of children available domestically dwindled, childless couples increasingly sought to adopt internationally, responding, in part, to what they saw as a global problem of children in need. Expansion in the international arena, particularly in Asia, took another jump after 1975, when Operation Babylift moved some two thousand South Vietnamese children into adoptive homes in the United States. (Many of the children adopted from Vietnam and Cambodia during Operation Babylift were not orphans, and disputes over the validity of those adoptions were legion in the mid-1970s.)[20]

While infants and children from Asia continued to find their way into American homes throughout the 1980s, adoptive parents also looked increasingly to Central and South America.[21] The fall of the Ceausescu regime in Romania in 1989 and the subsequent dissolution of the Soviet Union prompted a rush to adopt children from across Eastern Europe.[22] Beginning in the mid-1990s, the adoption of baby girls from China became a phenomenon in itself, as noted earlier.

During most of the 1990s and the first few years of the twenty-first century, between fifteen and twenty thousand children from other countries were adopted each year in the United States, although, as noted earlier, that number has declined very recently. These children have hailed from more than fifty countries, with children from China, Russia, Guatemala, and South Korea more or less consistently constituting the majority of that population, although very recently there has been a sharp increase in the number of children adopted

[19] *See* Ceniza Choy, *supra* n. 17.
[20] Tracy Johnston, "Torment over the Viet Non-Orphans," *New York Times*, May 9, 1976.
[21] The popularity of Asian children may be traceable to the "model minority" myth that children of Asian descent are likely to be intellectually superior to children adopted from other areas of the world. David Eng, "Transnational Adoption and Queer Diasporas," *Social Text* 21, no. 3 (2003): 1–37. Parents soon turned to other areas of the globe as well. *See generally* Peter Selman, "Trends in Intercountry Adoption: Analysis of Data from 20 Receiving Countries, 1998–2004," *Journal of Population Research* 23, no. 2 (2006): 183–204 and Peter Selman, "From Bucharest to Beijing: Changes in Countries sending Children for International Adoption 1990 to 2006," in *International Advances in Adoption Research for Practice*, eds. G. M. Wrobel and E. Neil (West Sussex, UK: Wiley-Blackwell, 2009): 41–69.
[22] Selman, "From Bucharest to Beijing," *supra* n. 21.

from Ethiopia.[23] Transnational adoptions currently account for the bulk of nonkinship adoptions in the United States, although the figures have varied considerably from year to year and have recently declined in total numbers.[24]

As noted, at various times over the last two decades, the transnational adoption world has been rocked by scandals, usually resulting in the sending country's suspension of the practice for some period of time; such suspensions have occurred in Russia, Vietnam, and Guatemala in recent years. International media interest in South Korea prior to the 1988 Olympics in Seoul generated several stories about the number of South Korean children adopted transnationally. Indeed, more than one story referred to South Korea's children as the nation's primary export.[25] Embarrassed by the coverage, the government suspended all transnational adoptions during the Olympics and subsequently announced its intention to discontinue all transnational adoptions by 1996. For a short period thereafter, South Korea allowed only special needs children to be adopted. Later, finding itself unable to place all children domestically, and facing deep economic setbacks, the government abandoned those statements and reopened its doors in the mid-1990s. As noted earlier, the South Korean government has struggled with how to deal with the issue as Korean adoptees have questioned the adoption policies in the last ten years: the nation continues to rank high among sending countries today, while opening its doors to Korean adoptees from the last thirty years who are now seeking reconnection.

Following the December 2004 tsunami in Southeast Asia, the Department of State and other aid agencies were inundated by offers from families hoping to adopt children "orphaned" by the catastrophe. The State Department quickly moved to halt adoptions because of concerns that many children were not orphans, but displaced persons who needed to be reunited with their families, a position that was largely endorsed by adoption experts.[26] Indeed, the State Department was careful to suggest that there might be a particularly compelling need to keep children within their communities to limit further trauma.

The same concerns surfaced following the 2011 earthquake in Haiti. To avoid the kind of confusion that followed the 2004 tsunami, international aid agencies quickly disseminated information reminding would-be adopters that

---

[23] *Id. See also* Rosman, Johnson, and Callahan, *supra* n. 9.

[24] Rose M. Kreider, "Internationally Adopted Children in the U.S.: 2008," in Rosman, Johnson, and Callahan, *supra* n. 9, 81–96.

[25] Tamar Lewin, "South Korea Slows Export of Babies for Adoption," *New York Times*, Feb. 12, 1990.

[26] U.S. State Department, "Update on adoption of December 26 tsunami victims," January 3, 2005.

aid organizations were taking immediate steps to locate the families of affected children, stressing that it was particularly important to provide as much in-place stability as possible for such children. Save the Children, for example, issued the following statement, calling for a moratorium on new adoptions:

> A large number of children may be separated from their parents or extended families due to death, injury or the sheer chaos created by the disaster.... These children are at risk of malnutrition and disease, trafficking, sexual exploitation and serious emotional distress....
>
> Save the Children has received many well-intentioned calls from people who wish to help the children of Haiti by evacuating them to foster and adoptive homes in other countries. While we realize this is a natural instinct, long experience tells us that it is almost always in the best interests of a child to remain with their relatives and extended family, when possible.
>
> Haiti's infrastructure has been severely damaged by the disaster, and with it the systems to ensure that children are correctly identified as orphans. The possibility of a child being mistakenly labelled as an orphan during this time is incredibly high.
>
> Save the Children is concerned about the mass movement of Haitian children to other countries, and we are asking governments and international organizations to respect Haitian law pertaining to the movements and adoption of children. Cases of children already taken for care should be screened and managed once they have arrived and suitable care options identified when the child is physically recovered.[27]

As this very brief overview suggests, there is little likelihood that the demand for transnational adoptions will abate in the near future (once the various parties have adjusted to the new regimes), and as the practice continues, the debate is likely to intensify.[28] The vast majority of prospective adoptive parents are motivated by humanitarian concerns and the belief that children available for adoption internationally are likely to have few life chances without adoption.[29] Some begin their search domestically, but turn to transnational adoption in

---

[27] Save the Children Statement on Adoption in Haiti, "Every Child To Be Given Best Possible Chance of Being Reunited with Family Members" (Jan. 21, 2010).

[28] It is too early to determine how the growth of new reproductive technologies will affect the demand for children to adopt transnationally. There is, for example, a booming new business in surrogacy, as parents essentially rent the wombs of women to carry their children. Amelia Gentleman, "India Nurtures Business of Surrogate Motherhood," *New York Times*, March 10, 2008. These practices raise difficult ethical questions that are beyond the scope of the discussion here.

[29] *See, e.g.*, Sara Dillon, "Making Legal Regimes for Intercountry Adoption Reflect Human Rights Principles: Transforming the United Nations Convention on the Rights of the Child with the

hopes that, while expensive, waiting times will be shorter and younger children will be available. Some parents pursue transnational adoption because parents believe it is easier than adopting domestically, in part because of a perceived reluctance among domestic agencies to place children transracially or because they view children who are available domestically as more likely to be damaged than children available transnationally.[30] Indeed, recent changes in U.S. law have facilitated transnational adoption by extending automatic citizenship to transnationally adopted children.[31]

The problem, however, is that there are relatively few healthy infants available internationally; those who are available can often readily be placed with adoptive families in their own countries or have a parent or close relatives with whom they are living.[32] Although many children globally may be living in orphanages, some have been placed in those institutions because of poverty, and have living parents and siblings who maintain contact and intend to reunite with them at a later date. The majority of children who are available for adoption internationally are five years of age or older, beyond the age that most attracts adoptive parents. Many of these older children have experienced trauma and exhibit the same behavioral problems as children who have experienced stress in the domestic foster care system.[33]

At the systemic level, nongovernmental organizations (NGOs) and those skeptical about transnational adoption worry that the practice draws attention away from the compelling moral obligation to provide economic and social assistance to families and communities in poor countries to eliminate the necessity of relinquishing children in the first place. Indeed, International Social Service, an NGO long active in adoption and foster care for children in need, specifically stated in its 2004 "Guidelines for Practice on National and Intercountry Adoption and Foster Family Care" that "[a]s a priority, the child shall be adopted within his/her own State. *Intercountry adoption can be considered as an alternative only after having ensured that a satisfactory solution for the*

Hague Convention on Intercountry Adoption," *Boston University International Law Journal* 21 (Fall, 2003): 179–256; *also*, Bartholet, *supra* n. 14.

[30] Christine Ward Gailey, *Blue Ribbon Babies and Labors of Love: Race, Class, and Gender in U.S. Adoption Practice* (Austin: University of Texas Press, 2010): 100–102.

[31] Child Citizenship Act of 2000, Public Law 106–395 (codified at 8 U.S.C. secs.1431–33).

[32] E. J. Graff, "The Lie We Love," *Foreign Policy*, Oct. 15, 2008. According to reports from UNICEF and Save the Children, "most of the children living in institutions around the world have a surviving parent or close relative, and they most commonly entered orphanages because of poverty." "Aid Gives Alternative to African Orphanages," *New York Times*, Dec. 5, 2009.

[33] Graff, *id.*; *see generally* Ana Teresa Ortiz and Laura Briggs, "The Culture of Poverty, Crack Babies and Welfare Cheats: The Making of the Healthy White Baby Crisis," *Social Text* 21, no. 3 (Fall 2003): 39–57.

child cannot be found within his/her state of origin,"[34] a position that the UN's Guidelines for the Alternative Care of Children, discussed *infra*, largely adopts.

Other critics charge that the demand for children has become the ultimate expression of global capitalism, with children becoming commodities transferred from poorer to wealthier nations under the guise of rescue.[35] Indeed, at their most strident, they argue that the practice has evolved into a status game involving the display of exotic children. As one author has noted, adoptive parents frequently make a point of noting that they can provide children with lives they could only dream of in their countries of birth, conveying the impression that the mere fact that they have resources should excuse them from any investigation into their worthiness as adoptive parents.[36] On this reading, transnational adoption seems to confirm the sense of entitlement enjoyed by adoptive parents from the West.

If transracial adoption is criticized domestically as devaluing parenting by persons (particularly mothers) of color while privileging parenting by wealthier white families, that concern is amplified in the transnational arena, where privilege is conspicuous and it is difficult to assess the processes by which children become available for adoption. On the global adoption stage, race, class, and gender hierarchies are arguably deepened.[37] Nor have Western nations worked very hard to assist in keeping families together; as Jacqueline Bhabha has pointed out, "[c]alls by developed states for social and cultural changes in the birth countries to minimize the pressures on birth mothers to separate from children are effectively non-existent."[38] Moreover, she notes, the surrender of girls in particular may shore up cultural beliefs in sending nations that devalue women. Western parents seek Asian or Latino children, particularly girls, in far greater numbers than black children. Bhabha points out that Ethiopia had significant numbers of AIDS orphans in 2002, but ranked far behind Russia and China in the number of adoptions processed during that year, although, as noted earlier, Ethiopia has very recently become a popular site for adoption.

The demand for transnational children is fueled by the myth discussed in Chapter 3 that children domestically available for adoption, especially coming from state care, are likely to be profoundly damaged and thus undesirable. The

---

[34] International Social Service, *Guidelines for Practice on National and Intercountry Adoption and Foster Family Care,* 2004 at 4.

[35] Smolin, *supra* n. 12.

[36] Gailey, *supra* n. 30 at 88.

[37] Jacqueline Bhabha, "Moving Babies: Globalization, Markets, and Transnational Adoption," *Fletcher Forum on World Affairs* (Summer, 2004): 181–195, 194.

[38] *Id.* at 187.

flip side of that myth, of course, is that children available transnationally are likely to be infants and to have suffered less emotional or physical abuse or neglect than might be expected from the pool of children available domestically. In fact, children available transnationally have often grown up in the midst of war or famine or simply poverty, and are "no more, and no less, likely to be dealing with the consequences of that trauma as they mature."[39]

Whereas the majority of families adopting children internationally may not be wealthy in their own countries, they almost invariably have funds far in excess of potential adoptive families in the sending countries. Because transnational adoption generates substantial currency, sending countries may direct the most adoptable children to international families, from whom agencies can reap the largest monetary rewards.[40] As a result, potential adoptive families in local communities find themselves simply sidelined. To deal with this claim, more sending nations and several international documents have accorded a preference to in-country adoption over transnational placement.

For children adopted transnationally, especially children whose racial or ethnic identity differs from that of their adoptive families, studies suggest that it is important to facilitate the children's understanding of the communities and cultures they have left behind.[41] These efforts, to date, have attracted their share of criticism, too, especially the "culture camp" approach that many adoptive parents, with the best of intentions, have utilized; the Donaldson report suggests that those measures may not, alone, be sufficient to meet children's needs.[42] There is also a concern that children are presented with sanitized versions of their cultures of origin, stripped of the context that is essential to any real understanding of cultural or communal difference. Indeed, in a deeper sense, these reconstructed cultures may be represented in forms that drain them of their potency as a challenge to dominant cultures. In any event, introducing a child to a culture of origin is problematic: culture is a lived experience and cannot really be instilled from the outside. Efforts to acquaint children with their communities of origin may simply be a way to police and contain these children's otherness, assuring assimilation while celebrating a cultivated difference.[43]

---

[39] Graff, *supra* n. 32.

[40] David M. Smolin, "Intercountry Adoption as Child Trafficking," *Valparaiso University Law Review* 39 (Winter 2004): 281–325.

[41] Hollee McGinnis, Susan Livingston Smith, Scott D. Ryan, and Jeanne A. Howard, *Beyond Culture Camp: Promoting Healthy Identity Formation in Adoption* (Evan B. Donaldson Adoption Institute, 2009) (hereafter *Beyond Culture Camp*).

[42] *Id.*

[43] A group of Australian scholars recently noted that intercountry adoption in Australia, while supported with a rhetoric of multiculturalism, has remained largely assimilationist. "[I]ntercountry

Few if any of the commentators regularly addressing adoption have focused on the impact of the loss of children on communities of origin, but those concerns must be addressed in any discussion of transnational adoption if the conflicts are to be resolved. Sending communities, both national and subnational, are increasingly vocal about what they perceive as the loss of their children, especially as it becomes clearer that these children often have families and kinship networks who might be able to provide care. Adoptees, as well, have developed active support groups to help them search out and reconnect with families and communities of origin (although, of course, the need to connect and with whom varies considerably from child to child).

As noted, concerns about transnational adoption are increasingly viewed in a human rights frame, focusing on how transnational placements affect particular communities in sending nations. Article 6 of the Draft Declaration on Indigenous Rights prepared by the UN Working Group on Indigenous Persons issued in 1993, for example, declared that "the removal of indigenous children from their families and communities *under any pretext*" could amount to violence or genocide that indigenous peoples had a collective right to resist.[44] In the final Declaration, adopted by resolution in the United Nations General Assembly in 2007, that language, now in Article 7(b) has been softened to state that "Indigenous peoples . . . shall not be subjected to any act of genocide or any other act of violence, including forcibly removing children of the group to another group."[45]

Proponents of transnational adoption acknowledge many of the criticisms outlined here, but argue that if adoption can save at least a few children from living their lives in institutions or under conditions of inhumane neglect, sexual abuse or torture, or simply wandering the streets, it is justifiable. Harvard law professor Elizabeth Bartholet, one of the most outspoken advocates for increasing both transracial and transnational adoption, argues that children's needs for permanent family placement should trump all other concerns.[46] Although there is certainly a global need to provide resources for impoverished families and children, she argues, there is an equal moral imperative

adoption has been understood as a way for mainly heterosexual, middle class white couples . . . to 'train' young, foreign-born children to be productive Australian citizens, as an alternative to immigration." Kate Murphy, Sarah Pinto, and Denise Cuthbert, "'These Infants are Future Australians': Making the Nation through Intercountry Adoption," *Journal of Australian Studies* 34, no. 2 (2010): 141–161, 156. It is not likely that individual adopting couples in most receiving nations are trying to supplant immigration, although the authors note that Australia has been struggling with a negative growth rate and has positioned itself as a nurturer of children in need.

[44] *Draft Declaration on the Rights of Indigenous Peoples*, U.N. Doc. E/CN.4/Sub.2/1994/2/Add.1 (1994).
[45] *Declaration on the Rights of Indigenous Peoples*, G.A. Res. 61/295, U.N. Doc. A/RES/47/1 (2007).
[46] *See* Bartholet, *supra* n. 14.

to provide immediate homes for children who need them. Indeed, Bartholet has been a strident critic of the human rights community's efforts, along with those of sending nations, to more strictly regulate transnational adoption, arguing that these efforts are typically a pretext to hide embarrassment over a nation's inability to care for children: "[O]pposition to international adoption that purports to be grounded in children's human rights tends to be more politically palatable and thus persuasive than arguments grounded in a country's nationalist claims of ownership rights over its children or nationalist pride in not appearing unable to care for its children."[47]

Supporters recognize that abuses may occur in the international adoption regime, but bridle at accusations that there is a market driven by the demand generated by potential adoptive parents; they are more likely to view scandals as individual aberrations than as problems as endemic to the practice. Thus, they assert, a more extensive international regulatory regime, such as that created by the Hague Convention, can limit extortionate fees and curb coercive and inappropriate practices and should be supported so long as those requirements do not unduly slow the adoption process.[48] In short, they worry that prohibition or even extensive regulation of transnational adoption may doom children to lives of extreme poverty or worse, as children without parents in many parts of the globe are at risk of being trafficked for labor or sex.

Finally, supporters assert that far from drawing attention away from systemic problems of poverty and global inequality, transnational adoption can bring those concerns into the public eye. Adoptive families in the global north are often acutely aware of the issues facing sending nations and the stories of adopted children become widely known, which can focus attention and concern. Indeed, they suggest that regulating and normalizing the global adoption process might reduce some of the race and gender disparity that continues to mark transnational adoption.

Adoptive parents and the agencies that facilitate adoptions, supporters note, are now learning about the need to provide children with exposure to their cultures of origin and the appropriate ways of inculcating such knowledge. Both agencies and adoptive parents today embrace the need to provide children with access to information about their origins in increasingly sophisticated ways, and scholarship has supported this endeavor.[49] The 2009 Donaldson Institute report noted earlier, for example, underscores the need to develop

---

[47] *Id.* at 251.
[48] *Id.; see also* Dillon, *supra* n. 29.
[49] *See generally* Barbara Yngvesson, *Belonging in an Adopted World* (Chicago: University of Chicago Press, 2010).

more comprehensive strategies to help children learn about their own transnational migration. These changes, proponents argue, can largely eliminate the troubling identity issues with which some adoptees struggle.

Just like critics of the practice, however, proponents rarely discuss the impact of the loss of children on the communities from which they originate, and efforts to connect children with their cultures of origin are only now beginning to be critically evaluated. As the debate over transnational adoption itself has moved into the sphere of human rights, however, concerns about the impact of removing children from their communities of origin are moving from the margins to the center of the discussion. The human rights documents provide no clear guidance, however: critics of transnational placement argue that the practice may violate the rights of the child under the Convention on the Rights of the Child to a family and community of origin, while proponents draw on many of the same provisions to argue that transnational placement furthers the fundamental rights of the child to a family and nurture. Increasingly, cultural communities have begun to claim that the removal of children violates their rights to self-determination, cultural identity, and protection, as discussed later. These sharp divides in the contemporary conversation about transnational adoption make conversation difficult. Proponents too easily overlook the serious problems generated by the emergence of a global adoption market with all of its shadowy possibilities for corruption and fraud; they also discount the extent to which families and communities may be pressured to surrender children. Critics, on the other hand, may advocate for community-based care with too little attention to how such communities are defined and whether those communities have sufficient resources to provide care. Recently, concepts of cultural and communal belonging have begun to take shape in the debate, providing a basis for discussing the emerging human rights concerns and changes in the international regime under the Hague Convention that flow from that awareness.

BELONGING, ROOTS TRIPS, AND CULTURAL CONNECTIONS

Transnationally adopted children feel the push and pull of belonging along several axes. As anthropologist Barbara Yngvesson has observed, adoptees are situated within two distinct narratives of belonging and return. The first portrays them as found babies, for whom adoption provides secure belonging, erasing their former "nowhere-ness."[50] The other narrative, according to

---

[50] Barbara Yngvesson, "'Going 'Home': Adoption, Loss of Bearings, and the Mythology of Roots," *Social Text* 21, no. 1 (Spring 2003), 7–27.

Yngvesson, is one of connection to the place of origin: identity is "associated with a root . . . of belonging that is inside the child . . . and unchanging," a root of belonging that is "outside" of the child in the sense that it is located in some distant place, but "is assumed to tie her to others whom she is like (as defined by skin color, hair texture, facial features, and so forth)."[51] Sara Dorow, a Canadian sociologist, has written a compelling ethnography of the adoption of Chinese girls by American parents that points out that the global transfer of children raises three "impossible contradictions" of identity and belonging: the child is at once both a commodity to be exchanged and an object of care and compassion; she both belongs and does not belong to her biological and adopted families; and she is both a citizen and forever alien.[52]

One significant response to these complexities of belonging for transnationally adopted children, therefore, has centered on connecting them to cultures and communities of origin – opening avenues that allow these children and their adoptive families to understand and embrace the ambiguities of belonging. That concern has been directed primarily at facilitating the adjustment of children to new adoptive families and communities by providing a bridge back to the child's community, and sometimes family, of origin.[53] Providing a child with information about his or her origins is now widely recognized as essential to promoting the child's adjustment and self-esteem, and is particularly important for children whose adoption is both transnational and transracial.[54]

This imperative to create connections has begun to draw the attention of both sending countries and distinct communities located within those countries – the former because they often face criticism at home and abroad for "outsourcing" the care of children, and the latter who have begun to give voice to the sense of loss that the transfer of children has imposed. As a result, some sending countries are now imposing more stringent standards to ensure that parents are counseled about the special issues associated with raising a

---

[51] *Id.* at 8, 13.

[52] Sara K. Dorow, *Transnational Adoption: A Cultural Economy of Race, Gender and Kinship* (New York: New York University Press, 2006): 16–23.

[53] It is not always possible to locate a child's biological family. In China, for example, information about birth parents is virtually impossible to discover, and in China and elsewhere transnationally, most adoptions are closed. The fact that most international adoptions are closed runs against the trend favoring open domestic adoptions, discussed in Chapter 3. This "clean break" model of adoption appeals to some prospective adoptive parents, because it appears to raise less potential for disruption of the new family. Gailey, *supra* n. 30 at 85–86. Closed adoptions, however, may decline in the future as the Hague Convention imposes greater recordkeeping responsibilities and may open the door to easier or more frequent connection with birth parents, families, and communities.

[54] *Beyond Culture Camp, supra* n. 41.

transnationally adopted child. Indeed, the Hague Convention itself appears to articulate such a requirement, although that requirement is relatively weak.[55]

The effort to connect children with their origins can arise at several points in the adoption process – from the pre-placement evaluation process of potential parents to post-placement efforts by agencies and adoptive parents on behalf of children. As noted earlier, many adoptive parents already take extraordinary steps to introduce children to their cultures of origin as they mature. Parents may enroll the children in classes or camps designed to introduce them to their cultures of origin while others work to introduce children to those communities through everyday efforts in books, visits to museums, and cultural events. Some may participate in "roots trips" that allow children to visit their communities of origin and, in some cases, reconnect with their biological families.[56]

These efforts raise complicated questions about cultural authenticity and belonging. Critics of transnational adoption view the loss of a child's (original) cultural or communal heritage as a concrete loss of identity and a rights violation; proponents argue that this loss is insignificant, especially for young children, who can gain their bearings from the new culture into which they are placed.[57] Attempts to make such connections are complicated, too, because, as noted earlier, culture is a lived experience, and it can be difficult to expose a child to a culture or community of origin in any meaningful way. Any exposure may be simply connecting to a "museum" culture that cannot impart the nuances of distinct cultural values and belonging. No matter how conscientious parents might be, it is virtually impossible for someone from one culture to transmit another, especially when that other culture is approached out of context. Over time, too, both parents and children may experience a sort of cultural fatigue. British sociologist Derek Kirton, for example, who conducted a lengthy study of race, ethnicity and adoption in the United Kingdom, relates the reaction of a South Asian adoptee when her (white) mother gave her a sari when she was sixteen: "I didn't know what to do with it. There didn't seem to be any meaning behind it."[58] Adoptive parents may be accused by

---

[55] Hague Convention, *supra* n. 13, art. 16(b) and art. 17(d).

[56] For a discussion of the complicated aspects of making these connections, *see*, Yngvesson, *supra* n. 51.

[57] *See, e.g.*, Jena Martin, "The Good, the Bad and the Ugly: A New Way of Looking at the Intercountry Adoption Debate," *Davis Journal of International Law and Policy* 13 (Spring 2003): 173–216.

[58] Derek Kirton, *"Race," Ethnicity, and Adoption* (Buckingham, UK: Open University Press, 2000): 53.

their children of appropriating the child's cultural experience, especially as children become teenagers and want to create their own sense of belonging and identity.[59]

Roots trips can have especially unpredictable results, as Barbara Yngvesson's work has demonstrated. She notes that these trips rarely produce a seamless whole for children: "[The] trips reveal the precariousness of 'I am,' the simultaneous fascination and terror evoked by what might have been and a longing for the safety of home," revealing what has been both lost and gained in the process of moving transnationally by uncovering the "interruptions, contradictions and breaks in creating the child's identity."[60] Although some adoptees may feel moments of closure, Yngvesson finds that "the moments of clarity are typically that – moments – in a process of self-constitution that is ongoing, painful, and turbulent, challenging any sense of a stable ground of belonging."[61] For some children, meeting members of a biological family or spending time in a community of origin may feel like a homecoming whereas others find themselves uncomfortably situated between worlds of poverty and plenty, between profoundly and irreconcilably contrasting value systems, and between different ethnic or racial groups in both their adoptive and original families.

Under these circumstances, some children may feel distinctly burdened by the obligation to "be" a member of a culture in which they have not grown up. Other children may appreciate such efforts as a corrective for feelings of loss, although they are unlikely to feel as if they belong to the community of origin. As Yngvesson notes, few of the adoptive children she studied reported feeling "completed" by the return to roots. Rather, she notes, these trips "reveal[] a kind of chaos, shaking up families in the world that created international adoption and that international adoption hoped to create."[62] Many adoptees are more ambivalent about tracing their origins than their adoptive parents, who often have difficulty with the dissonance of having a child who "belonged" somewhere else.[63]

At the same time, there is increasing evidence that transnationally adopted children need to be able to learn about their origins in greater depth than has previously been recognized. The *Beyond Culture Camp* report noted earlier begins with the assertion that it is necessary

[59] *Id.*
[60] Yngvesson, *supra* n. 51 at 9.
[61] *Id.*
[62] *Id.* at 18.
[63] *Id.*

to go "beyond culture camp" to provide children with ongoing experiences and relationships that promote positive racial (and adoptive) identity development. Our respondents valued cultural celebrations and other opportunities to learn about their origins, but such singular events appear insufficient. Instead, the research points to a need to move beyond strategies that promote cultural socialization to experiences that promote racial and cultural identification and comfort. Part of this work is to expand understanding of the importance of learning about one's origins, whether by traveling to birth country or by seeking out biological relatives.[64]

The report echoes the findings of numerous earlier studies indicating that a "child's loss of earlier relationships, along with all traces of their pre-adoption identity, is widely recognized as potentially damaging to some children."[65]

All of this work, however, focuses on assisting the individual child and adoptive family to cope with identity issues; none of these conversations about connecting to cultures of origin focus on the impact of the outmigration of children on their communities. Yet, among transnationally adopted children, the search for origins is often about finding that "lost" community as much as it may be about finding severed kinship ties. A child may be as much or more concerned with "being" Guatemalan or Cambodian as with finding a biological parent.

The criticisms voiced about transracial adoption in Chapter 3 – that the practice undercuts communities of color by suggesting that its members are inadequate parents – applies as well in the international arena. Sending countries like Guatemala, Ethiopia, or Vietnam are typically presumed to be too poor, disorganized, or corrupt to provide care for dependent children, when in fact there may be families within those communities with the means to adopt such children. Painting nations and communities as too stressed to care for needy children has specific political ramifications for those nations or subcommunities within those nations. The demonization of poor families – particularly poor women – multiplies on a global level, as sending countries fall further in international esteem. Proponents of transnational adoption may assume that any adopted child will be better off in the West than in their own communities. Adoptive parents are reassured that they are "rescuing" children from lives of abuse and poverty without close inquiry into the specific circumstances facing each child. This narrative diverts attention away from the deeper causes of children's neediness and the West's own responsibility for creating and maintaining global inequality.

[64] *Beyond Culture Camp, supra* n. 41, Executive Summary.
[65] Ya'ir Ronen, "Redefining the Child's Right to Identity," *International Journal of Law, Policy, and the Family* 18, n. 2 (2004): 154.

Sending communities also object to the ways in which transnational adoption becomes a project in cultural reconstruction. As discussed in Chapter 3, domestic adoption and foster care initially were lauded not only for providing loving homes for children in need, but for creating "normal" families and erasing children's ties to "unsuitable" parents and "unhealthy environments." Not only are the nations from which children originate often depicted as disorganized, callous, or irresponsible, but the reconstructed cultures to which children are reintroduced are carefully vetted and repackaged to contain the "otherness" of adopted children.

Under these circumstances, a child's return to a community of origin can be as unsettling to the community as it is to the child. The child comes back as a stranger who may have grown up believing that this community failed him, and the community may feel its own integrity has been attacked. Even if an adoptive family has done a superlative job of introducing a child to his or her origins, the adoptee will experience that connection in an attenuated fashion. At the same time, the child is familiar: the belonging on both sides tends to be uncomfortable. As one Swedish adoptee, originally from Ethiopia, reported to Yngvesson following a trip to that country that while she recognized the country because it was "as though all the older people I saw could be my mamma or papa," it was also difficult because "the physical and cultural difference is so great . . . the culture isn't exactly – if I could choose – it isn't the country I would choose to be from."[66]

EMERGING HUMAN RIGHTS DISCOURSES

Creating connections among children and their communities of origin has been largely unidirectional, as adoptees and, increasingly, their adoptive families have sought to uncover the child's origins. To date, most of those efforts have been carried on outside of a discourse of rights. The emergence of a constellation of identity rights for both individuals and groups, however, is now transforming that conversation by introducing a different set of interests. The idea that children have a cognizable set of "identity rights" to remain within or, at the very least, be provided with access to, their cultures of origin has gained currency under a variety of human rights instruments in recent years. The starting point is the Convention on the Rights of the Child (CRC).

Adopted by the United Nations in 1989, and ratified by 194 nations to date, the CRC articulates a wide array of political, economic, social, and cultural rights for children. All of those specific rights, however, are tempered by the

[66] Yngvesson, *supra* n. 49 at 148.

overarching principle, set forth in Article 3, directing that in all actions taken by State or private welfare providers, "the *best interests of the child* shall be a primary consideration."[67]

The CRC has broad international support and obligates signatory States to enact laws that further its provisions. A number of States have ratified the CRC, however, with reservations of particular importance for issues of belonging and identity by declaring that the rights of the child shall not be interpreted in ways that violate a State's specific religious or cultural values or that otherwise require States to recognize rights that go beyond those articulated in national constitutions and laws. For example, some Muslim countries interpret the Qur'an's prohibition on adoption strictly, whereas others interpret Sharia law more expansively and allow children to acquire full rights of filiation through the adoption process.[68] As International Social Services, a preeminent NGO engaged in analyzing transnational adoption, has noted, "These reservations often place transnational adoption in a disfavored position, since such placements automatically raise concerns about religious, ethnic, or other kinds of cultural continuity in a child's life."[69]

Protecting children's personal, familial, ethnic, and national identities is a theme that crops up repeatedly in the Convention. The Preamble, for example, nods to the importance of cultural and communal belonging when it declares that its provisions should be implemented taking "due account of the importance of the traditions and cultural values of each people for the protection and harmonious development of the child."[70] Article 5 similarly instructs signatory states to respect

> the responsibilities, rights and duties of parents or, where applicable, the members of the extended family or community as provided for by local custom . . . to provide, in a manner consistent with the evolving capacities of the child, appropriate direction and guidance in the exercise by the child of the rights recognized in the . . . Convention.[71]

[67] Convention on the Rights of the Child, *supra* n. 7, art. 3.
[68] ISS/ICR *Fact Sheet No.* 51, Dec. 2007. The Qur'an imposes an obligation, known as *kafalah*, to voluntarily care for orphaned and abandoned children. *Kafalah* endows the caregiver with parental authority and obligates that caregiver to maintain the child, while preserving the exclusivity of the caregiver's family bonds and the child's own family status at the same time.
[69] *Id.* The ISS is a social service NGO established in 1924 that is active in some 140 countries. Its mission statement notes that it is specifically focused on the adoption of children, placing those concerns in the context of preventing abandonment and providing support for families of origin and monitoring children placed in foster and residential care. www.iss-ssi.org/2009/index.php?id=3.
[70] Convention on the Rights of the Child, *supra* n. 7, Preamble.
[71] *Id.* art. 5.

As British legal scholar Geraldine van Bueren has pointed out, trying to define children's rights in international law is difficult because that body of law must be able to accommodate a variety of family and community forms while also articulating a constant set of rights for children themselves.[72] Because the definition of the family itself varies from culture to culture, and may be regarded as communal in some places, she points out, the drafters of the CRC tried to incorporate a definition that recognized local and customary childcare practices. Part of the reason for obligating signatory States to respect such a broadly defined family, she notes, was to afford children a variety of sources of protection, as in many communities, the obligation to care for children extends by custom beyond the nuclear family. But this expansive understanding of the family is not consistent throughout the Convention and is not always read into other provisions respecting responsibility for children.[73]

Article 8 of the Convention expressly recognizes the child's right to national and familial identity; Stewart has argued that this Article also implicitly protects personal and communal identity, pointing out that Article 8 originally came into force because of concerns about Argentina's disappeared children, which led Argentina to originally propose wording that would recognize a child's right to understand and hold onto his or her "genuine" identity.[74] To account for adoption, Article 8 of the Convention now declares that every child has a right to "nationality, name and family relations as recognized by law."[75] Article 30 affirms the rights of children belonging to ethnic, religious, or linguistic minorities, as well as indigenous children, "in community with other members of his or her group, to enjoy his or her own culture."[76] Article 9 protects a child from arbitrary separation from his or her parents, and Article 12 guarantees the child a right of access to information, which arguably includes information about a child's family and community of origin.

Articles 20 and 21 of the CRC are of particular importance as they address concerns specific to children without parents and children subject to adoption. The former obligates the State to provide "special protection and assistance," including alternate care, to any child "temporarily or permanently deprived of his or her family environment, or in whose own best interests cannot be allowed to remain in that environment," where the alternate care might include "foster

[72] Geraldine Van Bueren, *The International Law on the Rights of the Child* (The Hague: Martinus Nijhoff Publishers, 1998): 67–72.

[73] *Id.*

[74] George A. Stewart, "Interpreting the Child's Right to Identity in the UN Convention on the Rights of the Child," *Family Law Quarterly* 26 (1992–1993): 221–233, 225–226.

[75] Convention on the Rights of the Child, *supra* n. 7, art. 8.

[76] *Id.*, art. 30.

placement, kafalah of Islamic law, adoption or, if necessary, placement in suitable institutions for the care of children."[77] Critically, Article 20 continues: "When considering solutions, *due regard shall be paid to the desirability of continuity in a child's upbringing and to the child's ethnic, religious, cultural and linguistic background.*"[78]

Article 21 directly addresses adoption:

> States Parties that recognize and/or permit the system of adoption shall ensure that the best interests of the child shall be the paramount consideration and they shall: . . .

> (b) Recognize that intercountry adoption may be considered as an alternative means of child's care, if the child cannot be placed in a foster or an adoptive family or cannot in any suitable manner be cared for in the child's country of origin.[79]

Taken together, these provisions of the Convention raise questions about the nature of transnational placements and their relative status in the preferred hierarchy of care options. One line of analysis suggests that the right of a child to know his or her identity and the strong endorsement of family and communal ties may be read as a significant restriction on transnational adoption, because it may violate the child's basic right to remain connected to his or her family and community of origin. At best, it might be viewed as endorsing transnational adoption only as a last resort, lagging even behind institutional placement in the child's country of origin, because of the directive that "transnational adoption may be considered . . . if the child . . . cannot *in any suitable manner* be cared for in the child's country of origin."[80] In fact, as initially worded in a 1982 draft of the CRC, Section 20 contained only the language that States should facilitate adoption and foster care when alternative care for children was necessary; the more restrictive language contained in the final draft was added after delegates from a number of countries objected to foregrounding adoption over other forms of communal and extended family care.[81] These interpretations place primary emphasis on providing on-site services to needy children, thus retaining the child's links to his or her family, and his or her national, ethnic, or religious community of origin.

[77] *Id.*, art. 20.
[78] *Id.*
[79] *Id.*, art. 21.
[80] *Id.*, art. 21, emphasis added.
[81] *See* Sonia Harris-Short, "Listening to 'the Other'? The Convention on the Rights of the Child," *Melbourne Journal of International Law* 2 (2001): 304–350.

Alternately, these provisions can be read as neutral toward, or as positively endorsing, transnational adoption as one among several options for caring for children without parents. The 1986 Declaration that preceded the Convention, for example, appeared to set up a preference for permanently placing a child with a family, wherever that family might be located. Article 4 stated that "[w]hen care by the child's own parents is unavailable or inappropriate, care by relatives of the child's parents, by another substitute – foster or adoptive – family or, if necessary, by an appropriate institution should be considered."[82] Thus, Sara Dillon has argued that the 1986 Declaration endorsed transnational adoption over institutional or other care and that the changes in the final version of the CRC should be read as neutral on the issue. She argues further that the focus on providing "suitable care" in the current Convention is an implicit endorsement of family over institutional placement, even if the familial care must be obtained across international boundaries.[83] Van Beuren, however, has argued that the Convention protects children from interference with their families by state and private actors; it does not grant them a "right" to a family.[84] The question then arises whether placement in a permanent family serves the "best interest" standard articulated in Article 3 better than other forms of community-based care.

UNICEF itself has taken the position that transnational placement is appropriate in some cases:

> [E]very child has the right to know and be cared for by his or her own parents, whenever possible.... UNICEF believes that families needing support to care for their children should receive it, and that alternative means of caring for a child should only be considered when, despite this assistance, a child's family is unavailable, unable or unwilling to care for him or her.

> For children who cannot be raised by their own families, an appropriate alternative family environment should be sought in preference to institutional care which should be used only as a last resort and as a temporary measure. Inter-country adoption is one of a range of care options which may be open to children, and for individual children who cannot be placed in a permanent family setting in their countries of origin, it may indeed be the best solution.[85]

---

[82] *Declaration on Social and Legal Principles relating to the Protection and Welfare of Children, with special reference to Foster Placement and Adoption Nationally and Internationally*, G/A Res. 41/85, Dec. 3, 1986), art. 4.

[83] Dillon, *supra* n. 29.

[84] Van Bueren, *supra* n. 73.

[85] UNICEF's Position on Inter-country Adoption, www.unicef.org/media/media_41118.html.

Casting transnational adoption as a strategy of last resort, however, also commands significant weight in contemporary discussions of caring for vulnerable children in the international human rights community. In fact, the African Charter on the Rights and Welfare of the Child expressly disapproves of transnational adoption. Article 24 provides that "inter-country adoption in those States that have ratified or adhered to the International Convention on the Rights of the Child or this Charter, may, as the last resort, be considered as an alternative means of a child's care."[86] The American Convention on Human Rights, created under the aegis of the Organization of American States, does not contain specific provisions relating to children, but has endorsed the principles contained in the Convention.[87]

In 2006, the UN Committee for the Rights of the Child created a working group to develop international standards for protecting children without parental care. After several years of work and wide-ranging consultation by the working group, the United Nations General Assembly passed a resolution approving the "Guidelines for the Alternative Care of Children" on November 20, 2009, concurrent with the twentieth anniversary of the adoption of the Convention on the Rights of the Child.[88] The Guidelines are clearly oriented at keeping families together, emphasizing that poverty alone should never provide a reason to separate a child from his or her parents; they direct nations to put programs into place that will allow families to care for their own children in their own communities. If those efforts are unsuccessful, Section 2(b)6 of the Guidelines support finding other appropriate resolutions, including adoption or *kafalah* under Islamic law, directing States to identify and provide "the most suitable forms of alternative care . . . under conditions that promote the child's full and harmonious development . . . taking into account the full and personal development of [children's] rights in their family, social and cultural environment and their status as subjects of rights, both at the time of the determination and in the longer term."[89]

Section 10 provides that

All decisions concerning alternative care should take full account of the desirability, in principle, of maintaining the child as close as possible to his/her habitual place of residence, in order to facilitate contact and potential

[86] *African Charter on the Rights and Welfare of the Child*, OAU Doc. CAB/LEG/we.9/49 (1990) entered into force Nov. 29, 1999.
[87] *American Convention on Human Rights*, O.A.S. Treaty Series No. 36, 1144 U.N.T.S. 123, entered into force July 18, 1978.
[88] *UN Guidelines for the Alternative Care of Children*, A/HRC/11/L.13., Nov. 2009.
[89] *Id.*, sec. 2(b)(6).

reintegration with his/her family and to minimize disruption of his/her educational, cultural and social life.[90]

Although these Guidelines do not apply to children once placed with adoptive parents pursuant to a final adoption order, they do apply to "pre-adoption or probationary placement of a child with the prospective adoptive parents, as far as they are compatible with requirements governing such placements as stipulated in other relevant international instruments."[91] They specifically bind "all public and private entities and all persons involved in arrangements for a child to be sent for care to a country other than his/her country of habitual residence . . . for medical treatment, temporary hosting, respite care or *any other reason.*"[92]

The Guidelines favor family or community-based care over institutional options, embodying the common presumption that institutional care will always be inferior to family care. They specifically denounce institutional care for children under the age of three, creating an exception, however, for very young children who may be attached to siblings placed in institutional care. To that extent, the Guidelines support the position of proponents of transnational adoption that a child has a right to a secure, loving family, which right should trump all other concerns. But that conclusion is not the only one that may be drawn. The Guidelines as a whole argue that families at risk must be supported as a first priority and emphasize that decisions about children's placement must evaluate a host of concerns – such as maintaining ties with siblings and kinship networks – to determine what will best serve a particular child's best interests. The decision must always be contextual, based on a specific child's circumstances.

The Guidelines are constructed on a rights framework: they provide strategies for enforcing a child's *rights* under the CRC. As a rights document, however, the Convention does not stand alone. There are now a multitude of rights declarations and covenants that affect debates about transnational adoption and place the child's rights in conversation with the rights of the communities from which they originate.[93] Numerous ethnic, racial, and religious communities are now drawing on the language of rights to assert the importance of belonging and identity. Only one rights declaration, however,

[90] *Id.*, sec. 10.
[91] *Id.*, sec. 29(b).
[92] *Id.* sec. 136, emphasis added.
[93] As noted in Chapter 2, the enforceability of "group rights" is questionable. In fact, in refusing to approve the Declaration on the Rights of Indigenous Persons in 2007, the United States specifically raised questions about the nature and scope of "collective" rights.

the Declaration on the Rights of Indigenous Peoples, adopted by the UN General Assembly in 2007, speaks specifically to concerns about the removal and adoptive placement of children, as discussed below. The remaining documents give no specific guidance for dealing with conflicts over group membership, cultural belonging, and children, but all have the potential to significantly alter the landscape of transnational adoption.

The Declaration on the Rights of Indigenous Peoples contains language strongly condemning the placement of indigenous children outside of their cultural communities. The Preamble, for example, declares that "indigenous families and communities [have the right] to retain shared responsibility for the upbringing, training, education and well-being of their children, consistent with the rights of the child," and continues in Article 7 with the statement that "[i]ndigenous peoples have the collective right to live in freedom, peace and security as distinct peoples and *shall not be subjected to any act of genocide or any other act of violence, including forcibly removing children of the group to another group.*"[94] Article 8 imposes an obligation on States to

> provide effective mechanisms for prevention of, and redress for (*a*) Any action which has the aim or effect of depriving them of their integrity as distinct peoples, or of their cultural values or ethnic identities; [and] (*c*) Any form of forced population transfer which has the aim or effect of violating or undermining any of their rights; [or] (*d*) Any form of forced assimilation or integration.[95]

Article 33 grants indigenous peoples

> the right to determine their own identity or membership in accordance with their customs and traditions ... [and to] determine the structures and to select the membership of their institutions in accordance with their own procedures.[96]

Taken together, these provisions erect significant roadblocks to the adoption of indigenous children in the transnational arena, although there is some ambiguity about the scope of those provisions. The Declaration appears to speak to the systematic effort to erase indigenous groups that blot the histories of Canada, Australia, New Zealand, and the United States, rather than the removal of individual children because of alleged neglect or abandonment in particular cases. Those deliberate efforts, from the Indian Adoption Project in the United States to the Aboriginal Protection Acts in Australia, posed

---

[94] *Declaration on the Rights of Indigenous Peoples, supra* n. 46, Preamble and art. 7.
[95] *Id.*, art. 8.
[96] *Id.*, art. 33.

a serious threat to the very survival of indigenous populations and inflicted extraordinary damage on both children and their communities of origins. All of these countries refused to endorse the Declaration when it first came before the UN General Assembly in 2007, although the provisions just quoted were not the most troublesome for those four nations.[97]

Although these provisions might arguably be interpreted narrowly to prevent only the large-scale transfer of children with the specific intent to eradicate a population, indigenous children continue to be particularly at risk of removal from their parents across the globe as their families are often the least well-off in their own nations. The Declaration's strong endorsement of principles of self-determination for indigenous peoples thus presumptively challenges the transnational placement of indigenous children, at least unless such a placement is made by the community itself.

There is some movement at the international level to expand the definition of indigenous peoples to include a variety of minority groups.[98] While that expansion has been resisted by both indigenous groups and by various states, non-indigenous subnational minority groups are increasingly demanding greater state protection for fragile communities. The Declaration on the Rights of Persons Belonging to National or Ethnic, Religious, and Linguistic Minorities speaks in terms roughly similar to the Declaration of the Rights of Indigenous Persons: it begins by asserting that "States shall protect the existence and the national or ethnic, cultural, religious and linguistic identity of minorities within their respective territories and shall encourage conditions for the promotion of that identity."[99] Article 2 recognizes the right of individuals belonging to such groups "to enjoy their own culture" and grants such individuals, in common with others, "the right to participate effectively in cultural, religious, social, economic and public life."[100] Article 2 also confers a right "to participate effectively in decisions on the national and, where appropriate, regional level concerning the minority to which they belong or the regions in which they live," and "to establish and maintain, without any discrimination,

[97] The United States expressed significant discomfort with the nature and scope of collective rights in general, especially their potential for overriding individual human rights. All four nations expressed concerns about the self-determination provisions and the extent to which the rights granted to indigenous peoples might conflict with their own national laws, as noted earlier.

[98] *See* S. James Anaya, *Indigenous Peoples in International Law* (New York: Oxford University Press, 2004).

[99] *Declaration on the Rights of Persons Belonging to National or Ethnic, Religious or Linguistic Minorities*, G.A. res. 47/135, annex, 47 U.N. GAOR Supp. (No. 49), U.N. Doc. a/47/49 (1993), Preamble.

[100] *Id.*, art. 2.

free and peaceful contacts with other members of their group . . . as well as contacts across frontiers with citizens of other States to whom they are related by national or ethnic, religious or linguistic ties."[101]

It can be argued, of course, that invoking this language to limit a practice such as transnational adoption is beyond the plain meaning of the Declaration, which is, rather, intended to protect members of minority populations from directly discriminatory actions and to permit fragile communities and their members to live in accordance with the dictates of their own cultures. But the language is not so limited. The emphasis on protecting the rights of minority groups to perpetuate their communities and eliminating discrimination and violence can be compared to the language of the Declaration on the Rights of Indigenous Persons, which, as noted, defines the removal of indigenous children from their communities as itself an act of violence. Read against the general reluctance to endorse transnational adoption in the human rights community, such protection might be interpreted to require States to protect the children of minority communities in particular against removal.

Article 27 of the International Covenant on Civil and Political Rights protects the right of individuals belonging to ethnic, religious, and linguistic minorities to enjoy their own cultures. As Conte, Davidson, and Burchill point out, it is an individual right with a collective dimension: although the individual has the right to enjoy his or her cultural identity, that right is dependent on the ability of the group to maintain some cohesion and integrity.[102] Commentary on the Covenant noted that Article 27 was intended to protect minority identities.

Similar declarations of rights may be found in regional human rights documents. Article 5 of the Framework Convention for the Protection of National Minorities of the Council of Europe, for example, provides that its members shall

> undertake to promote the conditions necessary for persons belonging to national minorities to maintain and develop their culture, and to preserve the essential elements of their identity, namely their religion, language, traditions and cultural heritage.

> Without prejudice to measures taken in pursuance of their general integration policy, the Parties shall refrain from policies or practices aimed at assimilation

---

[101] *Id.*

[102] Alex Conte, Scott Davidson, and Richard Burchill, *Defining Civil and Political Rights: The Jurisprudence of the United Nations Human Rights Committee* (Burlington, VT: Ashgate Publishing, 2004): 183 *et seq.*

of persons belonging to national minorities against their will and shall protect these persons from any action aimed at such assimilation.[103]

The UNESCO Declaration on Cultural Diversity also articulates strong support for facilitating the continued cohesion of cultural groups. Although it contains no specific provisions respecting the rights of children or those of cultural communities, it endorses the concept of cultural rights defined in Article 27 of the Universal Declaration of Human Rights and in the International Covenant on Economic, Social, and Cultural Rights, as the right to "participate in the cultural life of the community."[104] Whereas the Inter-American Declaration of Human Rights does not contain any provisions regarding adoptive placement of children, the Inter-American Commission on Human Rights has recently noted that it is beginning to turn its attention to a

> third stage in the development of the regional system . . . where the primary challenge is the establishment of a comprehensive view of the protection of the human rights of children and adolescents that will lead to inter-American standards on the human rights of children and adolescents that have not yet been specifically dealt with by the organs of the system. Examples are issues related to protection of identity, adoption, [and] the right not to be separated from one's parents.[105]

All of these human rights documents endorse a degree of self-determination for members of minority communities. Just as with the Indian Child Welfare Act in the United States, however, strong enforcement of a right to self-determination is likely to become an intractable dispute. The Declaration on the Rights of Indigenous Peoples, for example, is not particularly clear about how membership might be determined in disputed cases. Moreover, there is neither any guidance for determining what the boundaries of various communities should be nor any mechanism for resolving disagreement when questions arise.

To date, no international tribunal has been asked to determine whether the transnational adoption of children interferes with the rights of groups to maintain their cohesion and identity or to determine whether children have identity rights that might allow them to connect with communities of origin. The European Court of Human Rights (ECHR) has entertained several

---

[103] *Framework Convention for the Protection of National Minorities* (1998) CETS no. 157.

[104] *UNESCO Universal Declaration on Cultural Diversity* (2001).

[105] *The Rights of the Child in the Inter-American Human Rights System*, Para. 61, www.cidh.org/countryrep/infancia2eng/Infancia2Cap2.eng.htm. There is no specific charter of children's rights endorsed by countries in Latin America, although all have endorsed the Convention on the Rights of the Child.

challenges to State decisions to terminate parental rights in individual cases, which cases typically charge that a State has failed to follow proper procedures or, more importantly for consideration here, that the State has given inadequate attention to all of the factors relevant to the assessment of the child's best interest. Cultural identity per se, however, has figured only marginally, if at all, in these cases, and has typically been raised as a defense to a State's assessment of abuse or neglect. Indeed, no tribunal has fully grappled with the exceedingly difficult question of defining who belongs to a minority group in the first place.

The ECHR has, however, begun to develop that jurisprudence in three recent cases examined by Julie Ringelheim.[106] *Sidiropoulos v. Greece* (1998) and *Stankov v. Bulgaria* (2001), as well as *Gorzelik v. Poland* (2001), all involved the efforts of self-designated members of a minority group to promote their communal identity – Macedonian in the first two instances and Silesian in the last. Both Greece and Bulgaria, in the first two cases, and Poland in *Gorzelik*, argued that the very claims to existence asserted by these groups constituted an assault on their national cultures. Greece and Bulgaria denied the existence of any distinct "Macedonian" population or culture, arguing instead that the populations were Greek and Bulgarian, respectively, and both voiced concern that such efforts were merely precursors to efforts of individuals in the region to demand secession. Poland, on the other hand, recognized the Silesians as an ethnic group, but not a minority group that could avail itself of the benefits deriving from legal minority status.

Ringelheim argues that these cases squarely raised the issue of what constitutes a cultural identity and how such an identity might be asserted; each case also raised questions about the ECHR's authority to render such decisions. Ringelheim notes that this self-identification was by no means uniform in the region: many people in these regions, "situated at the margin of the political entity they were part of, at the crossroad of various cultures," felt ambivalent about declaring a Silesian or Macedonian identity. The Court, according to Ringelheim, ducked the hard issues in each case, concluding that "the inhabitants of a region . . . are entitled to form associations in order to promote the region's special characteristics." The Court refused to opine on whether the applicants could "assert a minority consciousness," falling back on the position that people must be allowed to debate the issues, thus, according to Ringelheim, preserving the "fluid and ambiguous nature of cultural identities."[107]

[106] Julie Ringelheim, "Identity Controversies Before the European Court of Human Rights: How to Avoid the Essentialist Trap?," *German Law Journal* 3 (2002): www.germanlawjournal. com/index.php?pageID=11&artID=167.

[107] *Id.* at 11–15.

The fact that cultural identities are fluid and ambiguous only complicates questions about the adoptive placement of children. None of the human rights documents adequately addresses the question of who decides what community a child belongs to, nor who may make a final placement decision. The concern with preserving the cohesiveness of communities, however, suggests that at least some formal consideration of cultural identity and the impact of the loss of a child on the child's community of origin should be accorded during the adoption process.

To date, none of these conventions and declarations has been fully endorsed by the United States. As a result, many of the specific provisions currently do not affect adoptions by U.S. families. Nonetheless, they have been widely adopted elsewhere and hold significant potential for changing the international environment within which transnational adoptions take place. Ratifying the Convention on the Rights of the Child in the United States – the United States is currently only one of two nations that has not ratified the Convention – could raise very difficult issues, as the scope of parental rights under the U.S. Constitution is extensive and could conceivably conflict with some forms of recognizing a child's identity rights.[108] Of course, Article 3, as noted earlier, requires its provisions to be interpreted to protect a child's best interests, which mitigates that concern.

The interplay of the rights of adoptive parents and originating communities raises both an easy and a difficult question. Presumably, recognizing the right of a community to be involved in a placement decision predates the adoption finalization and the vesting of the adoptive parents' rights; it can be incorporated into the overall adoption process. If the rights declarations noted, however, are interpreted to confer an ongoing right to connect with a child, the potential for conflict grows. Some resolution may be possible by framing the responsibilities of the parties to the adoption carefully from the outset, which is in part what the Hague Convention, to which we now turn, tries to do.

THE HAGUE CONVENTION AND PRIVATE LAW

The Hague Convention on Intercountry Adoption was introduced in 1993, following close on the 1989 promulgation of the Convention on the Rights of the Child. The Convention, prepared by the Hague Conference on Private International Law, was intended to establish clear and uniform standards

---

[108] President Barack Obama declared, during a debate in the 2008 campaign, that the United States' failure to ratify the Convention on the Rights of the Child is "embarrassing," but it is not currently high on the political agenda.

governing transnational adoption and to regularize procedures from nation to nation. It is not a human rights document in itself, but the Preamble notes that it was drafted to assure that "intercountry adoptions take place in the best interests of the child and with respect to his or her fundamental rights as recognized in international law."[109]

The Convention's Preamble notes that although children "should grow up in a family environment" and that nations should accord priority to keeping families together, transnational adoptive placement may "offer the advantage of a permanent family to a child for whom a suitable family cannot be found in his or her State of origin."[110] The Preamble privileges domestic over transnational adoption but does not suggest that transnational adoption should be an option of last resort. At the same time, it stops short of taking the position that children have a right to be placed transnationally if that placement will secure to them a permanent family.

Indeed, the Hague Convention neither endorses nor condemns the practice of transnational placement per se. Its purpose, rather, is to ensure that when States choose to allow transnational adoption, the practice is sufficiently regulated and transparent to prevent coercion or abuse of any of the parties involved. Thus, the key provisions of the Convention obligate each nation engaged in transnational adoption to create a central authority with power to regulate the entire adoption process and reconcile the domestic requirements of sending and receiving nations. The Convention contains a number of substantive provisions to limit the unlawful separation of children and their biological parents, imposing duties on sending countries, for example, to ensure that parents have fully and freely surrendered a child for adoption and have not been induced to do so through unscrupulous financial incentives. It also obliges receiving nations to create a regulatory regime that will protect the child's interests by ensuring that parents are suitable for adoption and that the child will be able to permanently reside in the nation to which they are moved.

The Convention garnered considerable support in the decade following its enactment, although the most prominent sending nations (China, Russia, and Guatemala) did not immediately ratify the treaty, and the United States, the largest receiving nation, as previously noted, only ratified the Convention in 2007. To date, it is difficult to determine how effective the Convention has been in meeting its goals of regularizing the adoption process and reducing abusive practices. David Smolin, who has repeatedly expressed concern about

---

[109] Hague Convention, *supra* n. 13, Preamble.
[110] *Id.*

trafficking in the adoption market, argues that "rather than representing a comprehensive approach to Intercountry adoption, [the Convention] is primarily an anti-trafficking treaty, and a very incomplete anti-trafficking treaty at that."[111]

Leaving those issues aside, however, it is worth examining how the Hague Convention deals with issues of belonging and identity. On some counts, the Hague Convention is more explicit than the Convention on the Rights of the Child in obligating States to be sensitive to the issue of cultural and communal belonging: it specifically requires consideration of the child's ethnic and cultural background in the adoption process, in direct contradiction to the requirements of MEPA-IEP discussed in Chapter 3. On the other hand, it is less emphatic than the human rights documents discussed earlier in that it grants no right to an adoptee – and certainly no right or voice to the community from which the child originates – to create or maintain connections.

Article 5 requires that prospective adoptive parents receive appropriate counseling to prepare them for the special circumstances attendant on adopting a child transnationally, transculturally, and, often, transracially.[112] Article 16 requires receiving countries to prepare reports on potential adoptive parents that evaluate the ability of those parents to "undertake an intercountry adoption as well as [accommodate] the characteristics of children for whom they would be qualified to care," while, conversely, Article 17 requires sending countries to "give due consideration to the child's upbringing and to his or her ethnic, religious and cultural background" and, in light of that information, "determine, on the basis in particular of the reports relating to the child and the prospective adoptive parents, whether the envisaged placement is in the best interests of the child."[113] Article 30 requires that records relating to the child's background and history be preserved, with the idea that the child may later be allowed access to that information according to the laws of the

---

[111] David M. Smolin, "Child Laundering and the Hague Convention on Intercountry Adoption: The Future and Past of Intercountry Adoption," *University of Louisville Law Review* 48 (Spring 2010): 441–498, 452. Contrary to the claims of adoption advocates that the Convention imposes burdensome requirements that threaten to foreclose the ability of adoptive parents to secure homes for needy children, Smolin argues that the Convention has had relatively little impact on the practice, which is, in the last resort, determined by the domestic laws of both the sending and receiving nations. He worries, in particular, that the Convention cannot limit corruption so long as private, for-profit adoption is allowed. *See also* Judith Masson, "Intercountry Adoption: A Global Problem or a Global Solution?," *Journal of International Affairs* 55, no. 1 (Fall 2001): 141–166, arguing that the for-profit industry reduces the Hague Convention to an adult-centered document.

[112] Hague Convention, *supra* n. 13, art. 5.

[113] *Id.*, art. 17

receiving country.[114] The Convention does not require receiving states to otherwise ensure that adoptive parents will be attentive to the child's cultural, religious, or ethnic background, although follow-up reporting requirements imposed by sending nations could potentially become a vehicle for securing such assurances.

As Hollingsworth has pointed out, the Hague Convention largely leaves issues related to cultural identity and belonging to agencies engaged in assessing prospective adoptive parents.[115] Jena Martin has similarly pointed out that the Convention gives little notice to considerations of culture, "dismiss[ing] the importance of culture as a defining informative part of the child's identity."[116] As she notes, the Convention tends to defer to Western concepts of culture and Western standards in structuring the transnational adoption process. For example,

> in Western cultures, adoption is not just the placement of children in a new prospective home, but also the termination of parental rights by the biological parents. In contrast, . . . [some] non-Western states have a more fluid notion of adoption: rather than a choice of one family over the other, adoption represents a cooperative effort whereby both families are involved in the care of the children. . . . The Hague Convention, while allowing some national divergence, primarily tracks the Westernized version.[117]

Barbara Yngvesson has noted this limit of the Hague Convention as well, which, like the domestic laws of most Western nations, appears to be built around the dominant model of adoption, creating the "as if" family and erasing other bonds.[118]

At the moment, much of the value of the Convention appears to lie in the reassurance it can provide to adoptive parents: if a sending country asserts that the requirements of the Hague Convention have been met, an adoptive parent can assume that a child has been properly released for adoption. It is likely to be some time, however, before the Convention can be fully implemented, as many sending nations simply lack the governmental infrastructure to oversee the process, and the reassurance provided by the Convention may not be

---

[114] *Id.*, art. 30

[115] Leslie D. Hollingsworth, "Does the Hague Convention on Intercountry Adoption Address the Protection of Adoptees' Cultural Identity? And Should It?," *Social Work* (Oct. 2008): 377–379. Regulations under the U.S. Intercountry Adoption Act of 2000 and the Guide for Good Practice under the Hague Convention both require agencies to provide at least ten hours of training to adoptive parents to prepare them for various issues that can arise in the adoption process, which might include training on cultural identity, as Hollingsworth notes.

[116] Martin, *supra* n. 58 at 204.

[117] *Id.* at 205–206.

[118] Yngvesson, *supra* n. 49.

warranted without assurance that sending countries can curb corrupt practices. Moreover, the Convention does little to address the issues that lead many parents in poor countries to release their children in the first place, nor does it provide any mechanism by which a community can suggest options other than transnational placement for children in need.

THE COLLISION COURSE IN TRANSNATIONAL ADOPTION

Claims of community matter in the transnational adoption universe just as they matter domestically. They matter to adopted children, whose belonging reaches both backward and forward across national boundaries. Equally important, they matter for affected communities, whose interests in maintaining connections to children is rarely discussed except when those communities close their doors to adoption.

None of the human rights instruments give clear guidance on how issues of cultural belonging should be addressed when dealing with the transnational adoption of children; indeed, they occasionally directly contradict one another, or may, on occasion, contradict domestic provisions regarding adoption. Even the Declaration on the Rights of Indigenous Peoples, which contains the most pointed language concerning the placement of children, leaves room for interpretation. The Hague Convention is equally ambiguous. And the meta-debate between opponents and proponents of the practice often skates over the interests of both children in creating their identities as they grow and the interests of communities whose values deserve at least some consideration in the matter.

A few commentators have argued that the form of accommodation reflected in the Indian Child Welfare Act, which transfers jurisdiction to marginalized communities, can provide some direction in the international arena. Martin, for example, argues that the ambiguities in the Hague Convention provide some scope for introducing issues of culture, family, and sovereignty, and has suggested adopting a more flexible framework that would allow each side in the adoption universe to define what issues are most important, assuming that negotiation between the primary actors – the sending and receiving countries – would produce acceptable compromises.[119] Even Sara Dillon, a strong proponent of transnational adoption, has conceded that "in the case of endangered cultures characterized by small numbers of people and relatively large numbers of children historically taken out of the community," the fairest way to deal with issues of adoption may be to provide communities with

---

[119] Martin, *supra* n. 58 at 213–215.

the authority to make placements themselves.[120] Although simply transferring jurisdictional authority from one community to another may not prove an adequate resolution, at the very least, procedures that solicit a community's voice in meaningful ways in the adoption process could go a long way to easing the pain of seeing children moved transnationally and providing continuity and connections for the child.

There is also a need to bring more openness to discussing a wide range of community-based care options that would respond to the concerns of affected communities, which are too often foreclosed by adoption advocates who see such responses are inadequate. Save the Children estimates that of the at least eight million children living in institutions, 80 percent are not orphaned but have at least one living parent; children are placed in institutions because their parents have no other care options. Arguably, it would be difficult for many nations to provide a comprehensive program of high-quality institutional care, and there is always the risk that that corruption could undermine the effects of providing monetary assistance, but that is not a reason to dismiss all such options out of hand. In many impoverished nations, placing needy children with extended family can create risks for the child because of the additional financial burden that such an assumption of care can entail, but these problems can often be mitigated by providing limited stipends – of only a few dollars – to families who assume that care, for example, as some international aid organizations have suggested, in order to limit the number of children spending time in institutions.

An article criticizing institutional care, written for *Post* Newspapers in Zambia, recently discussed the surge in the number of orphanages in Africa over the last twenty years. The writer notes that "without romanticizing that era," most vulnerable children prior to the last two decades were cared for by extended family or community members. The AIDS epidemic changed that in an odd – but not surprising – way: money became available for orphanages, and communities were encouraged to send children to centers rather than care for children locally.[121] While not underestimating the scope of the problem of children in need of care, exploring all of the options communities have available for providing care is essential.

In addition, it is important not to paint all "institutional" responses as inadequate and inevitably traumatic for all children in need of care. The very idea of an orphanage conjures up Dickensian images of starving waifs, but some institutions can be highly effective and provide loving care. The *New York*

---

[120] Dillon, *supra* n. 29 at 221–222.
[121] Daphetone C. Siame, "Community Care or the Institution?," *Post* Newspapers, Zambia, (2007), www.crin.org/BCN/details.asp?id=13558&themeID=1002&topicID=1016.

Times, for example, recently reported on an innovative program at the Berega Orphanage in Tanzania that illustrates why a broader outlook on various forms of community-based care may be appropriate.[122] Tanzania has high rates of maternal mortality, which means many infants are left without adequate care if their mother dies at birth. The orphanage recruits a young woman from an orphaned infant's extended family to provide care for the child during his or her fragile infancy, spending two years at the institution. The program has seen marked success, as the young women develop ties to the children and care for them when they return to their extended families with the child. In addition, the young women develop communities of support and often receive educational and other training that creates security once they leave the institution.

Putting time and energy into exploring such options can go a long way to providing children and communities with the sense that their interests matter. Of course, transnational adoption should be included as one of the options available for caring for children. The currently polarized debate, however, could be moved forward by placing attention on a variety of responses and not adoption alone, and could incorporate the voices of communities and children more effectively.

---

[122] Denise Brady, "Fragile Tanzanian Orphans Get Help After Mothers Die," *New York Times*, June 24, 2009.

Conclusion

The discussion of adoption and foster care in the preceding three chapters may seem to wander far afield from questions about multiculturalism per se. But there are few arenas that place more questions about the need for dialogue, accommodation, tolerance, and respect than those touching on the family and children. Moreover, there are few issues that raise questions of belonging as starkly as the adoption and foster care arena, especially because the fact of belonging is wholly entangled in questions of race and ethnicity.

In the United States and abroad, the adoptive and foster care placement of children raises deeply unsettling questions about the position of historically disadvantaged communities whose children are so often at risk. All of those communities understand fully that many of their children are endangered. Globally, vast numbers of children live in desperate poverty, many of them on the streets, in nations that are in utter disarray or are hostage to communal norms that devalue children who are female or have special needs. Domestically, children live in communities decimated by poverty, substance abuse, or alcoholism, and, if removed from parents, find few lifelines in an underfunded, overcrowded foster care system that dooms most of them to life on the margins. It is no wonder that adoptive parents and others reach out to provide those children with warm, loving, permanent homes.

At the same time, looking to adoption as a one-size-fits-all response to the problem of abandoned and vulnerable children disserves children and contributes to the alienation of the communities from which such children originate. That emphasis allows more privileged communities to ignore the systemic problems that lead to large numbers of children without adequate care. More critically, it can sometimes sap the political will that could help to provide meaningful assistance for families and communities in need.

The adoption conversation, as has been emphasized throughout this book, is polarized and accusatory on both sides. "Children in need of families" becomes a large, amorphous population in these discussions and whole communities are painted as inadequate, which crushes more nuanced approaches to providing care and assistance that look at the particular circumstances of children and the historically determined status of their communities of origin. There are no formulaic resolutions, but there are steps that can begin to accommodate the variety of extant interests. Those steps can both build trust in communities that currently feel swept aside as they watch their children disappear and provide a greater understanding of the interests of children in learning about or connecting with their origins. As Annie Bunting, writing about cultural conflicts in contested custody cases in Canada, has observed:

> Questions of cultural identity need to be taken seriously in custody and access cases, but courts ought to resist neat equations or formulae for assessing the weight to be given to these factors. There are no simple presumptions, formulae, or tests that can capture the complexity and fluidity of the children's heritage as well as their families' and communities' interests. . . . [A] place to start in our judgments concerning culture is a laying bare of our assumptions in those decisions.[1]

Thinking through children's identities and communal interests in connecting with children is endlessly complex; there are few clear guidelines for understanding how to talk about protecting legitimate group interests and the interests of individual children in concrete cases. The fact of complexity, however, provides no excuse for glossing over the issues: they must be seriously considered in shaping regimes that facilitate children's movements among families, communities, and nations. As Bunting argues, the assumptions made must be laid bare – the assumptions, from one end of the spectrum, that any child for whom adoption or foster care is a possibility must be living in a lethal environment and must be placed as quickly as possible in a permanent "forever family," and from the other end, that continuity in a particular community and/or extended kinship network is the only key to providing the child with the secure grounding in order to grow into a healthy adult, even when such communities may be stressed beyond their ability to provide care.

In any decision affecting the care of vulnerable children, a best-interest standard should take precedence over all other concerns; that standard echoes, either explicitly or implicitly, through case law, domestic statutory regimes regulating the process of adoptive and foster care placements, and international laws and conventions. But determining what resolution will protect a child's

---

[1] Annie Bunting, "Elijah and Ishmael: Assessing Cultural Identity in Canadian Child Custody Decisions," *Family Court Review* 42 (July 2004): 471–484, 483.

best interest varies, depending on the circumstances in each case, the forum in which that decision is made, and whose voices are heard in reaching that decision.

This book has discussed adoption, and to a lesser extent, foster care, in three different contexts: domestic transracial adoption and foster care, domestic adoption and foster care involving American Indian children, and transnational adoption. Each sphere raises unique issues, and thus the three arenas do not map neatly onto one another. Nonetheless, there are important ways in which the problems in each arena overlap, and each sheds light on the others as well as on the theoretical problems involved in thinking through multiculturalism in general.

The domestic transracial adoption dispute implicates long histories that have viewed parents of color as less competent than white parents and communities of color as almost invariably toxic to children. In this area, arguments about cultural belonging are the most difficult to make, largely because of the porous boundaries between communities; assigning a child to a single community, or according an "appropriate" representative of the child's "dominant" identity to make a placement decision makes little sense across the board. There seems to be no compelling reason, for example, to deny a parent the ability to decide to surrender an infant or child to a family of his or her choice. It is important to respect the agency of a mother, for example, who has carried a child for nine months or who has cared for that child *ex utero* for some period of time and to trust that she is making a decision that she feels is in the child's best interests. Respecting the decision of a young woman, however, does not mean that other issues can be ignored: if a mother or father is surrendering a child simply because of poverty, the voluntariness of such a decision needs to be carefully considered.

In the domestic transracial foster care and adoption universe, however, the larger questions center on children whose paths traverse state child welfare systems, who comprise a distinct population of children in need of care. For those children, MEPA-IEP's directives to ignore race and ethnicity in placement decisions, coupled with ASFA's relentless push to terminate parental rights and place children in adoptive homes rather than in long-term foster care with relatives or others, can work substantial harm, particularly where those children have ties to a community or kinship system that can provide support and nurture. Both of those legislative solutions were framed around the promise that they would significantly assist in finding permanency for children in foster care, but although they have succeeded in moving larger numbers of young children into adoptive homes, they have not substantially changed the circumstances for older children. It is no wonder that marginalized communities feel that these pieces of legislation were simply a ruse to remove their youngest and most adoptable children to serve the interests of adoptive parents.

One small step to bringing the interests of both children and communities in connections would be adopting the recommendations of the Donaldson Adoption Institute to revert to the original wording of MEPA, which allowed the consideration of race and ethnicity as one among several factors in deciding where to place a child. While opponents worry that the reinstitution of that language would simply restrict adoptions, considering race and ethnicity should be available to meet the needs of particular children. The recommendations of the Donaldson Report dovetail with the recommendations of more and more professionals in the field, in the studies cited earlier, who have found that allowing children to maintain ties with families and communities, even when they have been removed from homes because of alleged abuse or neglect, is often helpful in providing the children with stability and a sense of continuity in their lives.

Revisions to ASFA are also in order, to provide better support for families and provide childcare workers with more options for placing children with extended kin or other caretakers without having to move in an expedited fashion to terminate parental rights. Although foster care drift is never an attractive option for a child, some forms of long-term foster care may be the most appropriate for a particular child. In addition, as noted in Chapter 3, providing more options for community-based care is essential; there are models for small group homes that can keep children tied to siblings, family, and community to meet the needs of those children in ways that the current foster care system cannot.

The situation is different for children whose placements are governed by ICWA. Once again, there is reason to be concerned with those provisions of ICWA that completely disregard the preferences of competent parents to place their children with families they know and trust; one alteration to ICWA might be to require tribes to defer to the wishes of parents in voluntary placements, which accords biological parents the rights generally granted to them as citizens of the United States in addition to their status as tribal members. That solution does not unnecessarily undermine tribal sovereignty, because a custody proceeding would still have to be conducted in a tribal forum, but it would limit the ability of a tribe to wholly disregard the interests of a biological parent. This alteration signals a slight retreat from the decision in the *Holyfield* case that places tribal interests on a parity – or even above – those of biological parents. Because such proceedings would be conducted in tribal fora, however, the interest of tribes would remain in the forefront. In addition, such proceedings would presumably also be tied to other social services provided by the tribe, which would minimize the chances that Indian parents would be unduly influenced by non-Indians in reaching such decisions.

Where Indian children have been involuntarily placed in foster or adoptive care because of alleged abuse or neglect of parents, conducting such proceedings in tribal courts once again allows a greater airing of tribal interests and provides a better space for understanding child-rearing practices and Indian values. ICWA was designed primarily to respond to the legacy of large-scale removals of children through deliberate government programs and to curb, in the present, the actions of state agencies responding to allegations of abuse or neglect with workers who misunderstood, or were actively biased against, Indian communities. In such cases, it is entirely appropriate to vest jurisdiction over the placements of Indian children in tribal courts. It is true that many tribes are plagued with problems, but there is no reason to believe that tribal courts cannot fashion appropriate solutions for children, or work with state agencies, as many do, to provide good outcomes for children when there are no immediate Indian placements available. Indeed, the fear that many non-Indians have about being treated fairly in tribal fora finds its counterpart in concerns that tribal members have long had about appearing in state courts that preconceptions of Indian life may equally color their judgments.

There is no easy answer to the most difficult question arising under ICWA, that of determining who decides who is an Indian child for purposes of the Act. There are certainly hard cases where tribal membership has been asserted as a way of defeating or setting aside adoptive placements after the fact when biological parents search for tribal connections that are extremely attenuated. Tribes have good reason to be wary about allowing state courts to determine who is an Indian child under the Act, through either a judicially created or legislatively mandated "existing Indian family" exception; they also have good reason to be concerned that state courts may overuse the good cause provisions in the Act to avoid transferring cases to tribal courts. At the same time, when state child protection systems work with families whose connection to tribes seems nonexistent, or with children whose identity is both Indian and non-Indian, there must be more flexibility in deciding where a case should be decided, rather than simply the either/or of jurisdictional allocation, and this may be an instance where Ayelet Shachar's concept of nonexclusive cogovernance may be appropriate. Shachar argues for "transformational accommodation," which is a form of power sharing however, centered on the idea that because national and communal (or *nomoi* group) memberships typically overlap, as they certainly do with American Indian children, the state and the *nomoi* group must, in essence, compete for the loyalty of its members, and can only do so by treating those members fairly.[2] Mechanisms currently exist that allow both state courts and tribes to engage, essentially, in a "significant connections" analysis, as tribes may decline jurisdiction where they choose to do so, although that approach has not been fully developed. Although cooperation has been evolving, there is still, however, considerable mistrust on both sides, which means that state courts will engage in various machinations to avoid communicating with tribes and tribes, in turn, may "grab" cases in order to assert their authority. Care needs to be taken, however, to ensure that open conversations about significant connections occur and do not simply become an excuse for evading tribal jurisdiction (or state jurisdiction, if the decision is initially being made in a tribal forum).

Of course, tribes may be unhappy about such a move, especially as attenuation of ties to tribes was in many ways deliberately engineered. Perhaps the best solution is to place jurisdiction in questionable cases presumptively with tribes, subject to challenge depending on a showing that a state forum will have better access to information about the child's needs, the history of the child's care, and information about important personal and communal connections. Both tribes and states need to be attentive to all aspects of a child's identity, especially for children whose lives are situated in two or more cultural communities, and neither should automatically trump the other.

The situation at the international level raises yet other questions. Transnational adoptions frequently do rescue children from lives of unimaginable hardship, but the focus on adoption as the primary answer to resolving the problems of millions of needy children is misplaced. Children caught up in transnational transfer are often those who feel most keenly the need to learn about their origins and their cultural histories. As Jacqueline Bhabha has noted, the current emphasis on reconnecting children to their roots generally serves adoptive families and not families and communities of origin; shifting focus to "acknowledge[] the importance and enduring presence of birth ties and of cultural heritage in the transnational context would reduce nationalist or racialized denunciations of transnational adoption as a new form of cultural imperialism."[3]

---

[2] Ayelet Shachar, *Multicultural Jurisdictions: Cultural Differences and Women's Rights* (New York: Cambridge University Press, 2001): 117–150. This may be a less than convincing argument when applied to children than to vulnerable adults, because children's loyalty is not necessarily a spur to accommodation for either tribes or states.

[3] Jacqueline Bhabha, "Moving Babies: Globalization, Markets, and Transnational Adoption," *Fletcher Forum on World Affairs* (Summer, 2004): 181–195, 195.

Transnational placement should be one of the tools, not the toolbox, for addressing the vast problems facing the world's children. Although adoptive parents are often vested in assisting other children in deprived areas following adoptions, more concrete assistance is needed. Moreover, it is time to face up to the fact that the system itself is rife with corruption: demand for young, healthy children creates incentives for trafficking that simply cannot be ignored. And the potential for corrupt practices exists regardless of the integrity of any particular agency, because such agencies have little control over how children end up in institutions available for adoption. Only when that fact is fully acknowledged can sending and receiving nations work toward resolving these problems; until that time, communities in sending nations will continue to view transnational adopters as stealing children. Few of these issues can be resolved through the articulation of rights to identity or group rights to preserve communities. But that discourse of rights is nonetheless taking center stage in the global community, and as the discussion around rights develops, it is likely to shape global adoption practices.

Recognizing the interests of groups in questions relating to the placement of children is essential to creating a more inclusive political community, both domestically and internationally, and is thus relevant to the broader discussions about creating multicultural societies. Many of the resentments that surface in discussions of adoption in all three arenas stems from the difficulty noted earlier by Waldron: claims of cultural difference can stymie discussion and accommodation, but are often advanced as a way of securing a voice that is otherwise too easily dismissed altogether.[4] Those claims need to be recognized, if not as rights, at least as legitimate concerns. The disputes are significant, too, because actions by dominant communities that affect children and family life are uniquely likely to incite distrust and resistance. Thus the adoption and foster care arena provides a significant forum in which to try to develop better mechanisms of accommodation and conciliation.

Perhaps even more than in larger conversations about multiculturalism, which tend to assume that the individuals affected by efforts to preserve identities and enhance group connections are adults, however, it is nonetheless important to understand the position of children. Children should not be unduly burdened with carrying forward any particular group's identities or claims. The interests of children, rather, should be framed in ways that understand their interests in exploring their origins as they mature.

---

[4] Jeremy Waldron, "Cultural Identity and Civic Responsibility," in *Citizenship in Diverse Societies*, eds. Will Kymlicka and Wayne Norman (New York: Oxford University Press, 2002): 155–174.

Parents who adopt transnationally and transracially are, for the most part, intensely attuned to the needs of their children. Indeed, over the last three decades, especially with the increase in transnational placements, adoption and foster care agencies are developing more sophisticated means of counseling parents on these issues. Developing such "culturally competent" practices, of course, requires soliciting meaningful input from children and the communities from which they originate.

Creating families through adoption is, indeed, miraculous. Even miracles, however, have their darker side. Caring for children, and attending to the interests of the communities from which they originate, requires understanding the chiaroscuro in the picture of adoption. Only when all of the interests are considered can the full picture be realized.

Index